The Raven Crown

The Raven Crown

The Origins of Buddhist Monarchy in Bhutan

Michael Aris

Michael Aris

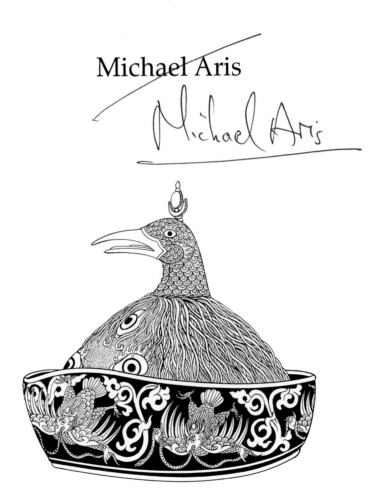

Serindia Publications, London

ISBN 0 906026 32 6

First Published in 1994 by
Serindia Publications
10 Parkfields, London SW15 6NH

British Library in Publication Data
A catalogue record for this book is available
from the British Library

Endpapers: Ugyen Wangchuk, his officers and
attendants, Punakha, 27 December 1907.
(Photo: H. Hyslop, private collection)

Printed by Biddles Ltd., Guildford

Contents

Preface 7

One The Changing Context 11

Two The Shabdrung's Legacy 27

Three The Black Regent 51

Four The Founding Monarch 75

Five The Second King 115

Six The Crown Past and Present 144

Appendix 1:
The Rulers of Bhutan, 1822-1972 147

Appendix 2:
British Photographs and Films of Bhutan, 1864-1949 148

Bibliographies 154

Index 156

Tables
1   Families of the religious nobility of central and
    eastern Bhutan claiming descent from Pemalingpa 22
2   The Wangchuk dynasty of Bhutan 50
3   The Dorje family of Bhutan 86

For Monica
and the memory of Fritz
and for their
children and grandchildren

Preface

This brief account of the development of monarchy in Bhutan could not have been written without the active support and encouragement I received from many friends both when I lived in Bhutan in the years 1967-72 and later after my return to England. My principal debt of gratitude is owed to Lobpön Pemala, known also as Lama Pema Tsewang, former Director of the National Library of Bhutan, whose own research has been a constant source of inspiration. His gift of an inscribed and greatly treasured proof copy of his major study of Bhutanese history written in literary Tibetan, for which I had been waiting close on twenty years, arrived in Oxford by courier just before I left for Rangoon to write this over a period of four weeks this summer. I have also used the transcript of a tape recording of Lobpön Pemala's memories of royal history made over a period of several days when he came to stay with us in England in 1976. I am also indebted for much guidance and wisdom to my dear friend the late Lobpön Nado, known also as Lama Tendzin Özer, who ended his career as abbot of the Tharpaling monastery. The sections of his own published account of Bhutanese history which deal with the monarchy proved invaluable. Similarly the work of that master of genealogy Dasho Lam Sangak also saved me from many pitfalls. To the late minister Sangye Penjor, best of friends and wisest of counsellors, I am grateful for the gift of the anonymous draft history of Bhutan submitted to the National Assembly in 1966 but never approved for publication.

Such merits as this short study may contain are truly owed to the labours of these kind scholars and friends. They were all born, not by random chance but by good karma, in that great centre of ancient culture and home of royalty, the central district of Bumthang. I came to know them well when I lived in the west of the country where they had all settled.

For the warm encouragement they gave me to explore the traditions of their kingdom I must also record my most sincere gratitude to members of the Royal Family of Bhutan, in particular His Late Majesty King Jigme Dorje Wangchuk and my former employer Her Majesty the Queen Mother Kesang Wangchuk. Their Majesties the Dowager Queens Püntso Chödrön and the late Pema Dechen also willingly shared their insights and memories with me on many occasions. During the course of a lengthy audience in 1989 with the present monarch, His Majesty King Jigme Senge Wangchuk, I received the same cautionary advice given by his late father when he made clear to me his own firm belief that history should be written as it truly occurred, free from panegyric.

The kind assistance given to me in 1984 by the Von Schulthess and Hoch families, true friends of Bhutan, enabled me to complete a preliminary survey of the British photographs and films of the country which survive in public and private collections in the United Kingdom. I have allowed myself the anachronism of using some of these images out of chronological sequence to illustrate some scenes which could have taken place at almost any time. I am most grateful indeed for the help and patience of the staff of the institutions where much of this material is now deposited. A summary of the survey is provided in an appendix. However, I cannot vouch for its total accuracy since I am aware that further documentation of some of this material has in the meantime taken place.

Her Royal Highness Princess Chökyi Wangchuk kindly allowed me to copy and use several photographs dating from the time of her father. The period I spent with her and her husband Dasho Topga Rinpoché at their home in the palace of Wangdü Chöling in Bumthang, scene of the early years of the monarchy, will always be remembered. I also recall with pleasure the time spent at the palace of Ugyen Pelri in Paro, which provided the setting for the early years of the reign of the third king. Photographs of his wedding to Queen Kesang Wangchuk and his later coronation have unfortunately not been available to me. I wish the book could have been brought to a close with images from that dawn of a new era.

The relatives of former British Political Officers in Gangtok and others who made tours in Bhutan and took photographs there all gave me unrestricted access to their collections. I am particularly grateful to the late Irma Bailey (widow of Eric Bailey), the late Margaret Williamson (widow of Frederick Williamson), Joan Mary and Maybe Jehu (daughter and grand-daughter of Leslie Weir), Eleanor Hopkinson (widow of Arthur Hopkinson), Dick Gould (son of Sir Basil Gould), Nicola Sherriff (grand-daughter of George Sherriff), the late Sir George Taylor, William Henderson and last but very far from least Hugh Richardson.

The early history of Bhutan I published in 1979 was based on my doctoral thesis and necessarily aimed at a specialist readership. The accurate transliteration of Bhutanese and Tibetan names used in that book inevitably caused difficulties to the general reader. In the first two sections of the present work, which present the context from which the monarchy arose out of theocracy, I have drastically summarized much of the ground covered in that earlier book, and throughout I have now used my own system of rendering Bhutanese names and terms to reflect the way they are actually pronounced rather than the way they are traditionally spelt in Bhutanese writings. My system, which employs the frequent use of umlauts, will certainly not please every-one, but in the absence of a universal standard it seemed better at least to aim for consistency. The tangle of names of the key figures who took part in the incessant feuding under the theocracy cannot be avoided without losing the thread of plot and counterplot. Common names are given in full rather than their colloquial Bhutanese abbreviations: thus Pema, Nyima and Zangmo, rather than Pem, Nyim or Zam. I apologize if some names, are put in an unfamiliar way.

Earlier published accounts in English of Bhutanese history in the nineteenth and twentieth centuries have depended solely on the testimony of the British records. For a country that only had sporadic contact with the British this has, it seems to me, provided a rather lopsided view. My principal aim here has been to try and reveal the indigenous perspectives gained from a reading of the Bhutanese chronicles presently available to me. These were all composed in the recent past by the scholars mentioned above, but they drew on earlier written compilations, biographies and the memories of witnesses. Lobpön Pemala is the only one to have carefully indicated the sources he used. The original Bhutanese archives dating from the period covered here — government edicts, official and personal correspondence, legal documents and the like — are with rare exception still closed, scattered or lost. My account has therefore had to depend on the chronicles, and while acknowledging their tremendous value I have been constantly aware that their objectivity is always to be questioned.

I have worked in some of the evidence and insights provided by British sources, but only when these seemed relevant. After the enthronement of the first king in 1907 they take on particular importance. However, this summer I have had to hand only a selection of the narratives and secondary works listed in my bibliography. For the evidence of the British Indian archives on Bhutan preserved in Delhi and London I have relied, except where indicated, on the excellent work of others. I hope this preliminary sketch will encourage others to better combine the internal and external views of the Bhutanese past.

Finally my brother Anthony is to be specially thanked, as my publisher, for his endless patience and constant encouragement — and Paddy Booz too for much practical help.

Rangoon
August 1994

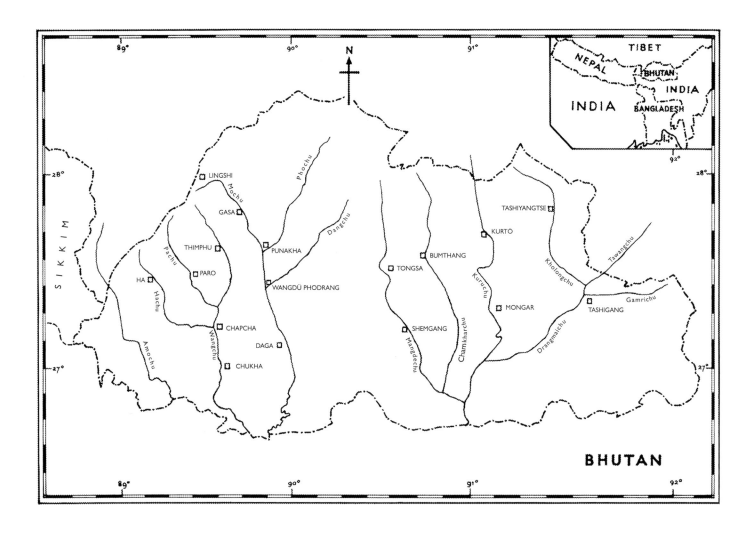

BHUTAN

One
The Changing Context

The Himalayan kingdom of Bhutan is an independent nation-state ruled since 1907 by the sovereigns of the Wangchuk dynasty, who serve both as heads of government and heads of state. Like the Hashemites of the Middle East, Bhutan's monarchs are therefore among the world's most recently established. Although the twentieth century has witnessed the total demise or radical weakening of numerous systems of kingship, it is sometimes forgotten that in this same period some new ones have taken root. The story of how the Bhutanese kings rose to absolute authority in their country is still among the least known of these echoes from an older world. In their combining of a secular role with a divine or sacred nature they further conform to many examples of past kingship. Their sacred character derives from their duty to protect the Buddhist faith and clergy and by virtue of their own divine descent. Bhutan is the only country in the world where Mahayana Buddhism is observed as the state religion, and her monarchy is Buddhist in the same way that Nepal's monarchy is Hindu.

Prior to the reign of Bhutan's first king Ugyen Wangchuk in 1907-26 and in the period following the country's first unification in the seventeenth century, Bhutan was governed by a Buddhist theocracy with a reincarnating lama as its nominal head. The system bears close comparison to that of Tibet under the Dalai Lamas. Bhutan's religious potentate is commonly known as the Shabdrung, but sometimes as the Dharma Raja or "King of Religion". In theory he delegated his secular powers to a regent called the Druk Desi who ruled in his name; this regent is sometimes referred to as the Deb Raja. My purpose here is to trace in brief outline the evolution of the present monarchy from its foundations in the theocracy of the past through to the final years of the second king Jigme Wangchuk, who reigned from 1926 to 1952. By that time the monarchy had survived a serious crisis and proved itself a viable and enduring institution. The two later kings, Jigme Dorje Wangchuk who reigned from 1952 to 1972 and his son the present king Jigme Senge Wangchuk, inherited unquestioned authority. Moreover, in their time the role played by British India as the external supporter of Bhutan as a buffer state has passed to independent India. The modern development of Bhutan, founded on the halting efforts of their predecessors, has become the main preoccupation of government. And recognition of Bhutan's sovereignty has been won from the international community. For all these reasons it seems right, in considering the origins of this Buddhist monarchy, to end with the reign of the second king and to leave aside the roles played by his modern successors.

The narrative unfolds in what is usually portrayed as a lost corner of the world. Yet it speaks to the universal and turbulent theme of state formation and nation building that continues to dominate the lives of everyone in the modern world. The reader is entitled to wonder at this point whether in view of Bhutan's long-established Buddhist religion and culture the story will perhaps be less violent and fraught than the history of past monarchies in other regions. It would be surprising if doubt remains on this score by the time the story is told. The ineffably peaceful Shangrila of Bertolucci's film "Little Buddha", which is set in the great monastic fortress dominating the western Bhutanese valley of Paro, does not as portrayed in the film evoke the stage for the turbulent struggles that brought the royal family to power.

For those with a European perspective it helps to know that this landlocked, mountainous country of long valleys and scattered villages occupying 46,500 square kilometres in the eastern Himalayas is larger than either Belgium, the Netherlands, Denmark or Switzerland but smaller than either Austria, Portugal or Hungary. However, if all its valleys were laid out flat the country would perhaps fill twice its area as the crow flies. Bhutan's population in 1990 was reckoned at only about 600,000, corrected from earlier estimates of over one million. In size of population it is almost equal to Arunachal Pradesh, the adjoining Indian state to the east, which however has an area half as large again as Bhutan's. The low population density of this section of the Himalayas must be contrasted with that of the western Himalayas and the Hindu kingdom of Nepal in particular. Nepal is three times the size of Bhutan but has a population of nineteen million. Its population density is therefore no less than an astonishing ten times that of Bhutan, which in turn appears to be more than eight times that of its northern neighbour across the main Himalayan watershed, the so-called Tibet Autonomous Region of China.[1]

To traverse the high mountains southwards is to pass from the almost barren, almost empty, high plateau of Tibet to a region of great ecological diversity. Descending the valleys of Bhutan from north to south one moves from the arctic, frozen north down through a temperate, alpine region filled with fields of rice and maize and forests of pine and rhododendron forming the heartland of the country, and still further south to the subtropical forests of the Himalayan foothills adjoining the teeming plains of West Bengal and Assam.

The relatively diminutive size of Bhutan and its population might lead one to expect a single people of the same language living within its borders. Nothing could be further from reality, for the true picture is one of a variety of ethnic groups and subgroups speaking diverse languages and dialects. Four major groups account for more than five-sixths of the population, and three of these groups speak languages of the Tibeto-Burman family, a branch of the broad Sino-Tibetan superfamily. The Ngalong of western Bhutan numbering 108,000[2] speak dialects closely akin to Tibetan or "Central Bodish". A polished version of their tongue has come to be termed Dzongkha, "The Language of the Dzong, or Fortress". It is widely used as a lingua franca and has been promoted by the government since the 1960s in a new written form as the official national language. Literary Tibetan in the past provided the sole

The high Himalayas of the Jomolhari range straddling the Bhutan-Tibet border as seen from near Dochen on the Tibetan side, with yaks in the foreground. (Photo: G. Sherriff, Royal Botanic Gardens, Edinburgh)

means of written communication among all groups. In the centre of the country, with its cultural heart in the Bumthang district, live a group of peoples numbering some 108,000 who speak a form of "East Bodish" in several dialects that are quite unintelligible to the Ngalong. A homogenous group in the far east of the country known to their neighbours simply as Sharchop, "Easterners", and numbering 138,000 speak Tshangla, a language unclassified within Tibeto-Burman and not understood by any other group. In between all these peoples and on the jungle and mountain fringes are some very small communities that preserve quite distinct local tongues, often only distantly related to the country's major languages.

The fourth major group is composed of Nepalese immigrants who began to enter and settle in the lower foothills at the end of the nineteenth century and who are thought today to number some 156,000. The Nepali language they speak is of the Indo-Aryan family and therefore unrelated to any of the Tibeto-Burman languages spoken in the rest of the country. It is not clear whether the figure provided for the Nepali population includes the many members of their community, and those claiming to belong to it, who have fled to refugee camps in Nepal in recent years to escape a wave of ethnic and political turmoil that has engulfed the south of the country. However, it should be understood that during the period covered here the "Nepali issue" lay quite dormant. A few farsighted individuals were aware that the policy of encouraging their

settlement would one day lead to difficulties in the life of the nation, but certainly during the first half of this century the problem did not exist. Except for a few scattered outposts, the jungle tracts adjoining the plains were rarely frequented by the Bhutanese of the north.

However, a complicating factor of the past not entirely unrelated to the Nepali issue of the present centred in the eighteenth and nineteenth centuries on the traditional rights won by the Bhutanese state over certain Indian communities in West Bengal and Assam. The approaches (*duars*, a word related to "door") which give access to the foothills from the plains were populated mainly by Indian tribal groups known as Kacharis and Mechis who paid tribute annually to the Bhutanese court and provincial magnates. The eleven *duars* of Bengal and the seven *duars* of Assam which the Bhutanese regarded as their rightful property became the cause of continuous conflict with the growing power of the British in India. It is clear that what was intended to be an orderly payment of tribute frequently degenerated into acts of plunder and despoliation by local Bhutanese unconstrained by the central government in the north. The steadily deteriorating relationship between the two govern-

The Himalayan peak of Gangphu (6797m) with its glacier and terminal moraine, east of the major peak of Jomolhari on the Bhutan-Tibet border, viewed from Gyangathang. (Photo: G. Sherriff, Royal Botanic Gardens, Edinburgh)

ments of British India and Bhutan came to a head in the Anglo-Bhutan war of 1864-6 which resulted in the whole tract being wrested from Bhutanese control.

With the removal of the only serious cause of lasting contention, relations with British and later independent India improved to the extent that they virtually supplanted the ancient ties of culture and politics which for centuries had linked Bhutan to Tibet in the north. The process also reflected broader geopolitical developments in Asia as a whole, and particularly those internal to China, which lay far beyond any conscious decision-making process in Bhutan or India. Yet to gain a true picture of Bhutan in any period it is necessary to review the ancient and fundamental contribution of Tibet to Bhutan's emergence as a distinct cultural and political entity.

Two critical transitions can be discerned in the life of the Bhutanese state. The first took place when the hierarchs of a Tibetan Buddhist school known as the Drukpa, beginning with Shabdrung Ngawang Namgyel (1594-?1651), founded a central government, established the present borders, and imposed a uniform set of institutions on the country. The theocracy then established, which lasted from the first half of the seventeenth century down to the opening years of the twentieth century, depended for its success on active support for the central government from the almost independent provincial magnates. It was more in the nature of a "galactic polity" than a unitary state since the provincial courts formed practically autonomous galaxies of authority, replicating the structure and purpose of the central government and constantly threatening it to the point of internal collapse. Although it was the achievement of the theocracy to bring about a real measure of cultural unity which began the steady process of eroding those ancient divisions of geography, race and language noted above, it was really left to the next key point of transition to usher in true political unity and national purpose. This came about after the apparently sudden decision to found a hereditary monarchy in 1907.

For their accounts of the earliest period of local history Bhutanese scholars have always depended on a number of legends deriving from Tibet, in particular those that look to the period of the Tibetan empire of the seventh to ninth centuries AD.[3] A great expansionary power under its own divine kings, the empire at its height controlled vast tracts of central Asia and threatened China itself under the Tang dynasty. It was in this period, too, that a late form of Indian Buddhism was introduced under royal patronage to Tibet, with enormous potential significance for its future history. Later chroniclers, who had limited access to genuinely early records or who chose to disregard them in the interests of piety, regarded the early kings primarily as promulgators and defenders of the faith rather than as empire builders. The truth is much more complex, the focus today of continuing research. However, it was the central, mainstream Tibetan view of their glorious past which the Bhutanese came to accept. Peripheral to the great empire of power and faith, yet never subjugated to it, the territory which became Bhutan was shown later after its unification to have been firmly linked in numerous ways to that essential source of divine legitimacy.

The Tibetan king Songtsen Gampo, who ruled from c. 627 to 649, is credited with building Buddhist temples to suppress a demoness whose spreadeagled form covered the whole land, preventing the conversion of the empire to the new faith. According to this scheme, recorded in texts of the twelfth century and later, two temples fall within Bhutanese territory: Kyerchu Lhakhang in Paro and Jampai Lhakhang in Bumthang. There seems every reason to believe that the temples do in fact date from this early period, and others can be added to make up a convincing list.

More important still are the stories surrounding the mythic figure of Padmasambhava, a Tantric wonder-working sage from the Swat valley of present-day Pakistan who took part in the consecration of Tibet's first Buddhist monastery at Samyé in c. 779. A great number of stories credit him with visits to the area of Bhutan, where he subdued local demons and concealed Tantric teachings in the form of "treasure texts" to be rediscovered in future times. One such story has him as the mediator between a refugee king from India called the Sindhu Raja who had settled in Bumthang and his enemy, another Indian king called Nauché. The guru is also found expelling from Tibet an evil prince called Khyikha Ratö to a site on the northern border, Khenpalung, which turned into a "hidden land" awaiting the faithful at times of future strife. Several such legendary arcadias are to be found in Bhutan, and many caves are pointed out where the divine guru is said to have meditated and around which temples were later built.

A widespread oral tradition claims that Padmasambhava introduced the early inhabitants of Bhutan to the (addictive and, it is now known, carcinogenic) custom of chewing betel nut as a substitute for cannibalism: the nut itself represents human bones, the leaf in which it is wrapped symbolizes human skin, and the lime paste applied to the leaf stands for human brains; an added herb called *rushing* is identified with flesh, and blood is replaced by the dark red juice produced when all these ingredients are chewed together. A national habit is thus linked and justified in legend

Taktsang, "The Lair of the Tiger". The famous complex of temples perched on a high granite cliff overlooking the northern part of the Paro valley, one of the oldest and most sacred shrines in Bhutan dedicated to the cult of the legendary Guru Padmasambhava, "The Second Buddha". The name of the shrine derives from the eighth and final aspect assumed by this Tantric saint as Dorje Drolö, who is always depicted in painting and sculpture standing on the back of a tigress. (Photo: H. Hyslop, private collection)

The temple complex of Kujé at the northern end of the Chökhor valley in Bumthang, 1933. The temple on the right, which is built around the sacred "Rock of Piled Vajras" where Padmasambhava is said to have left an imprint of his body, was founded by the text-discoverer Drimélingpa and enlarged to its present size by Ugyen Püntso, the Tamshing Chöjé, in the mid-nineteenth century. It was later restored by the present Dowager Queen Mother Püntso Chödrön. The temple on the left, dedicated to the form of the guru known as Sampa Lhundrup, "The Spontaneous Realization of Desires", was built by King Ugyen Wangchuk. The first three kings of Bhutan were cremated in front of these temples. (Photo: F. Ludlow, Natural History Museum, London)

to a founding figure having the status of national hero.

Before the unification of Bhutan in the seventeenth century a medley of clans claiming direct descent from a refugee Tibetan prince held sway in the east of the country among the Tshangla-speaking people of those parts. Prince Tsangma is known to have been a monk, the elder son of King Tridé Songtsen of Tibet who held the throne from c. 800 to 815. While the Tibetan sources claim he was expelled to Bhutan by his younger brother, the "apostate" Langdarma who brought about the end of the empire, the main Bhutanese source written in 1728 holds that he settled there and produced two sons from whom all the clans later descended. The chronicle slides from legend to reality in dealing with their later history, which is firmly grounded in historical fact.

The ancient nobility of Bumthang and adjacent areas of central Bhutan were termed Dung (spelt gDung). Their legendary origins derive from an early Tibetan conception of divine royalty which has their ancestral progenitor descending from the sky on a cord or ladder. Several variants of the story survive in the records, and the picture is further complicated by the appearance in Tibetan histories of the fourteenth century of a people also known as the Dung, divided into southern and eastern branches. They raided central Tibet on several occasions until subdued by the Sakya authorities who ruled under Mongol patronage in that period. Apart from the Dung nobility of central Bhutan who still survive, another group in the forested region of the southwest continues to preserve the name and are very likely the modern descendants of one branch of the early invading tribes.

The pre-unification history of the country only begins to take on real shape and colour with the arrival of prestigious Buddhist lamas from Tibet who came either as refugees or by the invitation of their local patrons in the area. Thus, while the east of proto-Bhutan is taken up with the emergence of clans and nobility having the status of "one-valley kings", the west sees the local establishment of branches of the main Tibetan monastic orders that developed during the period of fragmentation following the dissolution of the early Tibetan empire. From the eleventh century onwards there appears both in Tibet and Bhutan the figure that was to be a familiar model for all later centuries, namely the ruling lama who combined both sacred and secular authority over his spiritual disciples and lay followers. Whether his power was limited to a few villages or encompassed vast areas, a lama could, when circumstances allowed, represent ultimate sovereignty to his people.

Amid the contending rivalries of monastic principalities and estates there was always scope for the emergence of Buddhist teachers who were wholly dedicated to meditation, scholarship and teaching. However, the posthumous effect and prestige of these luminaries often tended towards founding or reinforcing secular institutions. This was made possible above all else by the fact that a Buddhist teacher was not necessarily a fully ordained monk. He could beget sons to inherit both his spiritual traditions and his worldly wealth; or if he were a full monk, these could be handed down within the same family through a line of uncles and nephews. The principle of reincarnation also came to be used to supply a line of rebirths who inherited the mantle

Monk with incense burner and two musicians performing on oboes (gyaling) for the formal welcome of the Linlithgow party at Rinpung Dzong, Paro, 1943. The photographer also painted a fine watercolour of the same monk in a similar pose. (Photo: W. Henderson, private collection)

and power of the founding lama. The picture is no different in "proto-Bhutan" than it was in Tibet.

Thus, several alternative and competing systems were simultaneously available to perpetuate the rule of a lama and his monastery in the absence of a universally recognized overlord in this long period of history. At the same time institutions were developed to separate the secular control and administration of a monastery's wealth from its primary, communal purpose of study, ritual and meditation — and in such a way that the latter retained a genuine degree of spiritual credibility. Yet despite a continuous tension in all periods between a lama's duty to transcend the world and his need and obligation to live fully within it, at many levels it came to be accepted that these various roles had in practice to be combined in a single person. Indeed, the simultaneous fulfillment of multiple responsibilities contributed ultimately to a lama's total charisma. Inconsistencies lay only in the eyes of the beholder.

At least four Tibetan lamas who are still household names among Tibetans left tangible traces in Bhutan. Milarepa (1040-1123) is revered as Tibet's greatest poet-saint, one of the founders of the Kagyüpa, "School of Oral Transmission". Longchenpa (1308-63) was the great synthesizer of the doctrines and methods of the Dzokchen, "School of Great Perfection". Thangtong Gyelpo (1385-1464) was the famous yogin who built iron-chain suspension bridges throughout the area, himself the founder of a school called the Chakzampa, "The Order of the Iron Bridge". Drukpa Kunley (1455-1529) was the best known of all the "mad saints" of Tibet and came from the main lineage of the school that was ultimately to win political supremacy in Bhutan, the Drukpa or "Thunder Dragon School".

The bodyguard of the Paro Pönlop, Dawa Penjor, in the courtyard of Rinpung Dzong, Paro, February 1910, during the final stages of its reconstruction following the fire of 1906. The Pönlop on this occasion tried to persuade Charles Bell to extradite some of his soldiers who had fled to Pedong in the Darjeeling district of West Bengal to escape punishment. Bell suspected the soldiers were in fact runaway slaves. (Photo: C. Bell, Merseyside County Museums)

The fifty-first Head Abbot of Bhutan, Jampai Tobzang (1851-1916), who occupied the abbot's throne from 1909 to 1912, seen here in the main courtyard of Punakha Dzong surrounded by monk dancers who had performed during the New Year festival of the Puna Dromchö in the presence of the Political Officer, Charles Bell, on 23 January 1910. Bell commented that the performance was "the best in Bhutan and better than any we have seen at Gyantse [in Tibet] or elsewhere". The present Head Abbot, Gendun Rinchen, recorded this comment on his predecessor Jampai Tobzang in his religious history of Bhutan: "Having listened to and meditated upon the stages of the path to maturation and release, he made the protective deities his servants". (Photo: C. Bell, Merseyside County Museums)

Milarepa left no immediate trace apart from a single song he is supposed to have composed while meditating at Taktsang but, as we shall see, the Kagyüpa school which stems from him emerged triumphant in the region through a branch of its sub-school of the Drukpa. Longchenpa founded eight local communities, and some sources speak of this saintly figure also leaving behind a son. The bridges of Thangtong Gyelpo were all standing until recently, and the descendants of his local disciple Dewa Zangpo were still to be found. While the memory of Drukpa Kunley's mad but sacred exploits became totally mythologized, those claiming to be his progeny rose to political prominence in the seventeenth and eighteenth centuries. In many ways besides these, the effect of religious and cultural penetration from the north in the eleventh to seventeenth centuries remains to this day. But the examples given here only derive from the achievements of the great and famous; the cumulative impact of the activities of many hundreds of lesser lamas whose names and schools are also known must have far exceeded the total impact even of these major figures. One effect of their efforts must surely have been the steady spread of lines of communication not only across the natural borders of the Himalayas but also laterally to link up some of the major valleys.

The Nyingmapa school which claims historical priority over all other orders but which never won concerted institutional authority became widely established and remains so to this day. It is best represented in Bhutan by the figure of the "text-discoverer" Pemalingpa (1450-1521), from whom most of the religious nobility of

Table 1

Families of the religious nobility of central and eastern Bhutan claiming descent from Pemalingpa

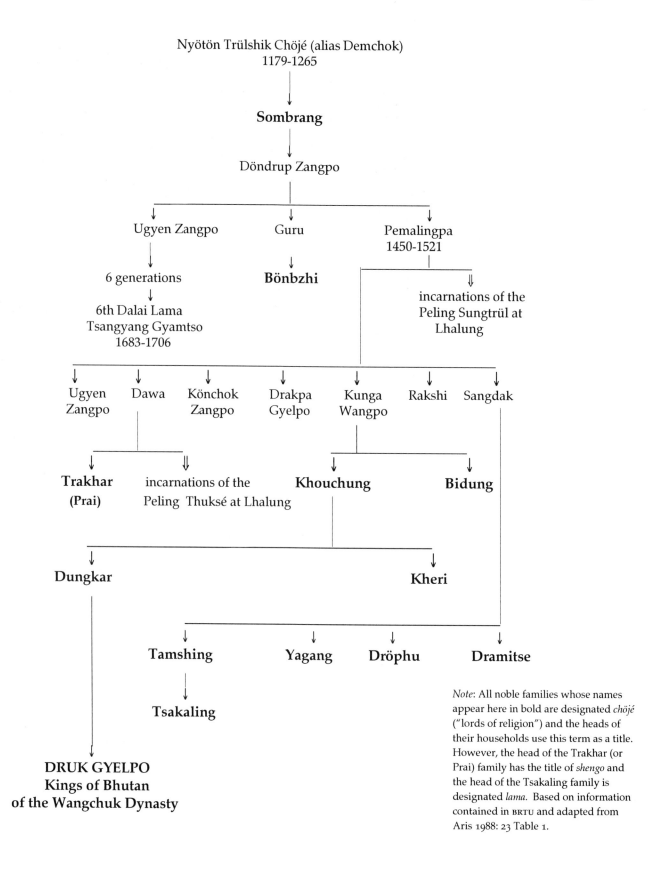

Nyötön Trülshik Chöjé (alias Demchok)
1179-1265

Sombrang

Döndrup Zangpo

Ugyen Zangpo | Guru | Pemalingpa 1450-1521

6 generations → 6th Dalai Lama Tsangyang Gyamtso 1683-1706

Bönbzhi

incarnations of the Peling Sungtrül at Lhalung

Ugyen Zangpo | Dawa | Könchok Zangpo | Drakpa Gyelpo | Kunga Wangpo | Rakshi | Sangdak

Trakhar (Prai) | incarnations of the Peling Thuksé at Lhalung | **Khouchung** | **Bidung**

Dungkar | **Kheri**

Tamshing | **Yagang** | **Dröphu** | **Dramitse**

Tsakaling

DRUK GYELPO Kings of Bhutan of the Wangchuk Dynasty

Note: All noble families whose names appear here in bold are designated *chöjé* ("lords of religion") and the heads of their households use this term as a title. However, the head of the Trakhar (or Prai) family has the title of *shengo* and the head of the Tsakaling family is designated *lama*. Based on information contained in BRTU and adapted from Aris 1988: 23 Table 1.

A fine example of a Buddhist "gateway" stupa (chöten) situated in a densely wooded side valley overlooking the main valley of Ha in western Bhutan. A mandala painted on the ceiling inside confers blessings upon travellers who take the path leading through the stupa. (Photo: A.J. Hopkinson, private collection)

central and eastern Bhutan, including the future royal family, claim descent.[4] The Kathogpa school of eastern Tibet operated from within the Nyingmapa and established an early branch in Bhutan. The Lhapa, who had close links with the Drikhungpa sub-order of the Kagyüpa, maintained a lineage that gained both religious and secular control of parts of western Bhutan. So also to varying degrees did the minor schools of the Barawa, the Nenyingpa and also the Chakzampa mentioned above. Of importance too was the Sakyapa, the school whose leaders functioned as viceroys of Tibet under Mongol patronage in the thirteenth and fourteenth centuries. However, their involvement in the area of what became Bhutan did not entail its political subordination to Mongol or Tibetan rule. The same holds for the few monasteries of the Gelukpa

"Yellow Hat" school which became established in the region before that school won supremacy in Tibet in 1642 under the Fifth Dalai Lama.

Of ultimately far greater importance for Bhutan than any of these was the Drukpa sub-order of the Kagyüpa, with the principal seat of its main branch established at the monastery of Ralung in the Tibetan province of Tsang. Named Drukpa after its first community founded at the monastery of Druk or "Thunder-Dragon", and given this name because thunder was heard during its consecration, the school was ruled by a line of hereditary prince-abbots who developed very close contacts with the future area of Bhutan. As we shall see, it was upon the basis of the many Drukpa monasteries founded in the region that the eighteenth in the line of prince-abbots, Shabdrung Ngawang Namgyel (1594-?1651), was able to bring unity to the country for the first time after he arrived there and settled as a refugee in 1616. It is for this reason that the same term Drukpa later came to be applied not only to the adherents of the order but also to the inhabitants of the country. The country itself came to be called Drukyul, "The Land of the Drukpa Order", often fancifully rendered as "The Land of the Thunder-Dragon". The much earlier term for the country, Lho, which means simply "The South", is still heard today, often in the form "The Southern Drukpa", Lhodruk. Another early term, Lhomön Khazhi, "The Southern Mön Country of Four Approaches",[5] is no longer used except in referring to pre-unification Bhutan. (Mön here is a general term used by Tibetans for many Himalayan regions inhabited by non-Indo-Aryans.) "Bhutan" itself is something of an Anglo-Indian misnomer, deriving from Bhotanta, an old Indian term for Tibet.

It would be wrong to conclude from the picture conveyed above that a movement of southward transmission from Tibet fell into an empty religious void or even that the traditions of Tibet wholly supplanted or displaced existing traditions and institutions. The widespread survival in Bhutan today of many local cults dedicated to placating and worshipping indigenous spirits, rites which long predate the later influence from the north, suggests that in fact several distinct religions manage to coexist although they are not formally differentiated or seen to oppose each other. Lay mediums, both male and female, of a quasi-shamanistic character are found acting as oracles in villages throughout the country. Elsewhere pre-Buddhist priests called *phajo* are active. In some areas the annual supplication of a mountain deity by the whole community is of primary importance. Every valley has its guardian divinity, some even still worshipped with blood sacrifices though they act as protectors of the Buddhist faith. Certain cults are found unique to a single village. At this level the cultural life of the country mirrors the fragmented linguistic picture, itself the product of geographical barriers that were for so long insurmountable. If one adds to this the complex pantheon and many alternative soteriologies available within Mahayana Buddhism as received in full in Bhutan, then one begins to gain an impression of the overall richness and diversity of the country's spiritual traditions.

Much of the real stuff of history both before and after the unification of the seventeenth century lies hidden and obscured beneath the overlay of religion, which is highly selective in what it records for posterity. The foundations of secular life —

The main Himalayan range looking north from Dungshing Gang, "The Fir Tree Mountain", south of Tongsa and west of the Mangdelung valley in central Bhutan. The mountain is the residence of the local protective deity Jowo Dungshing, "The Fir Lord", who is looked on with great reverence and some apprehension by the local population. (Photo: G. Sherriff, Royal Botanic Gardens, Edinburgh)

kinship organization and the structure of the household and the village, the pattern of land use and distribution, the interdependence of agriculture and pastoralism, the contribution of crafts and trade to the local economy, the nature of ethnic and community relations, and above all the attitudes and preconceptions of the laity as a whole—all these are usually projected backwards from the present on the assumption that they have not changed over the centuries. But change, if only of a slow and imperceptible kind, must certainly have taken place. When linked to major transformations in the structure of the state itself, then the speed of change as it affected both the main actors and ordinary people greatly accelerated.

Notes: Chapter One

1. I base these calculations on figures given in the 1992-3 edition of *Pear's Encyclopaedia*. The size of the Tibet Autonomous Region is said there to be 1,217,308 km² and its population 1,970,000, but some doubt attaches to the latter figure.
2. Population figures here and below are taken from Van Driem 1994.
3. The following brief summary is based mainly on Aris 1979, but specialists should also consult the recently published BRGI (see the Bibliographies for Bhutanese title abbreviations). Both works are based on a reading of numerous Bhutanese and Tibetan sources.
4. For my study of Pemalingpa, see Aris 1989; for the affirmation of the traditional view which it elicited, see PGLR. Table 1 (page 22) sets out the interconnections of the religious nobility claiming descent from Pemalingpa.
5. The term is first found in a Tibetan chronicle of the Nyö clan dated 1431, some two centuries before the political unification of Bhutan. Can this be taken to imply at least some degree of internal cohesion before the seventeenth century? The answer must await the discovery of more sources for the early period.

Two
The Shabdrung's Legacy

Shabdrung Ngawang Namgyel will always be remembered as the true founder of Bhutan.[1] Yet it was as a political refugee that he came south in 1616, and he spent the rest of his life there in exile. Although his position as prince-abbot of Ralung was not disputed, his claim to be the incarnation of the great Drukpa scholar Pema Karpo (1527-92) was opposed by the Tibetan ruler of this period, the Desi Tsangpa, who favoured a rival. There were other complications too, and the immediate bone of contention lay, literally, in a bone relic inherited from his forebears but claimed by his enemies. It later became the principal state treasure of Bhutan. Finally, a prophetic dream is said to have come to him during which the guardian deity Mahakala appeared in his raven form to guide him on the path south to Bhutan, which was now offered to him in its entirety by the deity as his "heavenly field" or "religious estate". As we shall see, the same deity appears much later as the kingdom's main protector surmounted on the royal crown of Bhutan, taking possession of its monarch and imbuing him with the character of "defender of the faith".

By the time the Shabdrung (he and his later incarnations are known by this title) died in about 1651 the whole country had come under his personal sway with the exception of the eastern regions that were in the process of being conquered. He had himself masterminded the campaigns which repulsed successive Tibetan invasions mounted against the new state, first by the Tsangpa and after 1642 by the Gelukpa rulers of Tibet. Five factions of local lamas are said to have opposed his rule in Bhutan,

Opposite:
Shabdrung Ngawang Namgyel (1594-
?1651), prince-abbot of the Drukpa Kagyü
school, founder and unifier of Bhutan. A
thangka from the collection of Paro Dzong.

The Head Abbot (Je Khenpo) of Bhutan, left,
supervises the unveiling of the state treasure
of the "Self-Created Karsapani", a relic image
of the bodhisattva Avalokitesvara, in the
presence of the king at Punakha Dzong. The
date is not known. (Photo: private collection
of HRH Ashi Chökyi)

and these too were defeated. In reward for the support and loyalty of his allies among the Drukpa nobility he conferred special privileges and tax exemptions. The magnetism and force of his personality comes across most vividly not in his official biography but instead in a narrative left behind by a Portuguese Jesuit who met him early in his career in 1627.[2] At that time the submission made to him by the inhabitants of the region was of a voluntary nature, encouraged more by his growing prestige than by acts of coercion, though doubtless these too later played a part. The effectiveness of his rule was demonstrated before his death by tribute missions from all over the country and by embassies from neighbouring Indian states, Nepal and several Tibetan principalities. Amidst all this activity the Shabdrung still found time for long periods of spiritual retreat. It must have been then that he developed the art of delegating his duties to capable subordinates.

There is no greater reminder of the presence and continuing legacy of the great Shabdrung than the colossal buildings dominating every major valley from which the country is still ruled to this day. The idea of enclosing Buddhist communities that combined both sacred and secular functions within massively constructed fortresses (*dzongs*) was not a new one. Several were founded in the region of western Bhutan in earlier centuries by the powerful Lhapa school.[3] For the Shabdrung it proved the ideal solution to the problem of continuous attack from both inside and outside the country. The fortresses also answered the need to further promulgate and entrench the Drukpa school in centres that could provide strong local administration. By this single measure more than any other, all came into his hands. Paradoxically, although initial unity was achieved by this means, in later times it was these same fortresses which encouraged the tendency towards regionalism and fragmentation. As seats of the powerful provincial governors, they provided the constant backcloth to all the struggles of later centuries.

The first dzong built in 1629 at Simtokha at the lower end of the Thimphu valley was more in the nature of a defended monastic palace for the Shabdrung himself. However, it controlled the road between the seasonal homes of the Wang people, who traditionally moved from their winter villages in Punakha to their summer villages in Thimphu. These two valleys were themselves secured later with the construction of capital fortresses in 1637 and 1641 respectively. Another located at Wangdü Phodrang south of Punakha was built in 1638 in the interval between the construction of the capital dzongs. With the completion in 1645 of the great dzong in the Paro valley, full control was gained over the whole of western Bhutan, the political and cultural heartland of the emerging country. Smaller forts at Gasa and Lingshi near the Tibetan border were built to protect the country from Tibetan invasion, and in the south Daga Dzong was established in 1650.

All the dzongs were built at strategic spots, either at the confluence of rivers or at important crossroads or on hillsides overlooking and commanding the centres of valleys. Many of them have external citadels, round towers which could act as points of final defence if the main dzong were lost to the enemy. All had a secure water supply, sometimes provided by a series of outworks leading down from the fortress

Simtokha Dzong at the lower end of the Thimphu valley, 28 January 1910. Constructed in 1629 by Shabdrung Ngawang Namgyel, this was the first dzong he built in Bhutan. The formal name of the building is Sangak Zabdön Phodrang, "The Palace of the Profound Meaning of Secret Mantras". It was restored in 1671 by the third Druk Desi, Mingyur Tenpa. The more than three hundred slate carvings of Buddhist saints and divinities displayed in the courtyard around the central tower are said to have emitted nectar while being consecrated by the fourth Druk Desi, Tendzin Rabgye (regn. 1680-95). New wall paintings were provided by Shabdrung Jigme Drakpa in 1753. Jigme Namgyel, father of King Ugyen Wangchuk, died here in 1881. (Photo: C Bell, Merseyside County Museums)

The Dzong of Ha, built in the early twentieth century to replace an earlier structure, was the seat of the local administrator known as the Ha Drung (or Drungpa). The office became hereditary in the Dorje family for three generations. Minor functionaries and attendants await the arrival in 1947 of the second king and the British Political Officer, for whom prayer flags have been erected in welcome (Photo: A.J. Hopkinson, private collection)

Drugyel Dzong, "The Fortress of the Drukpa Victory", guarding the northern approach to the Paro valley, in 1905. The central tier (utsé) of temples (left) rises from the inner courtyard. A purely defensive structure lacking a monastic community, the exact date of its construction in the later seventeenth or early eighteenth century is not yet known. The name of the fortress indicates that it was built to commemorate one or several Bhutanese victories over the Tibetans in this period. (Photos: J. C. White, private collection). The armoury of Drugyel Dzong, 1907, (right) with Samten Özer, the Drugyel Dzongpön and a close ally of King Ugyen Wangchuk, seated to the right. (Photo: H. Hyslop, private collection)

to a stream or spring. The fine cantilever bridges with strong bridge-houses at either end which straddle the major rivers in the close vicinity of many dzongs also formed an integral part of their defence. Immediate access to each fortress was gained by a single easily defended gateway leading to the main courtyard. From the beginning it seems the internal layout of every dzong was divided between an ecclesiastical wing occupied by the state monks of the Drukpa school and a civil wing where the business of government was transacted and where the grain tax and other levies raised from the public could be deposited in storerooms. The whole complex was dominated in every case by a tall, usually freestanding structure containing a set of temples on every floor. Thus the secular triumph of the Drukpa theocracy was actualized in a concrete and unambiguous form that all could see from miles around. The motto adopted by the new state in the words "The Glorious Drukpa Victorious in All Directions" must have struck a universal chord far removed from rhetoric and panegyric, for the victory lay there before all eyes.

The subjugation of central and eastern Bhutan was not the direct achievement of the Shabdrung but rather of the man he appointed as governor of Tongsa, Mingyur Tenpa. The chronology of the campaign to subdue all the communities of the east is uncertain but it seems to have begun before the death of the Shabdrung and completed by 1655. The fortunes of the campaign were faithfully recorded in a vivid chronicle that has survived.[4] Local jealousies and rivalries among the nobility of Bumthang and the clan rulers of the east were consciously exploited to the advantage of the invading force under the command of monk generals appointed from Tongsa. The speed of the campaign gathered momentum as more and more communities scrambled to make their submission. Six great dzongs were built in turn at Byagar, Lhuntse, Tashiyangtse, Shongar, Tashigang and Shemgang. It was only the power of the new Gelukpa government of Tibet under the Fifth Dalai Lama expanding south into the so-called Mönyul Corridor just east of Bhutan that contained the eastward movement of the Drukpa government and brought it to a halt. The border has remained much the same ever since. A similar expansion to the west into the area now occupied by Kalimpong took place in the 1670s, again masterminded by Mingyur Tenpa.

Little is known about how local administration was imposed after the construction of the dzongs. Taxes were raised only in kind in the form of grain and, in some areas, woven cloth, paper and other local products. Some of these levies, particularly the harvest tax of the autumn, were termed "initiation fees" (*wangyön*), the underlying theory holding that these went to support the monk communities which in turn conferred spiritual blessings and protection on the public. In fact the system of taxation as a whole consisted in a recycling of surplus wealth to support the country conceived as one huge monastic estate. Labour services, termed *ula* (a word of Turkish origin), also had the same ultimate purpose. These provided a fixed workforce to undertake specific tasks for the religious government on a regular or seasonal basis. Such compulsory *corvée* included the transport of government loads, the repair of roads, the construction and maintenance of government buildings, the supply of firewood and the entertainment of officials and guests. Military service at times of war was also

The monastic fortress of Rinpung Dzong in Paro, constructed by Shabdrung Ngawang Namgyel in 1645 on the foundations of the earlier Humrel Dzong, belonging to a branch of the Drukpa nobility. This photograph was taken in 1905, one year before it was burnt down in a fire and subsequently rebuilt. The covered cantilever bridge of Nyamai Zampa in the foreground was destroyed by floods in 1969 and also rebuilt. The restored citadel of Ta Dzong on the hill above, where King Ugyen Wangchuk was incarcerated in his youth, is now the National Museum of Bhutan. (Photo: J. C. White, private collection)

Tashichö Dzong, "The Fortress of Auspic-ious Religion", in the Thimphu valley in 1905, with a cantilever bridge over the Thinchu river in the foreground. From the time of its construction by Shabdrung Ngawang Namgyel in 1641 this building served as the country's summer capital. It was built on the foundations of an older fortress known as Dongön (or Donyuk) Dzong belonging to the Lhapa school. The structure was rebuilt from 1962 to 1969 as the main government secretariat of the permanent capital. How-ever, the state monks who occupy part of the fortress continue to migrate to Punakha for the winter. (Photo: J. C. White, private collection)

imposed on the public. Because all these obligations and the need to render taxes in kind fell on individual households, each reckoned as a single taxable unit, they must have acted as a strong deterrent to the creation of new households.

The idea of shared, communal labour, however, was not alien to society since even today in Bhutanese villages much agricultural and private building work is still done outside the aegis of government on a cooperative basis of reciprocity. Moreover it is certain that many communities had been providing taxes and labour to their individual masters before the unification. The decisive change came when these were instead given to a single recipient in the form of the Drukpa government. It is not clear at what point the further duty to supply sons as state monks and lay servitors was imposed on each household, but this became one of the essential features of the theocracy upon which its strength and continuity depended. The same held true for the provincial magnates established in each dzong since some at least of the tax revenue and labour, not to speak of monks and lay servitors, went to their support instead of to the central government. The apportionment could lead to much dispute.

With only a few minor changes and some additions, the offices created by the founding Shabdrung are essentially those which survive today in the structure of the modern government. The magnates in command of the fortresses in the winter and summer capitals in Punakha and Thimphu, also those located in the outlying provinces, were all called *dzongpöns*, "fort-lords" (now renamed *dzongda*, "fort-masters"), with the exception of the governors of Paro, Tongsa and Daga who were known by the more elevated monastic titles of *Pönlop,* "lord-teacher", or *chila*, "universal lama". Those of Paro and Tongsa are now reserved for the royal family as titular offices, while that of Daga is in abeyance. Beneath each of these magnates were a number of lesser

The great dzong *of Punakha seen from the south in 1906, built at the confluence of the Phochu and Mochu rivers in 1637 by Shabdrung Ngawang Namgyel whose mummified remains are still enshrined in a temple at the top of the central tower. This former winter capital of Bhutan, whose formal name is Dechen Phodrang, "The Palace of Great Bliss", suffered disastrous fires in 1780, 1798, 1802, 1831 and 1849, mainly as a result of the practically continuous civil conflict of this period. Serious damage was also caused by the earthquake of 1897. Each time the* dzong *was rebuilt or repaired by corvée labour to the same basic design. The two bridges visible in this photograph have since been washed away in floods. (Photo: J. C. White, private collection)*

Another view (left) *of Punakha Dzong, this one taken from the northwest in 1910. (Photo: C. Bell. Merseyside County Museums)*

officials who formed their court and who were known by monastic titles such as *zimpön*, "chamberlain", *nyerchen*, "storekeeper", and *drönyer*, "guestmaster". The central government also had a *shung drönyer*, "government guestmaster", whose duties remained vague and undefined, and sometimes a *shung kalön*, "government minister". Later a kind of semi-formalized cabinet came into being composed of the chief officers and magnates of western Bhutan, referred to sometimes as the *lhengye tsokpa*, "the corporate association". At the bottom of the scale were the *drungpa* and minor *Pönlop* in charge of groups of villages or smaller districts, each responsible to a *dzongpön* or major *Pönlop*. Below them stood the common village headmen known as *gap*. The land itself was divided into provincial units and sub-units, and each was given its own administrative designation on a Tibetan model.[5]

The state monks of the two adjoining capital dzongs and of the provinces had their own administration separate from that of the government and headed by a supreme abbot, the *je khenpo*, who supervised the appointment of the provincial abbots as he continues to do to this day. Then as now he came to office by a process of consensus reached among his senior brothers, who looked to age, rank and attainment in making their choice. Beneath him stood four senior "teachers", *lobpön*, who were in charge of tantric ritual, philosophical logic, grammar and chanting. Beneath them a host of minor offices rotated in the community. The state monks of the capitals always claimed formal precedence over their provincial brothers.

Although separated from the business of government, it was from the ranks of the monks that many of the government servants came to hold office, retaining their vows throughout their careers. Certainly at the beginning of the theocracy it seems that all senior officers were fully ordained monks. Later, when appointments were made from among the lay servitors conscripted from villages, these were compelled to take minor vows, assume a monastic name and at least temporarily renounce family life. Even among senior lay government servants of this kind, appointment by seniority acquired as a result of long years of service on a monastic model seems to have been the ideal. Inevitably favour and preference shown to close relatives and followers formed the alternative route to high office. This was so even during the years of the founding Shabdrung, and so the rival precedents of these alternative means of advancement were well established in the opening years of the theocracy.

Another powerful source of influence on secular life stemming from religious values centred on traditional concepts of loyalty. The word for a binding vow (*damtsik*) undertaken during an initiation bestowed by a religious teacher on his disciple came in popular usage to signify the ties of "pure loyalty" (*damtsik tsangma*) which linked a lord, who might yet be a monk, to his sworn follower, whether lay or religious. The personal bonds characterized by such loyalty, having much the same overtones of fear and reward surrounding a tantric initiation, gave rise to a network of competing feudal relations that were both the strength and weakness of the theocracy. When credible figures commanded universal respect and obedience in a manner similar to the Shabdrung himself, much could be achieved. In the frequent absence of such figures, endless imbroglios could and did result.

The dzong of Wangdü Phodrang situated at the confluence of the Phochu-Mochu and Dangchu rivers south of Punakha in 1931. It was built by Shabdrung Ngawang Namgyel in 1638 as the provincial capital of the Shar district. The beautiful cantilever bridge with its central island below the fortress is no longer standing. (Photo: J.L.R. Weir, Royal Geographical Society)

In the same way that the achievements of the first Shabdrung have remained before everyone's eyes down to the present, stamped indelibly on the landscape and on human institutions, so also the circumstances under which he chose to die closely determined the shape of history for the next two and a half centuries. Although he had a son, Jampel Dorje, born before he took his final vows, the Shabdrung never seems to have designated him as his heir. While a lineage of Jampel Dorje's own incarnations ultimately became established, none of them succeeded in replacing the founder in a convincing manner.

The last we hear of the Shabdrung is in 1651 when, at the age of fifty-eight by local reckoning, he decided to enter into an indefinite spiritual retreat, immuring himself for this purpose in his apartment in the main tower of Punakha Dzong. We are told that he entrusted the whole business of government to his precentor Tendzin Drugye, who thereafter ruled until 1656 as the first Druk Desi or regent.[6] He gave as his reason for this decision the need for complete solitude in order to devote himself to magical rituals intended to counter the threat of yet another invasion from Tibet. A corresponding passage in the autobiography of his enemy the Fifth Dalai Lama claims that at this time the Shabdrung actually died as a result of the lama's own acts of magic performed against him in Lhasa.[7] Whatever view we take of these claims, it seems likely the Shabdrung died quite early during the retreat. However, since the date is not known for certain it is safer to keep a question mark attached to the year of his demise.

Although the fact of his death was known or suspected at the Tibetan court, in Bhutan the fiction of the Shabdrung's continuing life was maintained for a period of up to fifty-four years until it was finally revealed in about 1705.[8] This strange device was made possible by several factors: the pretence of passing food through a trapdoor, the forging of his commands on a slate, belief in the enormous longevity of saints, the notion that even after physical death a lama's consciousness is still present until he chooses to expel it, the knowledge of the same ruse having been used to conceal the deaths of important lamas in the past, and perhaps above all the realization that if it were known that the Shabdrung had died then the new state he had created might quickly dissolve. There is some evidence indicating that towards the end of the period the pretence depended heavily on belief in the dead lama's "unreleased consciousness" still being present. However, the key source says in so many words that in c. 1705: "from the force of certain circumstances it became necessary to disclose the secret concerning the retreat".[9] By that time six regents had come and gone and various "representatives" (*gyeltsap*) of the founding Shabdrung had been elevated to rule in his place. The secret itself must have been shared between them and a small coterie of officials, the chief of them being the personal chamberlain of the dead founder. Even today in Punakha a chamberlain known as the *machen zimpön* is still appointed to watch over the remains, which have somehow survived no less than five disastrous fires in Punakha Dzong.[10]

The way ahead was clear at last to finding the Shabdrung's legitimate successor in the form of a recognized reincarnation, but there were several possible candidates. Over half a century after the secret had been disclosed and the dead lama's consciousness had finally departed in search of a new embodiment, the author of the first official

The monastic fortress of Chökhor Rabtentse in Tongsa and its main entrance, 1905. This dzong was constructed by the first Tongsa Pönlop, Mingyur Tenpa, in the 1650s on the site of a Buddhist retreat centre called Mön Drubdé founded a century earlier by a hierarch of the Drukpa Kagyü school, Ngagi Wangchuk (1517-54). The building came to serve as the provincial capital for all the districts of central and eastern Bhutan, and it later provided the power base for the emergence of the Bhutanese monarchy. The titular office of Tongsa Pönlop became hereditary within the Bhutanese royal family in the same way as the title of Prince of Wales was reserved for the heir apparent of the British royal family. (Photo: J.C. White, private collection)

A more distant view (below) of the dzong at Tongsa, 1931. (Photo: J.L.R. Weir, Royal Geographical Society)

history of Bhutan, the *lHo'i chos-'byung* wrote: "Now if I am to relate in truth what I have heard and come to believe — previously, at the time when the secret of the Shabdrung's retreat was disclosed, as soon as he arose from the meditative absorption in which he had been residing, three rays of light issued from his body, speech and mind and these came down at three places: Sikkim, Daganang [in southern Bhutan] and [the region called] Dranang in the Ü province of Tibet".[11] The child born to the ruler of Sikkim embodied the "physical principle" of the Shabdrung but was never brought to Bhutan and the line was never established. The "verbal principle" was found in Cholé Namgyel (1708-36) born in Daganang, and the "mental principle" in Jigme Drakpa (1724-61) born in Dranang. But the situation was even more complex.

The first forty years of the eighteenth century saw rival factions in western Bhutan supporting no less than five alternative "representatives" of the founding Shabdrung.[12] Each faction sought hegemony over the theocracy by advancing the claims of his candidate as the "true" incarnation of the founder. The extremely tangled struggles of the period came to a head when one side appealed in 1730 to the Tibetan ruler Pholhané (regn. 1729-35) for military assistance. This resulted in the only successful full-scale invasion of Bhutan by Tibet, and the last one that ever occurred. The campaign was in fact brought to an end more by an appeal for peace issued by the leading Tibetan lamas of the day than by outright conquest. A temporary truce provided for a division of the country into two states, each with a rival incarnation at its head to justify its legitimacy. Both sides then appealed in 1733 to the authorities in Lhasa, one side to the Tibetan ruler Pholhané and the other to the Manchu *amban*. A cease-fire was established by Sino-Tibetan mediation, and both sides were then authorized to submit the case to the emperor. Emissaries from both sides were duly despatched to the imperial court in Peking in 1734. Final peace was secured not only by imperial arbitration but also by the convenient deaths of some of the main Bhutanese protagonists in the conflict. The settlement was instrumental in reunifying the country under one theoretical head of state, the "mind incarnation" or "mental principle" of the founding Shabdrung (the Dharma Raja of the British records). The submission to Chinese mediation entailed a theoretical loss of ultimate sovereignty. At the same time it led to the establishment of formal diplomatic relations with Tibet that helped to guarantee the fact of Bhutanese independence. The word for the "annual tribute" (*lo-phyag*, pronounced "lochak") which the Bhutanese representative in Lhasa was meant to pay to the authorities there, and through them eventually to China, was at some time quietly replaced by the Bhutanese with a homophone meaning "annual mission" (*lo-chag*).

Not one of the six Shabdrungs who incarnated the mind of the founder wielded anything like his personal authority. Like the seven incarnations of the Dalai Lama who followed the masterful fifth embodiment, they were little more than ciphers in the hands of those who had secular power. In fact two of the Shabdrungs were compelled to serve very briefly and ineffectively as Druk Desi, combining their role with that of their own regents.[13] Two of the Shabdrung's "verbal incarnations" also had to serve in this way as regents,[14] likewise two of the incarnations of the most effective of the Shabdrung's earlier "representatives", Tendzin Rabgye, who had occupied the

Byagar Dzong, "The Fortress of the White Bird", provincial capital of the Bumthang district. This was the first of five fortresses built in eastern Bhutan during a campaign led by the first Tongsa Pönlop in the early 1650s. The round tower on the left has a purely defensive purpose, while the square tower on the right contains Buddhist temples. (Photo: Anthony Aris 1971)

Lhuntse Dzong, provincial capital of the Kurtö district in northeast Bhutan, 1949. The district is the ancestral homeland of the kings of Bhutan, who descend from the noble family of the Dungkar Chöjé. (Photo: G. Sherriff, Royal Botanic Gardens, Edinburgh)

regent's throne in 1680-95.[15] Despite these and other endless problems the line of the Shabdrungs supplied, albeit passively, the symbolic heads of state and provided legitimacy to the theocratic state as a whole.

Some quite long interludes of peace coinciding with the longer reigns of the more effective regents allowed attention to be given to questions of internal administration and to developing fruitful foreign contacts. Relations with Kuch Bihar had begun on a cordial note in the time of the founding Shabdrung but deteriorated in the next century in a way that brought the Bhutanese into contact with the British for the first time, as we shall see. The external recognition won by the first Shabdrung from various Tibetan authorities who opposed the rise of Gelukpa power in the centre of Tibet came to be formalized later when Bhutan was awarded monastic fiefs in the area of Kailash, Ladakh, Zangskar and Lahul. The appointment of a monastic official called the Gangri Lama by Bhutan to control the large estates given to it in the Kailash region began in the reign of the regent Mingyur Tenpa (1667-80) and continued down to the fall of Tibet to Communist China in the 1950s. The deputing of a regular emissary from Bhutan to the Tibetan court, known as the Drukpai Lochak, also continued from the settlement of the 1730s until 1959. Under the same regent, Mingyur Tenpa, Bhutan was presented with monastic estates by the Rajas of Gorkha, who won total ascendancy over Nepal a century later. Successive grants were affirmed in copperplates, and the appointment by Bhutan of another monastic official called the Balpö Lama to control these Nepalese monasteries and their land, also to hold the stewardship of the great Swayambhunath temple in the Kathmandu valley, continued down to the 1860s when they were withdrawn from Bhutanese hands. To the south in Assam the Bhutanese court maintained good relations with successive rulers of the Ahom empire from at least the middle years of the eighteenth century and probably from much earlier. Under the longest reigning regent Sherab Wangchuk, who ruled from 1744 to 1763, friendly contact was also established with the Nawab of Bengal.

In 1765, two years after the retirement of Sherab Wangchuk as regent, the Bhutanese began interfering in the succession to the throne of Kuch Bihar, whose military commander then appealed to the British for help in driving out the Bhutanese troops posted there who were also making incursions into neighbouring territories, Sikkim included.[16] By 1772 rival claimants to the Kuch Bihar throne were calling on the British and Bhutanese for assistance. The first Anglo-Bhutan war followed and in the course of it the Bhutanese were expelled from their border fortresses at Dalingkha, Chichacotta and Pasakha. The Gorkha ruler of Nepal, concerned about the rising power of the British, and the Bhutanese authorities both then turned for mediation to the Panchen Lama of Tibet, who interceded with Warren Hastings, Governor of Bengal, on behalf of Bhutan, which he claimed fictitiously as a vassal of Tibet. Under the resulting Anglo-Bhutan treaty of 1774 those lands appropriated from Bhutan during the 1772 campaign were restored, the Raja of Kuch Bihar and his brother who had been captured by the Bhutanese were released, trade was restored, and an annual tribute to be paid to Kuch Bihar by Bhutan was fixed at five "Tangun" ponies.

Members of the second British mission sent to Bhutan by Warren Hastings in 1783 and led by Samuel Turner. The mounted figure is probably Turner himself. He is accompanied by an attendant wearing the obsolete form of dress known as the pakhi. *Detail of a recently discovered watercolour painted in the Chukha district by Samuel Davis, who accompanied the mission as surveyor. (Courtesy: The Lawrie Group Collection)*

Warren Hastings seized the opportunity afforded by his contact with the Panchen Lama to send a number of missions both to Tibet and Bhutan with a view to opening up trade and discovering all he could about the countries of the north. Missions were led by George Bogle in 1774, Alexander Hamilton in 1776-7 and Samuel Turner in 1783.[17] For close on a decade thereafter a substantial increase of trans-Himalayan trade took place between Bengal and Tibet until brought to an end by the Sino-Nepalese war of 1792. Trade with Bhutan also increased in this period and continued sporadically into the nineteenth century. Of more lasting value were the vivid and sympathetic accounts of Bhutan and Tibet written by the members of these missions. In Bhutan's case the published reports afford a total contrast with those left behind by the British emissaries of the nineteenth century. These later ones were composed against a background of deteriorating relations along the whole Indo-Bhutanese frontier, constant civil wars in Bhutan, and a hardening of imperial and cultural attitudes on the part of the British. The relatively minor insurrections witnessed by both Bogle and Turner while they were in Bhutan had more the flavour of ritual encounters than major battles. Both were depicted by them as short-lived affairs aimed at reinstating Zhidar, the regent who had embroiled Bhutan in the affairs of Kuch Bihar and who had in the meantime fled to Tibet. Certainly they appeared to do little to interrupt the work transacted at the Bhutanese court or the daily life of the valleys visited by these missions. Nevertheless the regent of the period, Tritrül Jigme Senge (regn. 1776-88), who was the second incarnation of Tendzin Rabgye (1638-96), eventually retired and left on pilgrimage to Tibet, wearied with the continuing rebellions in support of his exiled predecessor.[18]

The thirty-seven years between the retirement of Jigme Senge in 1788 and the birth in 1825 of the Black Regent Jigme Namgyel, father of Bhutan's first king, provide a foretaste of the troubles facing the country throughout his youth and maturity, waves of insurrection in which he played the fullest part and from which he and his heirs were to emerge triumphant.[19] Fourteen regents fill these years, starting with the nineteenth in the line, Druk Tendzin alias Sangye Tendzin (regn. 1788-92). He came to the throne from the position of Punakha Dzongpön when the elders of the Wang people appealed to the state monks to find a convincing replacement for his predecessor. An outbreak of smallpox, traditionally blamed on the evil karma deriving from previous acts of violence, could only be brought to a halt by the appointment of a good ruler. This regent conformed in all traditional respects to that ideal, completing numerous acts of religious merit which marked him out as the potential equal of the great thirteenth in the line of regents. But he died in office after only four years on the throne. He was followed by his brother Tashi Namgyel alias Sonam Gyeltsen (regn. 1792-6), who shared the throne for some time with the precentor of the state monks known as Umdzé Chapchapa.[20] Sonam Gyeltsen retired in 1796 when faced with a rebellion apparently led by his own chamberlain Druk Namgyel (regn. 1796-1803). It was under this regent that Punakha Dzong was rebuilt after a fire and many of the finest Bhutanese blockprints of Buddhist classics and works of history were completed.[21] He was in turn killed in 1803 by his predecessor Sonam Gyeltsen, who now reoccupied the regent's throne till 1805. The followers of the murdered regent then proceeded to burn down Punakha Dzong once again, but this ruler succeeded in rebuilding it within one year before dying in office. He then was followed for less than a year by his nephew Sangye Tendzin, who shared the throne very briefly with the fifteen-year-old Shabdrung Jigme Drakpa the Second (1791-1830). Sangye Tendzin was forced to resign in the face of a further revolt led by Tsaphukpa Dorje, the Tongsa Pönlop, who long coveted the throne. The regent was not followed by the ambitious Pönlop, who only briefly achieved his aims later, but rather by the precentor known as Umdzé Parop (regn.

Tashigang Dzong, easternmost of the Bhutanese fortresses and the last to be constructed in the campaign of the 1650s. (Photo: G. Sherriff, Royal Botanic Gardens, Edinburgh)

1805-7) whom the state monks managed to get appointed. However, the Pönlop's rebellion continued, to be temporarily halted on the intercession of the head abbot, who forged a settlement that allowed a Tibetan lama, Pema Chödrak, to share the regent's throne with the precentor. But the lama and the precentor in turn fell out, the latter retiring after further ecclesiastical mediation in 1807, leaving the former to continue to hold the throne until 1808, when he was murdered by one Norbu of Tsamang. Norbu had first tried unsuccessfully to persuade one of the three highest lamas of this period, the Tritrül Tsultrim Drakpa (1790-1820), to seize the throne and give him the office of Shung Drönyer, but the lama had a frightful prophetic dream. The Mochu river of Punakha had dried up leaving all the fishes stranded, and into the space it had occupied there came swirling a great sea of blood that became the playground of evil spirits bearing weapons. The drying up of the river foretold the death of the lama regent Pema Chödrak, and the sea of blood the long feud which was now to break out.

Tsultrim Drakpa was after all prevailed upon to take the throne in 1808, but before long he and others succeeded in persuading the Shabdrung Jigme Drakpa against his will to occupy it, now for the second time. Recent incumbents, it was argued, "had been devoid of the eye of wisdom which can distinguish between what is religion and what is not religion, and they had brought immense suffering to their subjects by pursuing their own selfish desires". But when Tsultrim Drakpa's attendants heard that their master was to vacate the throne in favour of the Shabdrung, they planned their own insurrection. To make matters even more complicated the followers of Yeshé Gyeltsen, the "verbal incarnation" of the Shabdrung, installed him in Thimphu as a rival regent to the Shabdrung in Punakha. On the side of the "verbal incarnation" were lined up the Pönlops of Paro, Tongsa and Daga, also the Thimphu Dzongpön. In support of the "mental incarnation" stood the Dzongpöns of Punakha and Wangdü Phodrang and others.[22] After a number of engagements the headmen of the three major western valleys of Paro, Thimphu and Punakha turned to the retired and ruling head abbots of the state monks to use their good offices to mediate a formal settlement. This was reached in 1809 and provided for a joint regency by the rival incarnations. However, trouble continued to flare up. Shabdrung Tsultrim Drakpa, the "mental" embodiment, retired first but his chamberlain was soon killed by the Punakha Dzongpön, who in turn was murdered with his whole family by forces still loyal to the Shabdrung. Three or four years later the "verbal incarnation" also retired and departed for his seat in Paro, thus leaving the throne vacant to be occupied by the man regarded as the evil genius behind all this strife, Tsaphukpa Dorje, the Tongsa Pönlop. He succeeded in 1811 but only reigned for a few months before he in turn was killed by the Thimphu Dzongpön, Sonam Drugye, who thus came to power in 1812 and held it through an uprising of his predecessor's followers until he retired sick in 1817. It was during his reign in 1815 that Kishen Kant Bose, Bengali agent to the British, came to Bhutan and wrote a detailed report.[23] It helps to throw light on the pattern of revolt and counter-revolt which fill these years:

> The intestine broils, which so frequently occur in Bootan, are usually occasioned either by the Deb Raja doing something contrary to custom, or by his remaining too long in his office, in which cases the Zimpens [Dzongpöns], Pillos [Pönlops], &c. assemble and require him to resign, and in the event of a refusal battle ensues. If the Deb Raja resigns, or is defeated, the assembly, with the consent of the Dhurma Raja [the Shabdrung], choose some one of themselves to succeed him of the Sha [Shar] or Waa [Wang] tribe, and who has already attained the dignity of Zimpé or Pillo. These battles always take place at the annual poojahs in Assin and Phalgoon [the festivals of sacred dance held at Punakha in the winter and at Thimphu in the summer]. If there is no person in the assembly fit for the office of the Deb Raja, they select a Gylong [*gelong*, monk] ...[24]

> ... the Deb Raja strives, by removals and changes at the annual festivals, to fill the principal offices with persons devoted to his interest. The Booteahs are full of fraud and intrigue, and would not scruple to murder their own father or brother to serve their interest; but what is wonderful is that the slaves are most faithful and obedient to their masters, and are ready to sacrifice their limbs or lives in their service; while their masters, on the other hand, use them most cruelly, often inflicting upon them horrid punishment and frequently mutilating them.[25]

46

The processional band of the Paro Pönlop, Paro, 1931. These part-time musicians were drawn from a community of slaves descended from Indian captives brought to Bhutan in earlier centuries to serve the government and private families in perpetuity as menials. Their distinctive music, known by the onomatopoeic name of banga-tringtring, *and played on drums, gongs and oboes, traditionally accompanied the highest officers of state or their guests on journeys. All slaves received their manumission from the third king Jigme Dorje Wangchuk in 1956. (Photo: J.L.R. Weir, private collection)*

In fact there are no recorded cases of patricide or fratricide in the surviving records, and the "slaves" referred to are simply the lay followers of the rulers and magnates, quite different from the genuine slave class descended from Indian captives. Despite these reservations the account has value for the way it underlines not only the endemic nature of political strife under the theocracy but also the way that strife was always resolved, albeit temporarily, either by a process of corporate decision-making on the part of the "assembly" of senior officers (the *lhengye tsokpa*) or else by monastic mediation. The notion clearly existed that power was not to remain in the hands of any person longer than a certain unspecified number of years, perhaps three or four. This unwritten convention was clearly intended as a check to the development of an absolute and enduring autocracy that might deny others the fruits of power. However, the system also locked the state into cycles of conflict since practically every incumbent to the thrones of the regency and of the provincial magnates sought to test the limits of the convention.

Returning to the story of the contested regency, in 1817 Tendzin Drukdra came to the throne with monastic backing from his earlier posts of Punakha Dzongpön and Gongzim (chamberlain to the preceding regent). The Tongsa Pönlop[26] of this time planned his almost obligatory revolt by trying to win over the Shabdrung, but the latter wrote in response: "Even if victory is won now it will be the cause of being reborn in hell later, so don't wage war!" The Pönlop refused to listen and invested Punakha. The state monks then implored the Shabdrung to mediate but before he arrived with the aim of doing so the Pönlop was killed. There was nothing for the Shabdrung to do but perform the funeral and return to his retreat. Tendzin Drukdra then resigned as regent, "feeling total renunciation for worldly glory, perceiving it like the illusions of a dream", and left for a monastery. He was followed by Purgyel alias Chökyi Gyeltsen (regn. 1822-31), a monk who had risen to the post of Thimphu Dzongpön. True to form, he lasted only until Dorje Namgyel, the Tongsa Pönlop and nephew of his predecessor, unseated him with the help of troops sent by the Manchu amban in Lhasa.

In the meantime the man had been born who was destined to break the perpetual cycle of conflict by participating in it with a total ruthlessness that left almost no rivals. It is to his story that we now turn.

Notes: Chapter Two

1. The following is a summary of Aris 1979: 203 *et seq.*
2. The narrative is translated in Aris 1986: Text 4.
3. For a list of the Lhapa *dzongs*, see BRGI: 75.
4. See Aris 1986: Text 2.
5. These were: "The Thirteen *Dar-theg* of *Thed* (Upper Punakha)", "The Eight *Dar* of Shar (the Wangdü Phodrang district), "The Eight Great *Tsho* of Wang (Thimphu and Lower Punakha), "The Six *Bar-skor Tsho* of Paro", "The Eight Great *Yul-gling* of Daga", "The Upper *mKhar* and Lower *mKhar* of Gasa", "The Three *Gling* of Chapcha", "The Four *Tsho* of Mangdé", "The Four *sDe* of Bumthang", "The Four *mDo* of Kur(tö)", "The Five *Tsho* of (Tashi) Yangtse", "The Three *Ris* of Kheng", "The Seven *Tsho* of Shongar", "The Ten *Tsho* of Tashigang" and "The Three *mDo* of Khaling (and) Dungsam". The untranslated words in italics, rendered here in transliteration, are all variants for "district".
6. The British later knew the regents by the title of Deb Raja. "Deb" here is the common Bhutanese contraction of Depa (spelt *sde-pa*), the alternative term for Desi (spelt *sde-srid*) and conflated in Indian usage with Dev, "god". The title Desi was used by other potentates including Sangye Gyamtso, the famous regent of the Fifth Dalai Lama of Tibet.
7. I owe this information to Ariane Macdonald (Spanien) but have not yet been able to check the passage myself.
8. See Aris 1979: 233 *et seq.*
9. *Ibid.* 254.
10. During the civil wars the besieging troops are said to have always allowed the state monks to remove the Shabdrung's remains and other sacred objects to safety before setting fire to the dzong.
11. Slightly adapted from the translation in Aris 1979: 258.
12. This paragraph is based on the first of four brief case histories of mediation presented in Aris 1994, derived in turn from the detailed study of this most confusing period in Imaeda 1987: 187-230.

13. Jigme Drakpa the Second (1791-1830, regn. 1810-11) and Jigme Norbu (1831-61, regn. 1850-?2).
14. Yeshé Gyeltsen (1781-1830, regn. 1811-15) and Yeshé Ngödrup (1851-1917, regn. 1903-5).
15. Jigme Senge (1742-89, regn. 1776-88) and Tsultrim Drakpa (1790-1820, regn. 1809-10).
16. The best summaries of Anglo-Bhutanese relations which begin in this period are to be found in Collister 1987 and Singh 1988. Labh 1974 and Kohli 1982 should also be consulted.
17. For the report of Bogle, see Markham 1879. Turner's is contained in his publication of 1800. The diary and drawings of Samuel Davis, who accompanied Turner, are presented in Aris 1982. Hamilton does not seem to have left an account of his two missions to Bhutan. For an illuminating study of the way the British testimonies of the eighteenth and nineteenth centuries tie in with the Bhutanese sources, see Imaeda 1986.
18. During his reign Bhutanese complicity with Nepalese territorial ambitions in Sikkim had been secured with the promise of further land grants. The Bhutanese authorities seem to have been content to play both sides at the same time, for they offered some degree of succour to the defeated Sikkimese king Tendzin Namgyel.
19. The following summary of the reigns of the regents is based on BRGI 382-430.
20. The Balpö Lama appointed at this time to take control of Bhutan's monastic estates in Nepal is said to have saved some Nepalese soldiers from being killed by the inhabitants of Kyirong in Tibet, and he later helped to secure favourable terms for the Nepalese after their defeat by China in 1792.
21. Druk Namgyel is also remembered for refusing to give permission to Nepalese troops to invade Assam through Bhutanese territory.
22. Lobpön Pemala takes pains to point out that the three lamas who occupied the regency in this period were themselves unambitious for power. He maintains it was only their followers who embroiled them in strife, and they did this because they saw their status and benefit as wholly dependent on that of their lamas whom they regarded as "wish-fulfilling gems". Such followers were more than willing to pursue the secular advancement of their lamas to the point of death itself. BRGI 420.
23. See *Political Missions to Bootan*, 187-206. For the background to this mission, see Singh 1988: 298; Collister 1987: 44-50.
24. *Political Missions to Bootan*, 196.
25. *Ibid.*, 201-2.
26. It seems he is remembered only by his nickname which is spelt dPral-ba or dPral-chung and may mean "Baldy" or "Little Baldy".

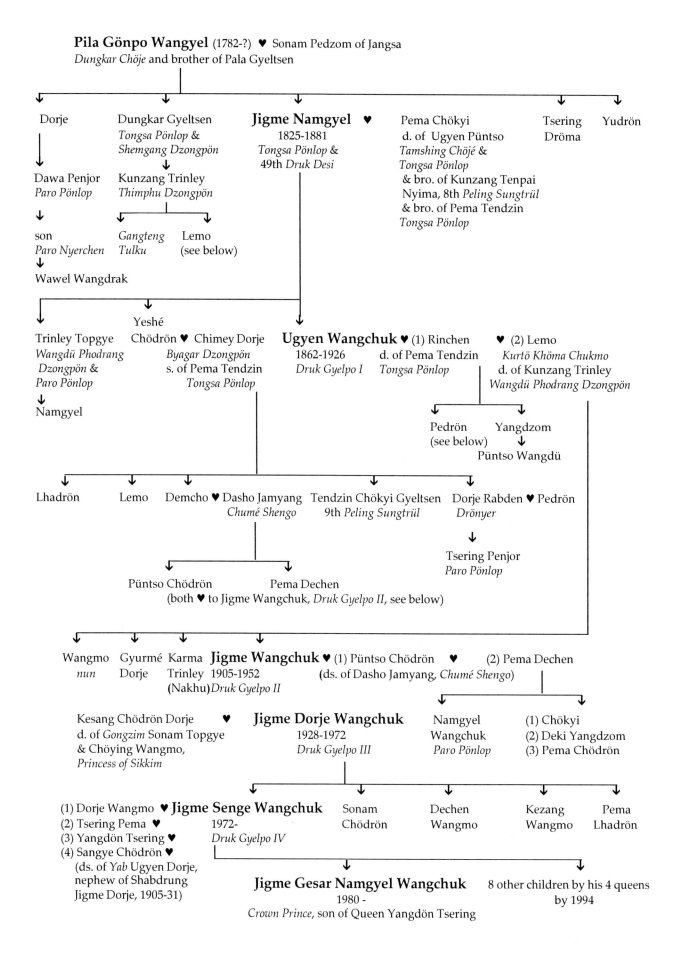

Pila Gönpo Wangyel (1782-?) ♥ Sonam Pedzom of Jangsa
Dungkar Chöje and brother of Pala Gyeltsen

Dorje

Dawa Penjor
Paro Pönlop

son
Paro Nyerchen

Wawel Wangdrak

Dungkar Gyeltsen
Tongsa Pönlop &
Shemgang Dzongpön

Kunzang Trinley
Thimphu Dzongpön

Gangteng   Lemo
Tulku   (see below)

Jigme Namgyel ♥
1825-1881
Tongsa Pönlop &
49th *Druk Desi*

Pema Chökyi
d. of Ugyen Püntso
Tamshing Chöjé &
Tongsa Pönlop
& bro. of Kunzang Tenpai
Nyima, 8th *Peling Sungtrül*
& bro. of Pema Tendzin
Tongsa Pönlop

Tsering   Yudrön
Dröma

Yeshé
Trinley Topgye   Chödrön ♥ Chimey Dorje   **Ugyen Wangchuk ♥** (1) Rinchen   ♥ (2) Lemo
Wangdü Phodrang   *Byagar Dzongpön*   1862-1926   d. of Pema Tendzin   *Kurtö Khöma Chukmo*
Dzongpön &   s. of Pema Tendzin   *Druk Gyelpo I*   *Tongsa Pönlop*   d. of Kunzang Trinley
Paro Pönlop   *Tongsa Pönlop*   *Wangdü Phodrang Dzongpön*

Namgyel

Pedrön   Yangdzom
(see below)
Püntso Wangdü

Lhadrön   Lemo   Demcho ♥ Dasho Jamyang   Tendzin Chökyi Gyeltsen   Dorje Rabden ♥ Pedrön
Chumé Shengo   9th *Peling Sungtrül*   *Drönyer*

Tsering Penjor
Paro Pönlop

Püntso Chödrön   Pema Dechen
(both ♥ to Jigme Wangchuk, *Druk Gyelpo II*, see below)

Wangmo   Gyurmé   Karma   **Jigme Wangchuk ♥** (1) Püntso Chödrön   ♥   (2) Pema Dechen
nun   Dorje   Trinley   1905-1952   (ds. of Dasho Jamyang, *Chumé Shengo*)
(Nakhu)*Druk Gyelpo II*

Kesang Chödrön Dorje   ♥   **Jigme Dorje Wangchuk**   Namgyel   (1) Chökyi
d. of *Gongzim* Sonam Topgye   1928-1972   Wangchuk   (2) Deki Yangdzom
& Chöying Wangmo,   *Druk Gyelpo III*   *Paro Pönlop*   (3) Pema Chödrön
Princess of Sikkim

(1) Dorje Wangmo ♥ **Jigme Senge Wangchuk**   Sonam   Dechen   Kezang   Pema
(2) Tsering Pema ♥   1972-   Chödrön   Wangmo   Wangmo   Lhadrön
(3) Yangdön Tsering ♥   *Druk Gyelpo IV*
(4) Sangye Chödrön ♥
(ds. of *Yab* Ugyen Dorje,
nephew of Shabdrung
Jigme Dorje, 1905-31)

Jigme Gesar Namgyel Wangchuk   8 other children by his 4 queens
1980 -   by 1994
Crown Prince, son of Queen Yangdön Tsering

Three
The Black Regent

Jigme Namgyel acquired his nickname on account of his dark countenance and because he wore black robes and rode upon a black horse. A man of enormous physical strength, his sinister appearance was matched by his reputation as a most determined opponent of all his enemies. The story of his life, however, shows that he had other qualities too.

He was born in 1825 into the eleventh generation of the family of the Dungkar Chöjé of Kurtö, which in turn descended from the fourth generation of the Khouchung Chöjé family founded by Kunga Wangpo (b. 1505), one of the seven sons of the famous saint of Bumthang, Pemalingpa (1450-1521). These *chöjé* ("Lords of Religion") families formed by this date a wide network of religious nobility stretching over central and eastern Bhutan, winning office under the central government and producing two Shabdrung incarnations in the Dramitse Chöjé family, a collateral of the Dungkar family.[1] (See Table 1,p. 22 above). Jigme Namgyel's own father Pila Gönpo Wangyel (b. 1782) and his uncle Pala Gyeltsen both supported the predecessor of these two, Shabdrung Jigme Drakpa, to whom they were closely related by marriage, in his struggle mentioned above against the rival "verbal" incarnation. Known as Pala and Pila, the brothers had the reputation of being great champions in arms. After taking part in that conflict Pila returned home to Kurtö, with an interlude along the way at Bonbzhi in Mangdelung where he left a son behind. He eventually settled down, married a girl called Sonam Pedzom from the village of Jangsa and produced a family of five children among whom Jigme Namgyel was the third.[2] (See Table 2 opposite)[3].

As a younger son Jigme Namgyel was not needed to maintain the family name and estate, so in his youth he set off to seek his fortune.[4] He was encouraged by a dream in which he was told to go off to Bumthang and Mangdelung. In lower Bumthang he would meet someone destined to help him and in Tongsa Dzong, centre of the Mangdelung district, he would find his master. On his way he stayed for some months in the house of the headman of the Naru village in the Tang valley of Bumthang. There he worked as a common herdsman before proceeding to Buli in the Chumé valley where he was befriended by the person who had been destined in the dream to help him, a lama called Shakya Namgyel. The lama gave him clothing and provisions and sent his servant, one Urukpa Döndrup, to show him the way to Tongsa. On arrival there they found Ugyen Püntso, the Tongsa Pönlop, at archery with his courtiers. Döndrup pointed him out to the young Jigme Namgyel, who prostrated before him three times and received his blessing. After enquiring about his home and family the

Table 2 **(opposite)**
The Wangchuk Dynasty of Bhutan
(Sources BRDK, BRGI, BRTU)

51

Pönlop gave him work among the lowest menials employed at his court fetching firewood and water. To follow the next turn of events one must consider briefly the history of the Tongsa governorship in this period.[5]

When Sonam Drugyel, whom we earlier met as the thirtieth regent, came to power in 1812 from his position as Tongsa Pönlop, he left behind seven children. Although he was from the Wang district in the west he had married a local lady called Norbu Drölma from the ancient family of the Byagar Dung in Bumthang when he was serving the Dzongpön there, who was his countryman. On coming to the regent's throne he succeeded in passing the Tongsa governorship to his own son Tsöndrü Gyeltsen. When the latter fell sick and requested his father's permission to retire, the regent consulted the omens in the presence of the Shabdrung's remains in Punakha and the choice fell upon his son-in-law Ugyen Püntso, the Tamshing Chöjé of Bumthang who was married to his daughter Rinchen Pemo. Thus the governorship of Tongsa came into the hands of the nobility, paving the way for one branch to rise to the monarchy.

When Ugyen Püntso died it should have been possible to have his son Pema Tendzin succeed him, but he was a minor and so instead his trusted follower Tsokye Dorje, the Chöjé of Ugyen Chöling and descendant of both Pemalingpa and Dorjelingpa, was appointed to the governorship. The young Pema Tendzin became his chamberlain. A person who played a key role in arriving at this settlement was a Tibetan lama called Jangchub Tsöndrü for whom the late Pönlop had conceived a great devotion and who was to exercise considerable influence in the years to come through repeated prophecies and admonishments. Indeed, it was at about this time that the lama is said to have foretold the triumphant rise of Jigme Namgyel, now aged eighteen.

Under his new master Jigme Namgyel was promoted from the ranks of the common menials (*tozen*, literally "food eaters") of Tongsa Dzong to that of *zingap*, a term which translates as "those who guard the master's chamber". Every magnate in Bhutan had a troupe of these to carry messages, fulfill minor commissions and, when necessary, act as bodyguards and soldiers. By the age of twenty-two Jigme Namgyel had risen through their ranks in Tongsa to be a personal attendant (*changgap*) of the Pönlop, holding the joint offices of junior chamberlain (*zimnang*) and the head of all the *zingap* called the *darpön* (literally "flag officer"). One of his duties was to accompany his master from Tongsa to Bumthang and supervise the performance of religious rituals in the government temples of the district, particularly those at Kujé, Byagar Dzong and Langmalung. He was then promoted to the post of trade officer (*tsongpön*) stationed at Tsampa on the route north from Bumthang to Tibet. On one of his journeys to Tibet he first met his future wife Pema Chökyi, daughter of his former master Ugyen Püntso. She had gone to the Lhalung monastery to visit her elder brother Kunzang Tenpai Nyima who had been installed there as the "verbal incarnation" of Pemalingpa. In 1848 he was made chief chamberlain (*zimpön*)[6] to his master and while occupying this post he went home to Kurtö and defeated in battle the Lhuntse Dzongpön who is said to have been oppressing the public. While he was there he had his first occasion to meet Jangchub Tsöndrü, the lama whom his earlier master had followed. Meeting the lama again later at Kujé he received teachings and initiations from him. The lama told him that if he aranged for a west-facing image of the deity Samvara to be made and installed in Tongsa Dzong he would become the "crown ornament" of the whole country. He resolved to do this. The image was surely intended to exert a powerful influence upon the centre of power located in the west of the country.

In 1849 the summons went out from the centre to Tongsa to provide labour for the reconstruction of Punakha Dzong which had been burnt down. Jigme Namgyel set off with the Pönlop to oversee the large numbers conscripted from Bumthang and Mangdelung for this purpose. It was the first of many such trips that involved him in the affairs of the west. All the chief magnates and their followers were gathered at Punakha. At that time it was the custom for each of the provincial lords to have in his retinue a man of exceptional strength and valour termed a *nyagö*, who acted as his champion in battle. In a friendly trial of strength among the assembled champions, Jigme Namgyel proved the victor at lifting boulders, throwing stones, chopping timber, leaping and the like. Getting wind of a plot among the other magnates to kill his master, he never let him out of sight. There is a vivid description of him peeping through the curtain of the door leading to the council chamber one day. When it became clear the other magnates were making ready to kill his master, who was shaking with fear, he went straight in with his hand on his sword hilt, took him by the sleeve and led him unopposed to safety. It was on that account that the Pönlop later made him a promise to bequeath him the Tongsa governorship when he retired, declaring that for saving his life he owed him more gratitude than his own son Tsöndrü Gyeltsen who would normally succeed him. After Jigme Namgyel had held the governorship for a number of years, the son could then follow him.

Upon returning to Tongsa the dzongs subject to the governor, namely those of Byagar, Lhuntse[7] and Shemgang, were found to be planning a rebellion and massing troops at Mongar. They were in league too with the three eastern dzongs and the border commissioner (Gyadrung) stationed at Dungsam in the southeast. Jigme Namgyel was further promoted to the post of Drönyer in 1850 and sent off to crush the revolt. On a day reckoned to be astrologically favourable he gathered the troops loyal to his master and set off to do battle. The enemy districts were conquered one after the other, and the Dzongpöns of Tashigang, Tashiyangtse and Shongar and the border commissioner were all taken captive and brought to Tongsa from where they were despatched to Punakha. Thus the whole of central and eastern Bhutan came into the hands of the Tongsa Pönlop, paving the way for total ascendancy.

The background to Jigme Namgyel's next adventure in the west must be explained. During the second reign of the regent Purgyel from 1835 to 1838 a revolt broke out led by Chakpa Sangye, the Dzongpön of Shongar. He and his men gained access to the dzong one night by using a tall prayer flag as a ladder. The regent took refuge with the state monks who arranged for him to retire without harm. The throne then passed to Chakpa Sangye's older brother Dorje Norbu, the Daga Pönlop, while he himself retained the position of chamberlain and Dzongpön of Wangdü Phodrang. Dorje Norbu, however, was forced to share the throne with his rival Tashi Dorje, a follower of the deposed regent who was serving as the Thimphu Dzongpön. This standard means of settling conflict, sworn to and sealed in the awesome presence of the images of the guardian deities of the state, held good for seven years until Dorje Norbu died a natural death. From 1848 onwards Tashi Dorje had the throne to himself. In 1849 he rebuilt Punakha Dzong which had suffered another disastrous fire. He fell sick, resigned and died in 1850. His successor Wangchuk Gyelpo came to the throne from the post of Thimphu Dzongpön but after only six months was faced with a revolt that led to his death at the hands of his successor as Thimphu Dzongpön, Tsaphukpa Tsewang. The details are difficult to follow but it is clear that the conflict waged by the Paro Pönlop Tsultrim Namgyel[8] against his own successor Tazik Drönma provided the background to the struggles in the capitals. Tsaphukpa Tsewang then met his death at the hands of Chakpa Sangye, the man who had helped install his own brother Dorje Norbu as regent in 1838 and who still held the post of Wangdü Phodrang Dzongpön. His killing of the Thimphu Dzongpön did nothing to stem the troubles, and he was unacceptable to the state monks and the retired but powerful Paro Pönlop (ally of the dead Dzongpön) as a candidate for the regent's throne. They therefore contrived to put on the throne the twenty-year-old Shabdrung of this period, Jigme Norbu (1831-61). The arrangement was meant to bring to an end a serious outbreak of smallpox that was seen as karmic retribution inflicted by the guardian deities disturbed by the violence of the constant feuding in recent years. But the Shabdrung was himself struck by the disease and retired to Paro after just four months on the throne.[9]

Chakpa Sangye was now able to realise his ambitions. He seized the throne in 1851 against the wishes of the monks and in the teeth of serious opposition from his enemies, not least the old Pönlop of Paro, Tsultrim Namgyel. When the latter called on the Tongsa Pönlop for help in ousting the regent he immediately responded by sending Jigme Namgyel off with two of his brothers at the head of a column of troops. The Pönlop was probably counting on the ties of family and regional loyalty that bound Jigme Namgyel to his own lama, the young Shabdrung who had just vacated the throne. Like his predecessor whom Jigme Namgyel's father had supported, this Shabdrung came from the Dramitse Chöjé family to which Jigme Namgyel was distantly related.

On arrival in Punakha the regent was found to have moved to the village of Norbugang, and not far away Jigme Namgyel had an encounter with the regent's champion, the "horse-master" (*tapön*) Mikthöm. He had been born at Mangdelung in the east to a woman who was said to have been impregnated by the local spirit Muktsen, the son thus conceived inheriting the spirit's qualities of violence. When Jigme Namgyel called out to him "You aren't a man of the west, so there's no need for you to take on duties like this here", the champion responded with "Haven't you heard that a dog growls from any place where he eats?". That night Jigme Namgyel and his brothers lay in wait for him as he returned from the regent's residence to his own lodgings. They slaughtered him on his path and took flight to the Shabdrung's seat of Talo close by. The lama was absent, presumably by this time in Paro, but his elder brother and chamberlain gave them refuge for three days before sending them off with a strong escort of sixty bodyguards as far as Gasa in the north. The old Pönlop of Paro who had called for their help is also said to have assisted their escape. From Gasa the brothers took a very long but safe road home, north into Tibet from Laya and thence round east back to the Bhutan border and south to Bumthang and Tongsa. Their escort, however, suffered a terrible fate at the hands of the regent, infuriated at the loss of his champion. The house where they were lodging at Karbjisa was set on fire and all sixty were burnt to death. But the old Paro Pönlop had his revenge in the end. He had a fine silk robe stitched up and gave it to a servant of his who had survived the dreaded smallpox. The servant made someone afflicted with the disease wear it for a time till it was thoroughly impregnated with germs. Still warm, he then packed it up and delivered it as a gift of reconciliation to the regent with a message from his master: "Please try this on to see if it fits. If it's too small there's some spare silk left. It can be made bigger and returned to you. Send a reply." The regent put it on and very soon died. The year was 1851.

Back in Tongsa the rumour spread around that the governor was planning to break his promise to Jigme Namgyel and hand over his post instead to his son Tsöndrü Gyeltsen. Pretending to be ill, Jigme Namgyel retired for a time to the nearby village of Laushong to await developments. In fact the governor was in due course prevailed upon by his confidants to honour his promise, and so it was that Jigme Namgyel succeeded him as Tongsa Pönlop in 1853. There was a clear understanding that after three years he would give way to the governor's son, who in the meantime took the post of Byagar Dzongpön. It was at this time that Jigme Namgyel had the west-facing image of Samvara made in Tongsa Dzong according to the advice of the lama Jangchub Tsöndrü. Its purpose was to bring the whole of western Bhutan under the control of the new governor and his heirs. He also at this time managed to obtain a specially powerful relic in the form of one of the vertebrae of the early Drukpa saint Tsangpa Gyaré which had taken the form of the female deity Vajravarahi. (It will be remembered that another of these vertebrae had been brought south by the founding Shabdrung.) This too he enshrined in Tongsa Dzong within a larger silver image of the goddess as the talisman of his future fortune. However, it was still some years before his destiny was to be revealed.

In the meantime Damchö Lhundrup, a highly respected senior monk, had been appointed regent in 1852 with the full support of the monastic community and the public. It was thought he could stem the tide of continuing conflict after the violent death of his predecessor, but unable to do so he retired. He was followed in 1854 by the incarnate lama Jamtrül Jamyang Tendzin (1831-55), but his predecessor was forced to return and share the throne with him as part of a settlement aimed at containing the opposition of Umadewa, the Thimphu Dzongpön. This did not work and the two regents found themselves beleaguered in Punakha Dzong with Umadewa and Kalön Kasha in control of the two bridges that gave access to the fortress. Jigme Namgyel again came over from Tongsa — not, it seems, to take part in the battle but this time to mediate. As a reward for his successful intervention he was given the right to appoint all the Dzongpöns east of Tongsa. Moreover it was agreed that he could retain for his own use four loads of rupees obtained annually as part of the British compensation for the annexation in 1841 of the Assam duars which previously the Tongsa Pönlop had been compelled to deliver to the central government.[10] In effect the whole of central and eastern Bhutan which he already largely controlled was made his personal fiefdom, though it was later to be again formally divided.[11]

Upon his return to Tongsa Jigme Namgyel was determined to invite his lama Jangchub Tsöndrü to receive again his blessings and teachings. The lama, however, declined. He was far away in Tibet, at Phari across the border from western Bhutan. Determined to have him change his mind, Jigme Namgyel undertook acts of merit and piety calculated to impress the lama with his sincerity. He issued orders that all hunting in the provinces under his control was to cease and he sent men to the great printing house of Narthang in Tibet to obtain two complete sets of the Buddhist canon. The lama at last relented and made the long journey from Phari to Tongsa. In the course of a long series of initiations bestowed on the governor he gave him further crucial encouragement to fulfill his ambitions for power.

By this time Jigme Namgyel had already married Pema Chökyi, daughter of his first master the retired Pönlop Ugyen Püntso. This accorded with the wishes of her brother, the Pemalingpa incarnation installed at the Lhalung monastery where he had first met her. It was still the custom for all Tongsa Pönlops to put their wives aside while they held office and this was expected of Jigme Namgyel too. However, the lama now absolved him of this obligation, explaining that Pema Chökyi had a special karmic bond with her husband that would enable her to assist him. Moreover, a son would be born to him who would benefit the kingdom.[12] Whereas it was traditional for a disciple to offer prayers for the long life of his lama, in this case the lama said the reverse was appropriate. It was at this time too that the lama designed and consecrated the famous headgear that was to be Jigme Namgyel's special symbol and bequest to his heirs. This first version of the Raven Crown was conceived more as a magical battle helmet than a symbol of royalty. Imbued with the essence of two of the forms of the great protector Mahakala, namely the linked pair of "enemy gods" (Dralha) called the Northern Demon (Jangdü) and the Raven-Headed Mahakala of Action (Legön Jarok Dongchen), it was intended to associate these gods permanently with its wearer. There was conscious allusion, surely, to the role played by the Raven-Headed Mahakala in the state's first unification under the founding Shabdrung. The victories which Jigme Namgyel won over his rivals within Bhutan and his success, albeit temporary, against the British in 1865 are still ascribed to its power. The later crowns which developed from this prototype shed its immediate purpose of giving advantage and protection in real conflict, domesticating its symbolism into that of triumphant royalty.[13]

When Tsokye Dorje, the previous Tongsa Pönlop, had retired in favour of Jigme Namgyel on the understanding that the post would fall to his son the Byagar Dzongpön Tsöndrü Gyeltsen after three years, he had left behind to guard his interests at Tongsa one Pasang, who held the senior post of Drönyer. This Pasang, whose loyalty to Jigme Namgyel was clearly in doubt and who had an overbearing nature, fell out with the other courtiers and was done to death by the governor's senior attendant, Kurtöpa Kolong, apparently with the full encouragement of his master. It became the

The Raven Crowns of Bhutan
Above: *The crown of Jigme Namgyel (1825-81), father of the first king Ugyen Wangchuk, now preserved at the National Museum of Bhutan, Paro.*
Below: *The crowns worn by the first and second kings (left) and by the third and fourth king (right). The earlier version is decorated with tantric skulls, the later with the mythological garuda bird. (Drawings by Robert Beer from original photographs.)*

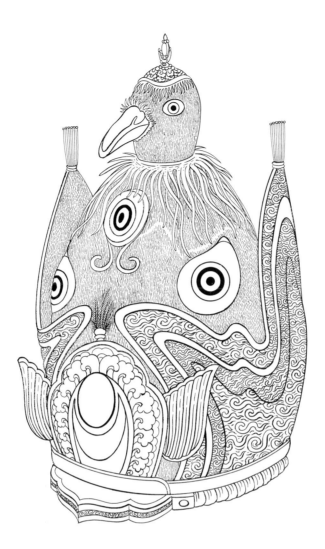

immediate cause of a feud which broke out in 1857 between Jigme Namgyel and Tsöndrü Gyeltsen, the latter supported by his father. Battle was joined in Bumthang with no clear result but with the advantage somewhat to Jigme Namgyel. Indeed the stalemate allowed him to build himself the fine palace of Wangdü Chöling on the land at Shamkhar occupied by his camp. This was located on the broad floor of the valley below Byagar Dzong, which was held by the enemy. Government troops summoned from Punakha to the side of the enemy failed to dislodge Jigme Namgyel and so in 1858 a high ranking delegation led by the head abbot Yönten Gyeltsen came to negotiate a truce. The Shabdrung's chamberlain who had earlier called for support from Jigme Namgyel also came from Dramitse to take part. The final peace settlement, celebrated with religious ceremonies at Kujé, provided for the nominal promotion of Tsöndrü Gyeltsen from Dzongpön to Pönlop and a division of the dzongs of eastern Bhutan between the two rivals. The arrangement had the short-term effect of weakening Jigme Namgyel's power, but it held good for a time and led to some measure of stability in the east that contributed to his ultimate success.[14]

Jigme Namgyel's next escapade in the west was to have an effect that long outlived him. The regent Umadewa had been killed in 1857 by the chamberlain of the man with whom he had been compelled for a time to share the throne. The regency then passed to Nadzi Pasang whose former office of Wangdü Phodrang Dzongpön was coveted by his ally Darlung Topgye, the Dzongpön of Punakha. When the new regent chose instead to reserve this post for his nephew, the embittered ally called on Jigme Namgyel and his erstwhile rival Tsöndrü Gyeltsen for military support from Tongsa and Bumthang. In 1863 battle was joined in Thimphu, the enemy defeated and the regent himself forced to resign. Darlung Topgye won the post of Wangdü Phodrang Dzongpön he had wanted so badly, and Jigme Namgyel appointed his kinsman Khasar Topgye to the office of Thimphu Dzongpön. The person who had held that post, Tsewang Sithub, was elevated to the regency but forced to share it with a monk Tsultrim Yönten till he was deposed and the monk died. In 1864 there followed briefly two more monks, the respected Kargyü Wangchuk, who had been in control of the Bhutanese monasteries in Nepal, and Tsöndrü Pekar, the teacher of philosophy of the state community. Both soon died and so in the same year Tsewang Sithub returned as the fiftieth regent. Jigme Namgyel, the real power behind all these appointments, was still present in Punakha both in his capacity as Tongsa Pönlop and with a new office he had given himself, namely chamberlain to the "verbal incarnation" of the Shabdrung, the young Yeshé Ngödrup (1851-1917), who was standing in as Dharma Raja for the discredited "mental incarnation", Jigme Norbu. The scene was thus set for a turn of events Jigme Namgyel could never have planned for.

Nor could the Honorable Ashley Eden, British envoy to the Bhutan court in 1864, ever have imagined the trouble he would have to face there. It is sure he would otherwise never have set foot in the country. In 1864 he was sent on a mission to try and resolve problems arising from a long series of "depredations" committed by the Bhutanese in the duars and to negotiate a treaty which would regularize future relations. He was accompanied by the Chibu Lama of Sikkim who had responsibilties

The palace of Wangdü Chöling, Shamkhar, Bumthang, 1970. The building was constructed in 1857 on the site of his battle camp by the Tongsa Pönlop Jigme Namgyel and later refurbished by his son King Ugyen Wangchuk. It was the principal residence of the second king, who bequeathed it to his junior queen Pema Dechen, and the home in his youth of the third king. A community of serfs (drap) attached to the palace gained the status of common taxpayers in the 1970s. (Photo: 1970, Anthony Aris)

both at the Sikkimese court and under the British in Darjeeling from where the expedition was planned. Despite a great number of warnings from Bhutan that the mission would not be welcome, Eden and his escort forced their way to Punakha with many obstacles and delays along the way. Almost the only person to offer him any help at all was the retired but still powerful Pönlop of Paro, who was opposed to the court in Punakha. Even in Paro they had deal with countless obstructions, but these were as nothing compared to the treatment received in Punakha.

There they found an extremely fluid and dangerous situation presided over by Jigme Namgyel. He is described in the most unflattering terms possible as the *de facto* ruler of Bhutan, an evil genius presiding over a court of his henchmen who mistrusted and feared him. Eden declared without reservation that he had "the worst and most replusive countenance I ever saw in any man of any country. He is said, by his own countrymen, to be utterly reckless of human life, and to be an avaricious, treacherous, unscrupulous robber".[15] The protracted discussions were conducted in such a way as to injure British pride very deeply, and indeed the only point of interest for Jigme Namgyel seemed to have been the return of the sequestered Assam Duars, a matter

A posed photograph of three Bhutanese, probably taken in Darjeeling or Kalimpong in present-day West Bengal in the 1860s. The man on the left is threatening to settle an argument with the use of his sword, but the impassive expressions on the faces of his adversary and the seated onlooker betray the artificial nature of the pose. From J. Forbes Watson and John William Kaye (eds.), The People of India: A Series of Photograpic Illustrations with Descriptive Letterpress *(London, India Museum, 1868), plate 43.*

The Chibu Lama who served as Sikkim Agent in Darjeeling and drönyer *to the Sikkimese ruler Tsukphü Namgyel, seen here with two Sikkimese guards. The photograph was probably taken in Darjeeling shortly after the lama returned there from accompanying the disastrous Eden mission to Bhutan in 1864. (Royal Geographical Society)*

which from the British standpoint was not negotiable. Far from being able to arrange a treaty favourable to British interests, Eden was forced to sign a document imposed on him under threat, doing so with the words "under compulsion".

This came after what must have been the low point of the whole mission. In Eden's words, "The Penlow took up a large piece of wet dough and began rubbing my face with it; he pulled my hair, and slapped me on the back, and generally conducted himself with great insolence. On my showing signs of impatience or remonstrating, he smiled and deprecated my anger, pretending that it was the familiarity of friendship, much to the amusement of the large assemblage of bystanders". On the same occasion the Wangdü Phodrang Dzongpön, the same Darlung Topgye whom Jigme Namgyel had helped install, "surpassed the Penlow in insolence; he took some pawn [betel nut] which he had chewed in his mouth and told Dr. Simpson [medical officer] to eat it, and on his refusing, threw it angrily in his face ... Dr. Simpson sat perfectly still without wiping the pawn from his face, showing clearly that the insult was felt and understood by us all".[16]

Imperial dignity had suffered a mortal blow. The mission retreated in disarray but managed to make its way back to Darjeeling from where Eden reported total failure. The treatment he had received and the continuing intransigence of the Bhutanese led directly to what is perhaps the most forgotten of all colonial wars. All remaining duars belonging to Bhutan were annexed by the British in the Anglo-Bhutan war of 1864-6. The date has special significance since it followed the mutiny of the Bengal army at Meerut in 1857 and the almost universal revolt against British rule in India that lasted down to 1859. Indeed, punitive measures had been planned against Bhutan as long ago as 1857 but had been abandoned in the face of the revolt. The contemptuous attitude of Ashley Eden for everything Bhutanese was in fact typical of the hardening of imperial feelings in this period. In Bhutan everything seemed to conspire to bring those feelings to boiling point.

There is another, more direct connection with the Indian mutiny that has escaped much notice. The "confidential advisor" to Jigme Namgyel at this time was a well-born Indian who had learnt to speak Bhutanese and who dressed in Bhutanese robes. He claimed to be a grandson of the great Ranjit Singh who had died in 1839 after creating the enormously powerful Sikh state in the Punjab. He had certainly come to Bhutan by way of Nepal in the aftermath of the revolt and he is still remembered in Bhutan by the title of "Padshah Raja" that is normally applied only to the Mughal emperor. Regarded with the deepest suspicion by Eden, who thought he may have been originally from Lucknow, it will probably never be known who he really was. The apartment in Tongsa Dzong which Jigme Namgyel reserved for his use is still pointed out and there is a tradition that he took part on the Bhutanese side in the conflict with the British.[17]

Jigme Namgyel played a decisive role in the war of 1864-6.[18] Despite the ultimate victory of the British, he never succumbed to defeat and went on from strength to strength. In particular he will always be remembered as the man who in February 1865 compelled the British to retreat from Dewangiri, inflicting heavy losses and capturing two canons which he took back to his fastness at Tongsa. According to Bhutanese memories of the war,[19] he had come down to the plains at the head of a column of troops, invoking the guardian deities at all the temples on his route. He had with him astrologers and special priests to summon the aid of the gods, principally the Raven-Headed Mahakala whose crown he now wore in battle. The account speaks of a first engagement during which the Bhutanese first retreated with the loss of Tsöndrü Gyeltsen, who still had the post of Byagar Pönlop. The Shabdrung's chamberlain, Sonam Döndrub, and Jigme Namgyel were able to pull back and attack once again, this time with the astrologer using a powerful ritual invoking the planetary god Rahula. Part of the story now takes on a legendary quality, with a British bugler's gullet severed in mid-note, an elephant of the enemy having its trunk sliced off, and Jigme Namgyel shooting down four or five of the assembled British officers with a single bullet while they were conferring at a table in their tent. It was the above-mentioned "Padshah Raja" who had identified to Jigme Namgyel the seniormost officer present, referred to by the Bhutanese as "the one-armed sahib". The shot is said to have been timed to coincide exactly with the point in the special ritual bestowed on him by his lama when

Rinpung Dzong in Paro, with the Nyamai Zampa bridge in the foreground and the citadel of Ta Dzong on the hill above. The earliest surviving photograph from Bhutan, taken during the mission of Ashley Eden who was delayed in Paro for sixteen days in February and March 1864. The photograph was probably taken by Dr. Benjamin Simpson who acompanied the mission as medical officer. (Royal Geographic Society)

the Raven-Headed Mahakala is summoned and exhorted to battle. Whatever view is taken of these stories, firm belief in the total support from the divine guardians must have played a major part in the Bhutanese success, which is confirmed in the official British accounts. Surrounded and with all their lines of communication cut off, they abandoned their weapons and much ammunition, also the many killed and wounded, and retreated. Malaria also took a heavy toll among the British forces both now and later.[20] All along the frontier similar attacks took place and it was not till the following month that the British began to retaliate with a success that depended on infinitely greater fire power. The forts of the Bhutanese overlooking the western duars were first taken in March, and Dewangiri was recaptured in April. The professional British soldiers who took part in the campaign formed a very different opinion as to the fighting qualities of the Bhutanese than that held by Eden and other civilians who had had dealings with them earlier. They were found to be immensely brave and disciplined fighters, resourceful in strategy and kind to their prisoners.[21]

Negotiations for peace were prolonged throughout the summer but finally culminated in the Treaty of Sinchula signed in November 1865. Among its terms it provided for the permanent annexation to British India of all the duars and the hill tract on the left bank of the Teesta still under Bhutanese control, in return for which an annual "subsidy" representing only a portion of the total revenue of these lands would be paid to Bhutan. However, Jigme Namgyel refused to acknowledge defeat or the validity of the treaty signed by the Bhutanese authorities in the west. Moreover, its terms could not come into effect until he had surrendered the cannons and prisoners he had taken off to Tongsa. (He is also said to have removed the head and remaining hand of the "one-armed sahib" he had killed for offering to the guardian deities in Tongsa Dzong.) So stubborn was his resistance that the British threatened to bring him to heel by sending two armies to invade the country from the west and east. In February 1866 one

Opposite: *"Inside a stockade in the Bala Pass". The abandoned bows and arrows of the defeated Bhutanese are seen scattered on the ground. From* Illustrated London News, *24 June 1865.*

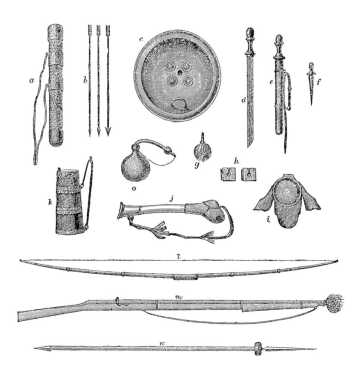

Below right: *"The war in Bhootan: The Bala Pass, stormed by the British forces on the 15th of February [1865]". The Bhutanese fortresses and stockades in the foothills of the southwest at Bala, Dalingcote (Daling Dzong), Buxa Duar (Pasakha) and Chamurchi were eventually taken by the British in the face of strong resistance to their vastly superior arms. From* Illustrated London News, *24 June 1865.*

Left: *"Arms, etc., taken from the Bhooteas at the storming of Dewangiri, Bhootan [in April 1865]". The key to the drawings reads as follows: (a) ornamental quiver; (b) three kinds of reed arrows, said to be poisoned; (c) shield; (d) long straight sword, the hilt ornamented with silver filigree work; (e) sword and scabbard; (f) dagger; (g) muzzle-stopper; (h) bullet-mould made out of soap-stone; (i) steel head-piece, thickly quilted; (j) trumpet, made out of a human thigh-bone; (k) water-bottle, made of wood and bound with figured brass; (l) bamboo bow; (m) matchlock; (n) colour pole; (o) powder-horn. From* Illustrated London News, *24 June 1865.*

expedition set off from Dewangiri and had to proceed as far north as Yongla Gompa south of Tashigang before Jigme Namgyel finally capitulated and returned the guns and captives.[22]

There followed a rare domestic interlude during which Jigme Namgyel passed the Tongsa governorship on to his brother Dungkar Gyeltsen. There was an understanding that after three years it would then come to Jigme Namgyel's brother-in-law Pema Tendzin. It is clear that Jigme Namgyel intended to remain the real power behind the scene. Retiring to his palace at Wangdü Chöling in Bumthang, where his wife, two sons and daughter were living, he occupied himself with a long-delayed plan of making a south-facing image of the deity Kalacakra ("The Wheel of Time") and new wall-paintings in the revered temple of Jampai Lhakhang. The plan again conformed to the advice of his late lama, who had foreseen troubles in the south. A fine copper-gilt roof ornament was placed on the temple, and the Pemalingpa incarnation was invited from Lhalung to perform the consecration. Jigme Namgyel then departed on pilgrimage to Tibet, visiting Lhasa, Samyé and Yarlung. Perhaps he had other plans there too but this is not known. Doubtless his main intention was to compensate for all the violent deeds he had committed by performing acts of piety.

There is a nice account of him on his return from Tibet going off on a hunting expedition for wild boar to the pass of Kyikyila. No boar was found and to cheer him up he asked his confidant, the nobleman (*shengo*) of Chumé called Sonam Thayé, to

The British camp at Dewangiri in 1865, by an unidentified photographer. It was here that the British were forced to retreat in January 1865, abandoning two cannons that were taken off to Tongsa by Jigme Namgyel, who was acting as commander of the Bhutanese troops. The position was finally recaptured by the British in April of the following year. (Photo: The British Library)

compose a poem. The result was: "On the pass of Kyikyila there is no game. / In the river of Chuméchu there are no fishes. / To the attendant Sonam Thayé there is no robe". Taking the hint, Jigme Namgyel said that if indeed there proved to be no fish in the Chuméchu his confidant would get a robe. A thorough search the following day proved the man right and he was duly rewarded.[23]

In 1867, just a year or so after the conclusion of war with the British and the brief interlude which followed, Jigme Namgyel found himself returning once again to the west, this time to avenge the murder of his kinsman Khasar Topgye whom he had installed as Thimphu Dzongpön. The feud had begun when the kinsman, in league with Tashi the Bastard who was Punakha Dzongpön, had abducted the wife of Darlung Topgye whom Jigme Namgyel had also brought to power as Dzongpön of Wandü Phodrang. Darlung Topgye succeeded in killing one of his wife's abductors, Khasar Topgye, and made his ally Kawang Mangkhel take the post of Thimphu Dzongpön which had thus fallen vacant. Against the two of them were ranged Tashi the Bastard of Punakha and his ally Shar Sigye, retired Dzongpön of Wangdü Phodrang. When these two were on the point of gaining the upper hand word was sent to Jigme Namgyel to avenge his kinsman and help oust his successor Kawang Mangkhel from the fortress of Tashichö Dzong in Thimphu where he was installed. He would have easily succeeded in doing this since the fortress's supply of gunpowder was soon exhausted. However, secret supplies were sent in by night by a traitor, the new Paro Pönlop, Trinley Zangpo, who was supposed to be on Jigme Namgyel's side. Eventually monks were summoned to resolve the stalemate, some kind of settlement was reached and Jigme Namgyel was able to return home to Bumthang.

The details of the truce are not known but it lasted no longer than two years. In 1869 Jigme Namgyel was summoned to the west once more, this time with his brother the ruling Tongsa Pönlop. He was destined to stay for twelve years and never return home, or so it would appear. The line-up on this occasion had his supporters Tashi the Bastard (of Punakha) with Sigye (retired from Wangdü Phodrang) facing the joint forces of Darlung Topgye (also by now retired from Wangdü Phodrang), Kunley Dorje (the latters's nephew and reigning Dzongpön of that place) and Kawang Mangkhel (of Thimphu).[24] When the ensuing battle at Wangdü Phodrang became so prolonged that neither side could win, Jigme Namgyel devised one of his clever tricks to break the stalemate. He sent two of his men secretly by night to burn down the capital fortress in Thimphu, thus causing the Dzongpön of that place, Kawang Mangkhel, to abandon the scene of battle to try and save his burning headquarters. This left the retired and reigning Dzongpöns of Wangdü Phodrang, Darlung Topgye and his nephew Kunley Dorje, holding the fort there without the help of their main ally and his troops. So they were compelled to sue for peace. Normally some arrangement could have been found to allow them to retire with dignity, but the chance of resolving an old feud now presented itself. Among Jigme Namgyel's retainers were two brothers who had earlier killed Darlung Topgye's brother who had killed their uncle, the regent Umadewa. These two now conspired with their master to use the opportunity afforded by peace talks to do away with their remaining enemies, the uncle and nephew, who believed a settlement was about to be reached in good faith. Both were slaughtered. Some would say they should by now have known better than to trust Jigme Namgyel.

It was now, in 1870, that the Black Regent finally assumed formal power as the fifty-first regent, replacing the totally ineffectual Tsewang Sithub who had held office since 1863. The master of Thimphu who had fled to save his burning fortress was now apparently reconciled to Jigme Namgyel. He, Kawang Mangkhel, gave up his post of Dzongpön to his younger brother Lama Tsewang, who was to become a trusted supporter of the victor. Felicitations were received by Jigme Namgyel from the Tibetan authorities and he appointed one "Fentook" (Phentok?) as the Bhutan Agent in India.[25] He spent ten months rebuilding and refurbishing the burnt fortress. The only other achievement of his short reign of three years for which he is remembered is the defeat of yet another revolt, this time led by Tsewang Norbu, the Paro Pönlop. Kawang Mangkhel took on the job of suppressing him on the condition that he would then be given the governorship of Paro. After he had done this, simply by persuading the Pönlop to flee to India, he naturally expected his desire would be fulfilled. However, Jigme Namgyel gave encouragement to his officers to assassinate the would-be successor. It had been pointed out to him that with one brother installed in Thimphu and the other in Paro "... the enemy might appear from within, not from without". Kawang Mangkhel's head was duly severed and thrown down from the high balcony of Paro Dzong. The Paro governorship then reverted to the former incumbent, Nyima Dorje.[26]

He retired as regent in 1873, passing the throne to his cousin and trusted confidant Dorje Namgyel who had served as his chamberlain during the regency.[27] The throne itself must have had few attractions. Setting up his own quarters close by at Simtokha Dzong rather than returning home to Bumthang, he clearly decided it would be easier to contain the further revolts that were bound to follow if he did not have to make the long journey all the way over from the east each time they broke out. He was in fact able to continue dominating the scene till his death eight years later — but not without serious crisis.

The first outbreak of trouble after his retirement was quickly dealt with when the Punakha Dzongpön, Damchö Rinchen, was removed and replaced with one Ngödrup. The fact that the former was allowed to survive his attempted coup, and with his feelings of bitterness hidden but festering, was to have important consequences later. Meanwhile a serious feud had broken out in the east when, true to form, Jigme Namgyel's brother Dungkar Gyeltsen, the Tongsa Pönlop, refused to honour his promise of giving up his governorship after three years to Jigme Namgyel's brother-in-law, Pema Tendzin, who held the fort at Byagar. When Jigme Namgyel refused to take sides after receiving appeals from both of them, merely saying he would support whichever of them came out on top, he thus managed to alienate even his own brother who had supported him loyally in all the battles of the past. The scene was well set for a conflagration.

It was sparked off in 1877 by the ousted master of Punakha inciting his relative by marriage, the reinstated governor of Paro, to kill the man whom Jigme Namgyel had

Two of the ceremonial bodyguards of the Paro Pönlop sharing a meal, Paro, 1931. (Photo: J.L.R. Weir, private collection)

left there to guard his interests. The murder meant that the whole of Paro would be lost unless quickly reconquered. Jigme Namgyel set off with the government levy of troops, taking with him his son Ugyen Wangchuk, the regent and Lama Tsewang, the Thimphu Dzongpön. They had managed to capture the Ta Dzong citadel above the main fortress in Paro when news came in that a general revolt had begun in Punakha and Wangdü Phodrang. The new Dzongpön of Punakha had installed the "verbal incarnation" of the Shabdrung, Cholé Tulku Yeshé Ngödrup, as a rival regent. At the same time Kawang Sangye, Jigme Namgyel's appointee as Wangdü Phodrang Dzongpön, had been murdered by that man's subordinate, Angdruk, as part of the uprising. It seems to have been carefully planned to coincide with the trouble in Paro. Since that was now overshadowed by the insurrection in the east, Jigme Namgyel left his son Ugyen Wangchuk in charge of the citadel and, undaunted, withdrew to his quarters at Simtokha to plan his next move.

Lama Tsewang told his master he could deal with the insurrection and departed for Punakha. The rebels were then joined by a force from Tongsa led by one Chözim Dawa on behalf of the disgruntled brother of Jigme Namgyel, the ruling Tongsa Pönlop. At the first engagement Lama Tsewang's champion was killed, a disaster that normally presaged total defeat. Hearing of this, Jigme Namgyel hastened from Simtokha to bring the lama relief at the place where he was surrounded on all sides. Together they drove off the rebels and then divided their forces so that one column could invest Punakha, the other Wangdü Phodrang. This in turn precipitated the rebels to adopt a typical diversionary tactic. The ousted master of Punakha, Damchö Lhundrup, made a pretense of abandoning the rebellion and going off on pilgrimage. Instead he went straight to Paro, captured Ugyen Wangchuk and imprisoned him within the citadel he had been holding. Jigme Namgyel's reaction was swift. He seized Damchö Lhundrup's sister and eleven more of his relatives, imprisoning them at Mendelgang. He then sent word to his son's capturer saying all his family would be put to death if Ugyen Wangchuk were not released unharmed. There was little choice, and Ugyen Wangchuk was safely handed over to the regent who was still trying to take Paro Dzong. The rebel's family was in turn released, perhaps to their surprise. Paro Dzong was eventually captured by having its water supply cut off, causing the rebel governor to give up and flee to India in the same way as his predecessor.

Shortly thereafter Punakha Dzong was also taken from the rebels. The Dzongpön took off on the route to India[28] and his puppet regent departed for his monastery in Paro. The scene then shifted to the other centre of opposition, the fortress of Wangdü Phodrang, where the murderer of Jigme Namgyel's appointee was still holding out. When this Angdruk found the odds were all against him he made preparations to burn down the fortress by placing kegs of gunpowder at key points within. Perhaps he thought he might escape in the commotion or maybe he had decided to die in a way that would give only a hollow victory to his opponents. When all was ready to go up in flames he made the mistake of listening to an offer from one of Jigme Namgyel's supporters, the senior monk who was master of chanting in the state community. This monk assured Angdruk he would save his life by smuggling him out of the fortress through the wood store. Suspecting no treachery, Angdruk accepted the offer — and was immediately captured. For twelve days he and eight of his followers were kept prisoners, and then one by one they were led off to be drowned from the famous bridge below the fortress. If the fading memory of how the executions were performed can be believed, the prisoners were led off to their end bound with ropes and with full ceremonial music being played. At the bridge, still bound, they were served a meal before they were pushed off into the river. The sin is deemed to have been lessened since no blood was shed. Later in life Jigme Namgyel used to say, with regret, that he had waited as long as possible for the head abbot to come from Punakha to intercede for the lives of his [22] prisoners. But the abbot never came and so eventually, to avoid the shame of waiting still longer, he had been forced to amass evil karma in this way.

The revolt was finished. He summoned his son Trinley Topgye from the monastery of Lhalung in Tibet where he was a monk and appointed him to the vacancy at Wangdü Phodrang. His younger son Ugyen Wangchuk he made Paro Pönlop. He himself resumed his life in retirement at Simtokha Dzong, but in 1881 on his return there one day from a trip to Punakha he was thrown from the yak he was riding. He suffered serious head injury and was carried down in a litter. Five days later as he lay dying at

Simtokha he summoned those closest to him to hear his last will. Present were his two sons, also two young men he looked on as his adopted sons.[29] They were, he said, to remain on close terms and support each other through any troubles that might face them ahead. He then died.

Notes: Chapter Four

1. They were Shabdrung Jigme Norbu (1831-61) and Shabdrung Jigme Chögyel (1862-1904).
2. In fact he was given the name Samdrup at birth and only later acquired the name by which he is remembered. For the names of his siblings, see Table 2; for their later fortunes and heirs, BRTU 283-4.
3. The information supplied in Table 2 is far from exhaustive, and BRTU should be consulted for full genealogical details. Only official marriages (marked ♥) affecting the direct line of succession have been noted. The titles Dasho (male) and Ashi (female) can precede all names in the Table except in the case of the kings and Pönlops who have their own titles. Children do not necessarily appear in chronological order.
4. The account of the life of Jigme Namgyel which follows is based on BRDK 172-88; BRGI 479-505; BRTU 285-6; SMLJ 58-62. One of the principal sources used by these authorities was the unauthorized and therefore unpublished history of Bhutan by Dasho Püntso Wangdü (see Table II) to which I myself had brief access when I lived in Bumthang but which is not now to hand.
5. See esp. BRDK 166-72.
6. In 1864 Ashley Eden recorded an account of Jigme Namgyel's promotion to chamberlain that is not found in the Bhutanese records. It is claimed this happened as a reward for his murdering the chief opponent of a regent who had summoned the Tongsa governor to his aid. See *Political Missions to Bootan* 101-2; *Papers Relating to Bootan* 218.
7. BRDK 174-5 maintains that Jigme Namgyel was also appointed as Dzongpön of Lhuntse at this time. He left his own representative Tangpa Rabgye there to act in his place and returned to Tongsa where he received further injunctions from the lama Jangchub Tsöndrü: "After the ruler's fortune has been exhausted / A short man with moles on his face will hold the throne. / When troops invade Tongsa / Have the Buddhist canon read three times".
8. He is better known as Agi Hap, "The Old Man of Ha". His rival had the alternative name of Yönten Rinchen.
9. After his retirement as regent Shabdrung Jigme Norbu was looked after by his patron the old Pönlop of Paro and the retired head abbot Sherab Gyeltsen at the latter's monastery of Gorina in Paro. It was at this time that he was deprived of the revenue deriving from the Bhutan *duars* that was traditionally reserved for the Shabdrung. From Paro he left on a long

trip to Tibet where he wrote some very expressive letters in verse to the Bhutanese authorities. The letters have survived. He is said to have broken his vows and had affairs with a lady of Adang in central Bhutan and a daughter of the head of the Sakya school in Tibet: BRGI 447-57, 460. In 1864 Ashley Eden reported that "the late [Dharma] Raja, whilst absent in Thibet, forgetful of his Lamaic vows of chastity, entered into a liaison with a Thibetan woman, and had two children by her, a boy and a girl; the boy is about eight years old ... brought up carefully in a monastery, and is treated with considerable veneration": *Political Missions to Bootan* 100; *Papers Relating to Bootan* 217.

10. According to BRDK 179 this payment constituted the "land price" of the Indian district of "Kumarkatra", a place I cannot identify. For the background to the annexation of the Assam Duars, see Singh 1988a: 307-9.

11. BRDK 178-9 suggests this settlement took place during the brief reign of Kunga Pelden in 1855.

12. The prophecy must have related to Ugyen Wangchuk, born in 1862, rather than his elder brother Trinley Topgye, born in 1856.

13. For an essay on the historical significance and symbolism of the Raven Crown, see BRGI 559-62. Lama Jangchub Tsöndrü died in 1856 in Tongsa. His funeral took place at Jampai Lhakhang in Bumthang.

14. If we are to believe the evidence of Ashley Eden, Jigme Namgyel's predecessor Tsokye Dorje continued to regard the Tongsa governorship as his by right and in 1864 was still trying to regain it for himself, not for his son: *Political Missions to Botan* 102; *Papers Relating to Bootan* 218.

15. Eden made the mistake of claiming Jigme Namgyel to be of "low extraction", his father having been a menial of a former Tongsa Pönlop: *Political Missions to Bootan* 101; *Papers Relating to Bhutan* 218. Eden failed to realise the absence of external signs distinguishing the nobility from the common peasantry. Nor did he know anything of the custom which required the nobility to render common service in their youth.

16. *Papers Relating to Bootan* 153-4. Although Darlung Topgye was seen to be acting as Jigme Namgyel's chief supporter at the time of the mission, no sooner did it depart than he planned a nationwide uprising against him. It failed. *Ibid.* 218.

17. *Ibid.* 153, 156-7, 218; BRGI 490.

18. For full details of the war, see esp. Eden 1864; Rennie 1866; MacGregor 1866; *Papers Relating to Bootan*; Warren 1867; Grey 1912; Kohli 1982; Labh 1974; Collister 1987; Singh 1988a.

19. See in particular BRGI 490-2.

20. It is possible that more died of malaria on the British side than were killed in the conflict on the Bhutanese side. "Future travellers in these parts will wonder whose are the rows of graves, who could have been the men to risk the deadly nature of this climate ... Of those who served in the last of England's little wars, there are but few whose health and constitution have not been broken and impaired. But the price paid would not be grudged by the victims were it certain that the history thereof taught a lesson or pointed a moral": Warren 1867: 160.

21. See in particular Warren 1867 and Grey 1912.

22. The final showdown finds no mention in the official reports of the campaign, presumably because it was seen as damaging to official pride. However, there is a lively account of this last expedition by the man who led it, concluding with: "We had nothing to show for all the cost and trouble save these two guns! We got back our prisoners, too, and a bedraggled lot they were. Men who had declined to fight and surrendered by hundreds were not cause of much rejoicing": Grey 1912: 78.

23. BRGI 494-5. A local tradition holds that the saint Pemalingpa had used his powers to bless the river in such a way that fish would never live there. (Fishing is regarded as specially sinful.) Sonam Thayé is said to have made his Indian slave Dombu transport live fish from the Chamkhar river in Bumthang to Chumé hoping they would breed there, but they never did.

24. Both sides appealed to the British for military assistance but they refused to intervene. On the other hand the Chinese authorities in Tibet sought to become involved. A Sino-Tibetan mission was sent to Thimphu, but mainly to dissuade the Bhutanese from contact with the British. Labh 1974: 117-18, 121-2; Kohli 1981: 113-18; Singh 1988a: 327, 331.

25. Kohli 1981: 118-19.

26. Although Nyima Dorje was the uncle of the one who had fled to India, he was thought to be well disposed towards Jigme Namgyel. As we shall see, that trust was in fact misplaced for he too later turned to rebellion.

27. Dorje Namgyel met the Lieutenant-Governor of Bengal, Sir Richard Temple, at Pasakha (Buxa) in 1875. The new regent was overruled by Jigme Namgyel in his desire to accede to the British request to open up a road from Bhutan to Sikkim. The rebels in the next insurrection hoped to arrange for this, counting on British military support in return, but they failed. Kohli 1982: 122-4.

28. Jigme Namgyel wrote to the British asking for the return of those who had fled to India. He got a polite letter back from Ashley Eden, now knighted and the Lieutenant-Governor of Bengal, saying the British would observe neutrality and only return criminals, not political refugees. It is not sure if Eden realised that the person to whom he was writing had rubbed wet dough on his face in 1864. The refugees were disarmed at Pasakha and allowed to settle in Darjeeling with a living allowance. Two years later circumstances allowed their repatriation. Labh 1974: 118-19; Kohli 1982: 124; Singh 1988a: 331-2.

29. They were Püntso Dorje, born on the same day as Ugyen Wangchuk to the sister of one of Jigme Namgyel's attendants at Wangdü Chöling, and Alo Dorje, the son of Jigme Namgyel's enemy Kawang Mangkhel but nephew to his ally Lama Tsewang. Püntso Dorje, who had shared Ugyen Wangchuk's imprisonment in Paro, was made Shung Drönyer at the time Ugyen Wangchuk was appointed Paro Pönlop. The latter was soon to appoint Alo Dorje as Punakha Dzongpön.

Four
The Founding Monarch

Ugyen Wangchuk inherited the strengths and weaknesses of his father, but he seems to have rearranged these into a decisive new pattern. He consolidated the hold his father had gained on the country, using to begin with some of his father's methods, but early in his career he turned, crucially, from tactics of blunt coercion to those which promoted harmony and consensus. By doing so at a time when the shifting balance of power in Asia favoured the emergence of Bhutan as an independent buffer between India and Tibet, he was able to introduce constitutional changes that left him and his heirs triumphant and the country's survival as a sovereign state assured. As the founder of the Bhutanese monarchy he certainly ranks equal with the Shabdrung as the creator of the theocracy.

The accounts of his early youth which have survived only tell us about one aspect of it, namely the way he had to work his way up the ladder of responsibility, starting on the very lowest rung.[1] Though he studied basic reading and writing under his maternal uncle, the eighth Pemalingpa incarnation of Lhalung, from the age of eight he was in daily attendance on his father.[2] As such he had to labour with the lowest menials of the court, collecting a daily load of three large bundles of firewood. Moreover, he was compelled to eat his meals in a line with the other servants; this is traditionally done with the youngest and most junior served last. He was forbidden to receive a single extra bowlful, even from his mother. At the age of eleven, the year his father resigned from the regency, he worked with other attendants as a labourer on a new road in Thimphu from Luntenzampa to Samardzingkha. Like his father who spent time in his youth herding animals in Bumthang, there would have been little to distinguish him at this time from an ordinary peasant. But there is no inconsistency here between his birth in a noble family descending from Pemalingpa and the hard training received in his youth. Something of the same tradition certainly continued under his descendants in the next two generations, and in the present too there is a general attitude that promotion and high office has to be earned from the bottom of the ladder. The speed with which it is climbed, however, can depend on several factors.

It has been seen how Ugyen Wangchuk at the age of sixteen took part in his father's campaign to reconquer the fortress in Paro. His capture by the enemy and imprisonment in the citadel was followed by his release, secured by his father who had taken a whole family hostage for his life. The retaking of the main fortress in Paro and the quelling of the whole rebellion were then followed by his elevation to the high office of Paro Pönlop. Again, there are many precedents for the trusted son or close relative

Ugyen Wangchuk wearing the Raven Crown and the insignia of the KCIE at Punakha, 1905. He is barefoot not only because this was his habit and preferance but more particularly because the investiture ceremony in the main temple of the dzong required this gesture of humility in the presence of the ecclesiastical dignitaries who were presiding. (Photo: J.C. White, private collection).

of a ruler or magnate receiving an appointment like this at a very early age.[3] Hard physical training and close observance and participation in earlier strife must have equipped him with the qualities of strength needed for holding the post. The judgement and statecraft came later.

In 1882, a year after Ugyen Wangchuk had performed the funeral ceremonies of his father, the regent Chögyel Zangpo died in office. Ugyen Wangchuk was instrumental in securing the appointment of his successor, Lama Tsewang, the son and brother of former Dzongpöns of Thimphu and a close confidant of Jigme Namgyel in his later years. He had in fact changed to Jigme Namgyel's side during the great rebellion of the 1870s and remained loyal ever since.

However, just as Ugyen Wangchuk's inherited authority is demonstrated by this appointment, so also is his potentially tenuous hold on power shown by the murder of another of his appointees, the Daga Pönlop.[4] The deed was done by that person's own senior officer, who had presumably held the same post under a previous master. He fled to the sanctuary of the Talo monastery where the nineteen-year-old Shabdrung Jigme Chögyel (1862-1904) was installed as Dharma Raja. The outcome is not mentioned in the records, but it was not long before Ugyen Wangchuk had to face much more serious trouble. Meanwhile, the first inkling that he would later adopt very different methods from those of his father is revealed in his handling of another case. When one of his father's enemies, the Kalön Ashang Wangya, returned from exile in India and presented himself at the fortress of Thimphu, the attendants of the late Jigme Namgyel were incensed and ready to do away with him. Ugyen Wangchuk, however, refused to give way to any instinct for revenge. On the advice of the regent, the former enemy went to Ugyen Wangchuk and made him a peace offering of his daughter Ludrong Drölma. Though it is not known how long Ugyen Wangchuk's liaison with the girl lasted, it must have become clear to him there were happier ways of resolving conflict than those previously employed.

In that same year, at the age of twenty, he had to face and take full part in the first of two major disturbances. It was a family affair, a story of bitter feuding and revenge that was to have far-reaching consequences. The cause is traced back to the promise made by his paternal uncle Dungkar Gyeltsen to vacate the office of Tongsa Pönlop after holding it for three years and pass it on to his, Ugyen Wangchuk's, maternal uncle Pema Tendzin, the Byagar Dzongpön. Dungkar Gyeltsen, like some of his predecessors, refused to step down when the time was due. At this point Pema Tendzin, who was now determined to unseat the Pönlop, promised to appoint one Senge Namgyel his seniormost officer if he carried out the attack successfully. But after the defeat of Dungkar Gyeltsen,[5] he broke the promise and the office went instead to the brother of his junior wife. Senge Namgyel therefore plotted to kill his master, the new Pönlop, who now held the governorship for three years. His later downfall was ascribed by some to the fact that during his tenure he refused to make revenue payments from his province to the central government. Such payments traditionally went to provide butter for the lamps used to placate the guardian divinities during annual ceremonies. The gods wreaked their revenge in the plot that was to follow.

The palace of Lamé Gönpa, Bumthang, 1933. First named Lam Pelri, its construction began in the 1880s as the residence for the Byagar and later Tongsa Pönlop, Pema Tendzin, who was assassinated in 1882. It remained in his family, passing to the descendants of King Ugyen Wangchuk's first wife Rinchen, the daughter of Pema Tendzin. (Photo: F. Ludlow, Natural History Museum)

The embittered Senge Namgyel enlisted for his purpose two local men who had been dismissed from employment at the site of the new palace of Lamé Gönpa that was being constructed in Bumthang for his enemy, the new Tongsa Pönlop. In 1882 these two men killed Pema Tendzin, and Senge Namgyel made himself governor in his place. To win the support of the region he issued an edict abolishing all taxes for one year except those paid in the form of grain and wood.

The murder had taken place at the fortress of Byagar within sight of the Wangdü Chöling palace where Pema Chökyi, sister of the dead Pönlop, was living. She immediately sent a runner to the west to summon her son Ugyen Wangchuk and his cousin Kunzang Trinley. On arrival they attacked the fortress and after some days succeeded in capturing its water supply. But they hesitated to attack the main building because Senge Namgyel now took as hostage Ugyen Wangchuk's aunt and cousins, the wife and children of the dead governor. He also had gunpowder set ready to burn down the dzong in case of attack. Ugyen Wangchuk withdrew to plan his next move.

His mother Pema Chökyi came up with a plot. She approached the Pönlop alone, saying that with her brother and husband both dead she now had absolutely no one else to turn to for the support of her daughter and estate. Her brother had brought his death upon himself. She harboured no ill will. Senge Namgyel, suspecting treachery, made her take an oath to swear to the truth of her declaration. She did so, he believed it, and so he was softened up in this way for an approach by her son with similar protestations of loyalty and forgiveness. Some days later, at a time fixed by astrology, Ugyen Wangchuk and his men paraded into the fortress bearing gifts, and so the plot was easily accomplished.[6] Senge Namgyel was slain and the two men he had employed to kill Pema Tendzin were also cut down. Their hearts were removed and placed in a new stupa by the river. It was consecrated by Ugyen Wangchuk's uncle, incarnation of Pemalingpa, in a special ritual designed to vanquish all future enemies. The dead Pönlop's "flag officer" was executed in the river by the drowning method. The property of Senge Namgyel was permanently confiscated from his family.

Ugyen Wangchuk further secured his homeland, long neglected by his father, by making himself Tongsa Pönlop. He gathered and delivered the revenue from the province which his uncle had withheld from the central government for three years. His elder brother Trinley Topgye, the former monk, he appointed to replace him as Paro Pönlop and to hold the joint office of Wangdü Phodrang Dzongpön. A year later when his brother died from a fall from his horse at the bridge in Paro, he nominated his second cousin Dawa Penjor to the Paro governorship and his relative Ashang Jampa to the post at Wangdü Phodrang. Dawa Penjor had been dismissed from service by Jigme Namgyel for poor performance in one of his battles, but Ugyen Wangchuk chose now to bring him back into favour.

Family ties were immensely strengthened now by his decision to marry his cousin Rinchen, daughter of the murdered Pönlop whose death he had avenged, and he further arranged for his own sister Yeshé Chödrön to marry the Pönlop's son Chimey Dorje. He then appointed his brother-in-law to the post of Byagar Dzongpön previously held by his father and restored to him his family's property and followers. To his sister he further entrusted the family estate of Wangdü Chöling and all its wealth. This pair of cousin marriages brought together for the second time the powerful families of the Dungkar Chöjé and Tamshing Chöjé, securing for Ugyen Wangchuk a stable base for all his future advancement.[7] But he lost his mother at this time. She is said to have died from the pollution caused by breaking her oath of loyalty to the dead enemy.

The second, much greater disturbance began when Ugyen Wangchuk learnt in 1884 of a plot to kill him. The men who planned this were none other than his own adoptive brothers Püntso Dorje and Alo Dorje, the Dzongpöns of Punakha and Thimphu. It will be recalled that Jigme Namgyel on his deathbed had enjoined his real and adoptive sons to support each other in all future conflict. Ugyen Wangchuk had therefore placed these two in positions of high trust and responsibility. But while he was attending to the troubles at home Püntso Dorje abducted the wife whom Ugyen Wangchuk had taken while residing in the west. This lady, Dechen Zangmo, he installed in his own house at Samtengang. Püntso Dorje then gave his sister as wife to Alo Dorje, it seems because he was looking to him for support should his abduction of Dechen Zangmo lead to trouble with Ugyen Wangchuk.

Dawa Penjor, the Paro Pönlop and second-cousin to Ugyen Wangchuk, surrounded by the officials of his court, Paro 1905. The virtually independent authority of the Paro Pönlop in this period is reflected in the varied official headgear seen here. The sipaho *standard held by the attendant behind bears a medley of astrological symbols to bring good fortune on the governor and his principality. The rug in the foreground is a fine example of Bhutanese appliqué work. Hyslop, writing two years later, noted that: "The Penlop is an old man, he has got a bad reputation as a ruler, for he squeezes his subjects rather too much, but he appears now to have rather broken up and is getting more lenient in his old age". (Photo: J.C. White, private collection)*

Having thus strengthened their adoptive relationship by ties of marriage, it is said "a demon possessed them" to hatch a plot against Ugyen Wangchuk. They installed their own candidate, the state monk Gawa Zangpo, as regent and sent a letter and large bribe to Ugyen Wangchuk's senior officer with instructions to kill his master. Instead the man revealed all. Ugyen Wangchuk responded by saying he had already heard rumours of the plot but that if war were declared without thoroughly investigating the situation first it could bring needless misery on the public. Far better, he said, to try and restore good relations. He sent an invitation to the plotters to meet him in the Shar district and went there bearing valuable gifts. When they failed to turn up as arranged, it became clear to him they were resolved on their course. A further cause of conflict lay in the refusal of the central government, now in the hands of his enemies, to hand over to him what he regarded as his rightful share of the annual subsidy paid to the government by the British as compensation for the annexation of the duars.[8] He replied in kind by withholding revenue payments. There was nothing for it but to fight it out.

Ugyen Wangchuk first made a tour of his province. At each temple he swore an oath to the guardian deities: "If my enemies are destined to bring benefit not only to the teachings of the Lord Buddha in general and in particular to those of the Glorious Drukpa but also to all the subjects of Bhutan, and if on the other hand I am doomed to cause them injury, then may my own vital organs come into their hands. If, on the other hand, I am the one destined to bring benefit and my enemies doomed to cause injury, then may their vital organs come into my own hands".[9] He arranged for a mass levy of 2,140 men, fully armed and equipped, and with battle standards flying and processional music playing he set off in 1885 to lead his troops into what was to be Bhutan's last civil war.[10]

When the head abbot and senior state monks arrived at his camp with an offer of mediation, he instead gave them the wherewithal to conduct a ceremony that would quickly reveal the identity of the state's real enemy. The first indication that the gods were fully intent on punishing his own enemies was seen when their followers tried to kill a battle champion on their own side whom they wrongfully suspected of treachery. Desperately looking for support, and getting none from their own puppet regent, the conspirators went to the Shabdrung's father, Könchok Wangdü, and offered him a massive bribe to take on the regency himself. But he refused, pointing out that he was related to many of those fighting on the side of the invading force and in any case he had no wish at all for the regency. He was from the same family of the Dramitse Chöjé, collateral of the Dungkar Chöjé, that had produced the earlier Shabdrung incarnation Jigme Norbu. He also happened to be the current Tamshing Chöjé by marriage. He was the father of no less than four important "state" incarnations, including one whose photograph has survived.[11]

Battle was first joined at Punakha in 1886 when Ugyen Wangchuk took his main force there by foot across the river, holding on to each other and using their bows as staves to steady themselves against the current. After two engagements the enemy retreated in a body to Thimphu, pursued by the invaders who tried to take a short cut over the mountains through a forest. Alo Dorje's men closed this route by setting fire to the forest, so the invaders diverted to Simtokha and quickly overpowered the guards left there. At the first engagement the enemy was driven back, "as if a stone had been cast into a flock of birds", and they retreated into the dzong.

A fortnight after Simtokha had been taken the head abbot and state monks began to play their customary role of trying to mediate a truce. A time and place was set for a meeting of representatives from both sides. Dawa Penjor, the Paro Pönlop, came in place of Ugyen Wangchuk while Püntso Dorje agreed to stand for the rebels. When next morning the latter was riding towards the place chosen for the meeting, Chang Limaithang, his horse refused to cross the stone bridge in between. His attendants saw this as the most evil of omens presaging death and tried to dissuade him from proceeding, but Püntso Dorje insisted. Since strife would in any case continue in Bhutan in his lifetime, he said there was no point in desisting now.

The Paro Pönlop duly arrived with food sent by Ugyen Wangchuk for the whole meeting, but it quickly turned to bloodshed. A commotion in the lower ranks of the

The incarnate lama of Tango (with goitre), Kunga Drakpa by name, standing in the main entrance to the monastery of Talo, situated on the western slope of the Punakha valley. This monastery was the seat of successive incarnations of the Shabdrung, Bhutan's head of state before the emergence of the monarchy. This Tango Tulku was the younger brother of Shabdrung Jigme Chögyel (1862-1904), whose embalmed remains he installed in a stupa within the monastery in 1905, the year this photograph was taken. The Tulku had charge of the monastery in the interregnum between the death of his brother and the discovery and installation of his successor, Shabdrung Jigme Dorje (1905-31). The monastery was the scene of that later Shabdrung's unhappy demise. (Photo: J.C. White, private collection)

attendants suddenly led to Jigme Namgyel's senior officer drawing his sword, intending to kill Püntso Dorje, but the sword got stuck in his sash. The Pönlop rushed to his defence and cleaved Püntso Dorje's head in two. Hearing of this, Alo Dorje and his chief supporters took off for safe refuge in Tibet.[12] Their troops were disarmed and made to pass beneath an arch of weapons held up by the victors. By this ritual the good fortune of the enemy was meant to be permanently destroyed.[13]

It would not appear that a great number of people died in this last civil war. It had much of the flavour of ritual engagement observed by the British in the earlier conflicts of the eighteenth century. Certainly the common troops do not seem to have fought with that desperate courage and determination that so impressed their British opponents in the Anglo-Bhutan war of twenty-one years earlier.[14]

The fortress of the winter capital was taken over by Ugyen Wangchuk. The regent whom his enemies had installed, but who had done nothing to assist them, was allowed to retire to a monastery.[15] Ugyen Wangchuk decided to replace him with another monk, Sangye Dorje, his late father's close supporter. To overcome strong opposition to his nominee from the council of state he is said to have taken the simple expedient of seizing the Shabdrung's seal, traditionally used to confirm the regent's appointment. He refused to give it up till all had agreed.[16] He then awarded himself the post of chamberlain (*gongzim*) to the new regent and made his cousin Kunzang Trinley the new Thimphu Dzongpön. All power thus came into his hands and was to remain there for his life. He had defeated all enemies of the east and west and filled all key appointments with his own trusted relatives. He was only twenty-four.

There remained the unsettled matter of his first wife Dechen Zangmo whom the dead Püntso Dorje had stolen from him. Here the story turns to what looks like a fairy tale but there must be many elements of truth in it. Ugyen Wangchuk ordered six of his retainers to go and fetch her to Bumthang. On arrival at Püntso Dorje's house at Samtengang she begged them to be allowed to remain for a week so she could prepare for the journey. She made her six maid servants entertain the attendants with singing and dancing during the day and she had them sleep with the visitors at night. They were plied with abundant food and drink. While they were thus distracted she had her most precious objects hidden in the ground and arranged for the rest of her things to be packed up. She sent these off to Tibet together with a son she had borne. (It is not clear who the father was.) On the night before she was to be led off to Ugyen Wangchuk

Ugyen Wangchuk at Wangdü Chöling, Bumthang, 1905. Standing next to him are his sister Yeshé Chödrön and two of her daughters, Lemo and Lhadrön, who were both married to Dasho Drupa, the Dungkar Chöjé. Dorje Rabden, son of Yeshé Chödrön, is to the left. The other ladies in the photograph are the family's serving maids and weavers from the ancestral home in Kurtö. All the ladies wear fine examples of the kushütara *weave from Kurtö. (Photo: J.C. White, private collection)*

Ugyen Wangchuk at Wangdü Chöling, Bumthang, 1905, with his two daughters by his first wife, Pedrön on the left and Yangdzom on the right. His sister Yeshé Chödrön stands in the centre behind with one of her daughters, Lemo, to her left. The lady on her other side is Ugyen Wangchuk's second wife, also called Lemo. The child she is holding is probably Pedrön's son, Tsering Penjor, the future Paro Pönlop. (Photo: J.C. White, private collection)

in Bumthang she had herself tied and sealed up in a sack and carried off under the noses of the exhausted attendants. The load was taken by way of Thimphu, Paro and Ha across the Tibetan border to Phari where it was finally unsealed. There Dechen Zangmo caught up with the party of losers who had fled from the battleground at Thimphu. Together they proceeded to Lhasa to enlist Tibetan support in making a comeback. The Chinese authorities in Tibet attempted to impose their own settlement by summoning a conference at Phari in 1886. However, the Tongsa and Paro Pönlops refused to attend or receive the insignias of rank the Chinese wanted to confer on them. It came to nothing in the end.[17] Later, as we shall see, some of them were allowed back to Bhutan but it is not known what happened to the resourceful Dechen Zangmo.

Ugyen Wangchuk spent most of the years from 1886 to 1904 in Tongsa and Bumthang. Clearly matters were sufficiently stable in the capitals to allow him to go home. The traditional centre of power in the country had few attractions for him, and throughout his adult life he only ever seems to have spent time there when he really had to. Little is known about the events of the period immediately following the civil war. The uncle who first taught him his letters, Kunzang Tenpai Nyima, the eighth incarnation of the speech of Pemalingpa, died in 1900. Ugyen Wangchuk went across the border to Lhalung for the funeral. He arranged for the great lama who was supervising the obsequies, Khamsum Yongdröl, to come south to Bumthang to construct an enormous new image of Padmasambhava at the temple of Kujé. The image took the form of the saint known as "He who Subdues the Phenomenal World with his Brilliance" (Nangsi Zilnön). It was completed in 1894 to serve as "the field of merit of all the people of Bhutan".

In 1897 both he and his wife Ashi Rinchen suffered serious illness. Many religious ceremonies were performed for their recovery but Rinchen died in 1900. She had borne him two daughters and three sons, but all the sons had died in their infancy.[18] It must have been at this time that he began to think of passing on his authority to his nephew, Dorje Rabden, whom he later married to his daughter Pedrön. He was also to make him the chief officer (*drönyer*) at his court. But before Rinchen had died she had insisted her husband should take a new wife to maintain the direct lineage. It is known that at this time he had a brief liaison with one Ngödrup Pemo and other women too,[19] but a monk called Geshé Mindruk who was close to him came up with a highly suitable candidate. This was Lemo, daughter of Ugyen Wangchuk's cousin Kunzang Trinley, the Dzongpön of Thimphu, who had married a noble lady of Khöma in Kurtö. Ashi Lemo was introduced to her second cousin and future husband on a day fixed by the astrologers. She brought with her the gift of a sacred pill for Ugyen Wangchuk's long life which had been made by a lama he greatly revered. Lemo had with her own hands stitched and embroidered the bag in which it lay. A poem was recited with allusions to the marriage of the ancient king Songtsen Gampo of Tibet to a Chinese princess. Four years later she was to give birth to a son.

It was some time in the last years of the nineteenth century that Ugyen Wangchuk became acquainted with a man who was to have a decisive effect on his own fortunes. He had heard that a certain Bhutanese trader from Kalimpong called Ugyen Dorje had presented very valuable gifts to the Shabdrung at Punakha. He sent word for this person to come and see him in Bumthang. It transpired he was the son of a retired Dzongpön called Pünchung whom Ugyen Wangchuk's great-uncle Pala Gyeltsen had fathered "on the side" while staying with a lady of the village of Tsendong in the Paro valley. Ugyen Wangchuk soon came to have a high regard and trust for Ugyen Dorje and later would refer to him as his elder brother. The first commission he appears to have entrusted to him was to negotiate the return of the exiles who had fled to Tibet in 1886.[20] He was sent to Lhasa on what seems to have been the first of many such trips. Eventually the border districts of Dungnak, Ha, Gasa, Lingshi and Lamgong were apportioned between the exiles. A clear division was made between their jurisdiction and responsibilities and those of the central government. It seems that Alo Dorje himself remained in Chumbi, perhaps because the district of Dungnak he had been given held no attractions for him. In order to dissuade him from fomenting trouble across the border it was agreed that Dechen Zangmo's younger brother Tsewang and others close to Alo Dorje should take up residence with Ugyen Dorje in Kalimpong.

Ugyen Dorje, the most trusted confidant and supporter of King Ugyen Wangchuk, in a formal studio portrait taken in Darjeeling or Kalimpong circa 1914 shortly before his death. (Photo: private collection of Dasho Topgye Dorje)

Table 3 The Dorje family of Bhutan

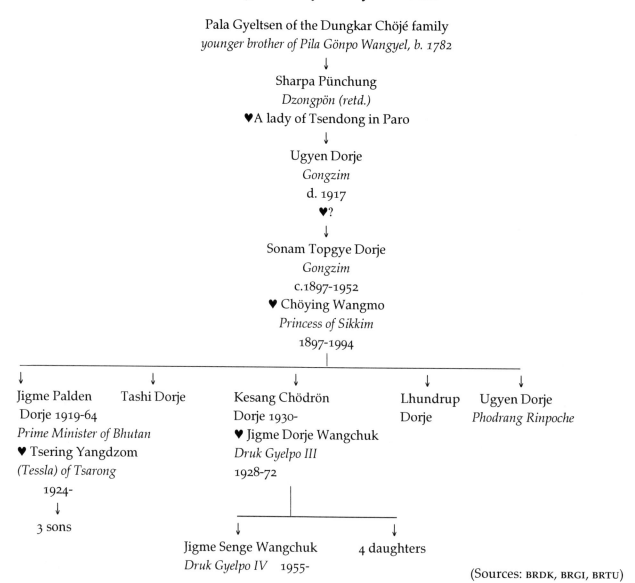

Pala Gyeltsen of the Dungkar Chöjé family
younger brother of Pila Gönpo Wangyel, b. 1782
↓
Sharpa Pünchung
Dzongpön (retd.)
♥A lady of Tsendong in Paro
↓
Ugyen Dorje
Gongzim
d. 1917
♥?
↓
Sonam Topgye Dorje
Gongzim
c.1897-1952
♥ Chöying Wangmo
Princess of Sikkim
1897-1994

| Jigme Palden Dorje 1919-64 *Prime Minister of Bhutan* ♥ Tsering Yangdzom *(Tessla) of Tsarong* 1924- ↓ 3 sons | Tashi Dorje | Kesang Chödrön Dorje 1930- ♥ Jigme Dorje Wangchuk *Druk Gyelpo III* 1928-72 | Lhundrup Dorje | Ugyen Dorje *Phodrang Rinpoche* |

Jigme Senge Wangchuk   4 daughters
Druk Gyelpo IV   1955-

(Sources: BRDK, BRGI, BRTU)

Though hostages, they were maintained very kindly.

In 1898 the British authorities began to use Ugyen Dorje as a go-between with the Tibetans as part of their continuing efforts to secure trade concessions. He had already been appointed Bhutan Agent by the British a year earlier. When he visited Lhasa in that year with gifts from Ugyen Wangchuk to the Dalai Lama he was asked to make overtures on behalf of the British. Ten years earlier British troops had attacked the Tibetan fortress of Lingtu in the aftermath of the unsuccessful Macauley mission which had been aimed at securing trade conditions favourable to British India.[21] Ugyen Wangchuk had at that time declined a Tibetan request for assistance on the grounds that the British would withhold their subsidy. After the arrival in 1899 of Lord Curzon as the new Viceroy, British determination to obtain better trade with Tibet became entirely bound up with a forward policy designed to counter Russian expansion in Central Asia. It was thought, wrongly as it turned out, that Russia had serious designs on Tibet. Ugyen Dorje did his best to explain to the British that conditions in Lhasa were far from being ready to accommodate their interests. However, in June 1901 he agreed to try and deliver a letter from Curzon to the Dalai Lama while escorting to Lhasa two elephants, two peacocks and a leopard which the Tibetan ruler had purchased in India. Fearful of angering the Chinese, the lama declined to receive the letter, and when Ugyen Dorje returned with the letter still sealed Curzon decided that he must after all be a Tibetan spy. It was only years later that Ugyen Dorje managed to clear his name completely in British eyes.

Meanwhile, in 1900 Ugyen Wangchuk had appointed Ugyen Dorje government agent (*kutsap*) for the whole of southern Bhutan with headquarters at Pasakha (Buxa). From then on he was to serve two masters since he continued to retain the earlier post of Bhutan Agent given to him by the British in 1898. In particular Ugyen Wangchuk now gave him sole responsibility for the settlement of Nepalese in southern Bhutan with authority to levy taxes from them. The edict appointing him made it clear that the office would become hereditary within Ugyen Dorje's family if he rendered good service. Among the seals fixed to the document were those of the Shabdrung, the regent, the Tongsa Pönlop and the Wangdü Phodrang Dzongpön.[22]

The last in the line of regents, in fact the fifty-seventh incumbent, was put on the throne by Ugyen Wangchuk in 1903. Yeshé Ngödrup, the fifth embodiment of the "speech" of the founding Shabdrung, had found himself used earlier in 1864 by Jigme Namgyel as a stand-in for the real Dharma Raja and he had acted as a rival puppet regent briefly in 1877. He was a politically ineffectual figure who yet had ambitions of his own, as we shall see later. Though credited with some religious attainments, he is not remembered for achieving anything during his regency, which continued till 1906.

By 1903 Curzon had convinced himself the Russians were moving into Tibet with full Chinese compliance. The refusal of the Tibetan authorities to deal with him directly made him decide there was a single course open to him. A mission led by Colonel Francis Younghusband would proceed under armed escort and if necessary fight its way to Lhasa, destroy the power of the monks who were blocking negotiations, and then proceed to secure British interests in the form of a binding treaty.[23] The importance of obtaining Bhutanese support in pursuit of these aims was quickly apparent to those planning the mission. Spies carried rumours that the Bhutanese were planning to aid the Tibetans. Curzon wrote of his worries concerning the "incomprehensible hierarchy who preside over the hills" of Bhutan.[24] Whether these worries were well grounded or not, logistics seemed to demand quick access to Tibet through Bhutanese territory.

In fact it transpired that Ugyen Wangchuk had indeed offered help to the Tibetan government, promising to close all roads into Tibet and ordering the production of many thousands of arrows to defend it. Suspicious and fearful of all outside contact, the Tibetans declined his offer, but Ugyen Wangchuk's order for arrows was then changed to one for iron in case of future need for weapons.[25] The Paro Pönlop, whose district fell on the frontier, made preparations that could either have been for attack or defence. What seems eventually to have turned the Bhutanese to the British side was

Cholé Tulku Yeshé Ngödrup (1851-1917), the fifth incarnation of the "speech principal" of Shabdrung Ngawang Namgyel (1594-?1651), who served as the fifty-seventh and last in the line of civil regents (Druk Desi) before Ugyen Wangchuk's accession as first king of Bhutan in 1907. He is seen here in his apart-ment in Punakha Dzong in 1905. Later he also served as fifty-third Head Abbot (Je Khenpo) of Bhutan from 1915 to his death in 1917. (Photo: J.C. White, private collection)

the threat to withhold the subsidy. Younghusband, who had taken charge of relations with Bhutan, made this very clear to Ugyen Wangchuk, reminding him of Bhutan's treaty obligations for friendship with India. He indicated that the subsidy would only be paid once Bhutanese compliance with the aims of the mission had been obtained. Ugyen Wangchuk's cousin and father-in-law, the Thimphu Dzongpön Kunzang Trinley, amply demonstrated this when he delivered to Younghusband a permit for the British to build a road to Tibet from India up the Amochu and Dichu valleys. Although carefully surveyed, in the end an alternative route was found.

The British and Bhutanese records all agree it was the trusted Thimphu Dzongpön who persuaded Ugyen Wangchuk to offer his services as mediator between the British and Tibetans. With growing intransigence on both sides there was a role to be played by anyone who had close relations with Lhasa while dealing with the British. The Bhutanese, moreover, had a long history of using mediation as a means of political and social conciliation.[26] Ugyen Wangchuk appears to have been playing both sides at the same time before he came down decisively for the British, though he did this in a way calculated to leave the door wide open to Lhasa. As Fleming puts it: "His mission was to mediate, but he made no pretence of impartiality and can only have been regarded by the Tibetans and Chinese as a puppet or collaborator of the British. He was however much respected by the Tibetans, and Bhutan's good offices — like those of Nepal, whose Maharajah had just renewed his attempts to make the Tibetans see reason — were of great value to the Mission, because both states possessed that rare amenity, a well-established, two-way channel of communication with Lhasa".[27]

Moreover, Ugyen Wangchuk had some very endearing qualities. He was "a jolly, astute individual who was the *de facto* (and later became the *de jure*) ruler of his country. He possessed a golden crown of great splendour ... The British soldiers called him 'the Tonsil', as they later called the Amban 'the Hambone'; but what with his *embonpoint*, his vivacity and his little imperial beard there was something vaguely Gallic about him, and to the officers he was known as 'Alphonse'. He brought with him a numerous and predatory retinue, whose looting caused distress to the Tibetans and embarrassment to the British ... Younghusband liked the Tongsa Penlop; he found him straight and possessed of a natural authority".[28]

By the time the mission had fought its way to Gyangtse with heavy and pitiful losses on the Tibetan side, their representatives had made it clear they would not come to the table unless Ugyen Wangchuk was present. The Dalai Lama himself had entrusted him with the task of persuading the British to turn back. Younghusband therefore called him up from Chumbi where he had earlier arrived, and so he rode into Gyangste on 2 June 1904 with two hundred of his men. He was the main go-between in the negotiations whose failure resulted in the British storming the Gyangtse fort on 6 July. When the fort was taken he was asked to bring in the Tibetan councilors, but they had all retreated. Ugyen Wangchuk at this time received two more letters from the Dalai Lama asking him to use his influence and saying that new delegates from his side were coming to Chaksam. With the collapse of further talks there the mission proceeded relentlessly to Lhasa. Ugyen Wangchuk led the grand entry into the sacred

Opposite: Ugyen Wangchuk at the conclusion of peace in Lhasa, 1904, with the Raven Crown revealed for the first time in this photograph. To the right stands his distant relative and chief supporter Ugyen Dorje, the Bhutan Agent, and to the left his cousin and father-in-law Kunzang Trinley, the Thimphu Dzongpön. (Photo: Johnston and Hoffman, British Library)

Ugyen Wangchuk, the Tongsa Pönlop, robed in silk brocade, rides through the Chumbi valley of Tibet in 1904 on his way to act as mediator between the British and Tibetans. The Raven Crown on his head is hidden by a cloth wrapper to protect it from the dust of the journey. (Photo: C. Bell, Merseyside County Museums)

city wearing his Raven Crown for the occasion and accompanied by ceremonial musicians and all his men. Fearing conflict, however, he pulled them back: "... the Bhutanese saw to it that they lay a bad second to the mounted infantry".[29] The Dalai Lama had fled and in the protracted negotiations which followed Ugyen Wangchuk took joint lead as chief negotiator with the Nepalese representative. He was constantly employed to explain to one side the terms the other was trying to secure and, on his own initiative, he sought to lessen the excessive indemnity the British sought to impose on the defeated Tibetans. In Younghusband's own words, Ugyen Wangchuk was "highly instrumental in effecting a settlement. A year ago the Bhutanese were strangers, today they are our enthusiastic allies".[30] In the final agreement the British won the trade concessions they had long been working for. They were not to forget the part played in this by Ugyen Wangchuk, who attended the signing ceremony "in full regalia, attended by myrmidons scarcely less ornate".[31]

The effect in Bhutan of Ugyen Wangchuk's mediation in Tibet was to count for a very great deal. For the first time since 1750, when a peace mission had been sent from Bhutan to Tibet to intervene in a civil war, the chance was presented of settling external rather than internal conflict. Both in Bhutan and in Tibet the traditional figure of the mediator is one of enormous prestige, standing above the contending parties and winning great honour from both sides. However, he declined the new official head-gear offered to him by the Tibetans, saying he would stick to his own crown. In Bhutan he was welcomed home like a conquering hero. The Shabdrung composed a poem in his honour,[32] and a minor verse epic recounting the whole story of his mediation is said to survive in some people's memories.[33]

To convey formal appreciation for the role he had played the British decided in 1905 to make him a Knight Commander of the Indian Empire. John Claude White, the Political Officer in Sikkim who had taken part in the Younghusband mission, was deputed to Bhutan for this purpose. In this way the prestige Ugyen Wangchuk had earned for himself abroad was demonstrated vividly to all those in his country who had till then only heard rumours of it. That British recognition certainly played a part in his ambitions is demonstrated by the fact that at this time he wrote to Lord Curzon, the viceroy, seeking assistance in making arrangements that would allow him to hold the post of Tongsa Pönlop for life. He had already held it probably for longer than anyone else in history. Doubtless there were no serious calls for him to give it up at this time, but with hindsight we can see he tried to formalize the Tongsa governorship as a step towards the higher goal of hereditary monarchy. The official British response, however, indicated that they were not going to abandon their policy of observing neutrality in Bhutan's internal affairs.[34] Curzon himself noted: "I should think it a most unwise thing to support or guarantee one of the Pönlops (even the ablest) against either of the [Dharma or Deb] Rajas. If he is the strongest man, he will support himself".[35] Ugyen Wangchuk must have soon realized he could count on British blessings but not on much practical support in achieving his long-term aims.

The need to further develop good relations had certainly been understood by the British side, hence the decision at this time not to take over a strip of territory on the

Ugyen Wangchuk in Lhasa, 1904. He was known to the British soldiers there as "The Tonsil", from his title of Tongsa Pönlop, and nicknamed "Alphonse" by the British officers on account of his little Gallic beard. This is the first visual record of that combination of the Bhutanese male robe (go) with Western shoes, stockings and headgear that has remained in vogue ever since. (Photo: F. M. Bailey, Royal Geographical Society)

The zhudrel *installation ceremony at Punakha Dzong in 1905 when Ugyen Wangchuk was presented with the insignia of Knight Commander of the Indian Empire as a reward for his services of mediation during the Younghusband Mission to Lhasa. The ceremony was presided over by the nominal regent Yeshé Ngödrup, seated on the throne at the back with the head abbot Rigdzin Nyingpo to his left. The British party was led by John Claude White, on the right, and included F.W. Rennick and A.W. Paul. The ever-present Ugyen Dorje stands behind Ugyen Wangchuk, and to his left sits his cousin, the Thimphu Dzongpön. (Photo: J.C. White, private collection)*

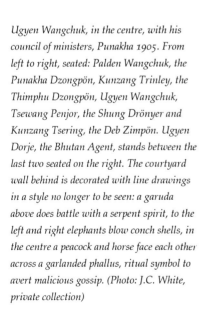

Ugyen Wangchuk, in the centre, with his council of ministers, Punakha 1905. From left to right, seated: Palden Wangchuk, the Punakha Dzongpön, Kunzang Trinley, the Thimphu Dzongpön, Ugyen Wangchuk, Tsewang Penjor, the Shung Drönyer and Kunzang Tsering, the Deb Zimpön. Ugyen Dorje, the Bhutan Agent, stands between the last two seated on the right. The courtyard wall behind is decorated with line drawings in a style no longer to be seen: a garuda above does battle with a serpent spirit, to the left and right elephants blow conch shells, in the centre a peacock and horse face each other across a garlanded phallus, ritual symbol to avert malicious gossip. (Photo: J.C. White, private collection)

Ugyen Wangchuk, wearing silk brocade imported from China, with nine members of his ceremonial bodyguard at his seat in Tongsa, 1905. The guards are typically equipped with chain mail helmets, two swords each, and rhino-hide shields decorated with brass bosses and symbols of the sun and moon. Behind Ugyen Wangchuk stands the Bhutan Agent, Ugyen Dorje, and to his left, with only his head visible, Ugyen Wangchuk's nephew and sometime heir apparent Dorje Rabden, who was at this time the Tongsa Zimpön (chamberlain). (Photo: J.C. White, private collection).

Ugyen Wangchuk in Bumthang, 1905, with his three British guests who had come to attend the investiture in Punakha and who had then accompanied him to visit his family in Bumthang: John Claude White, the Political Officer in Sikkim, standing; Major F.W. Rennick of the Intelligence Department, centre; and A.W. Paul, retired from the Indian Civil Service, who had travelled out from England for the trip on Ugyen Wangchuk's invitation. (Photo: J.C. White, private collection).

Tendzin Chökyi Gyeltsen (1894-1925), the ninth Peling Sungtrül (incarnation of Pemalingpa's "speech principle"), surrounded by monk attendants at his monastic seat of Lhalung in the Lhodrak province of southern Tibet. He had recently come here from his home in Bumthang and was being visited by his uncle Ugyen Wangchuk when this photograph of the twelve-year-old was taken in 1906. The elderly monk on the left is probably the young lama's tutor, Pema Tsewang, who had been a close disciple of the boy's previous incarnation. (Photo: J.C. White in Sir Thomas Holdich, "Bhutan: Strange Hill Folk and their Inchanted Land", in J.A. Hammerton (ed.), Peoples of All Nations, *i, London, c. 1908, p. 429.)*

Sikkim border controlled by the Bhutanese which should by rights have been ceded to India in 1865. More than anything else, however, it was the personal rapport which developed between Ugyen Wangchuk and White that ensured a strong footing for future relations. In 1906 he accompanied Ugyen Wangchuk to the great monastery of Lhalung across the border in the Lhodrak province of Tibet. It was a private journey to meet Ugyen Wangchuk's nephew, his sister's child, who had been discovered and installed at Lhalung as the incarnation of that sister's brother, the eighth embodiment of Pemalingpa's "speech principle", the same monk who had taken charge of Ugyen Wangchuk's early education. It can be seen how the lines of reincarnation were thus actively reinforcing the blood lines in a familiar manner. White's enthusiastic descriptions of his journeys with Ugyen Wangchuk and of the country as a whole stand in the same degree of contrast to those of Ashley Eden and his predecessors in the nineteenth

century as those in turn do to the accounts of the eighteenth-century travellers.[36] Again this is just as much a reflection of changing British attitudes as a mirror to the internal situation of the country.

The momentum given to Anglo-Bhutanese relations in 1904-5 was maintained by the formal visit of Ugyen Wangchuk to Calcutta to meet the Prince of Wales and the viceroy in 1906. It was the first of only two visits he ever paid to India. The regent Yeshé Ngödrup was also invited but pleaded the excuses of religion. Present in Calcutta too were the ruler of Sikkim and the Panchen Lama of Tibet. Ugyen Wangchuk was received in the manner of an Indian prince and he seems to have been more than content to accept that role. He was saluted with the fifteen guns reserved for such a prince and he presented the traditional *nazar*, a gift of gold coins symbolizing allegiance. The letter he brought to the viceroy declared: "As the stars and constellations never fail in loyalty attending on the sun and moon, so do we the entire Bhutanese nation resolve to do likewise to the Supreme Government, hoping that as the sun and moon are like the parents of the whole world, we also will enjoy the blessings of their beneficent rays for ever and ever till the cessation of worldly existence".[37] Was this no more than the sort of flowery and complimentary formula expected of him? Can he or others in Bhutan have intended the full implications of these words? A general declaration of allegiance like this one carried no constitutional validity, but if nothing else it meant Bhutan was now operating firmly within the British sphere of influence.

A group picture taken at Hastings House, Calcutta, during the visit in 1906 of Ugyen Wangchuk, the Tongsa Pönlop of Bhutan, and Thutop Namgyel, the Chögyal of Sikkim. Front row, seated from left to right: D.E. Holland, Ugyen Wangchuk, John Claude White, Thutop Namgyel and his consort Yeshé Drölma. Standing from left to right: Bhutanese guard, Capt. Henry Hyslop, Ugyen Dorje, Lobsang Chöden, Jerung Dewan, Burmiak Kazi, Bhutanese guard, Sikkimese guard. (Photo by unidentified photographer, print from Fondation Alexandra David Neel, Digne)

The enthronement of Ugyen Wangchuk as first hereditary king of Bhutan (Druk Gyelpo), Punakha Dzong, 17 December 1907. Left to right: John Claude White, Ugyen Dorje (standing), Ugyen Wangchuk, and the Head Abbot Jampel Shenyen. The seating arrangement reflects the disposition of power and authority. Whereas in 1905 Ugyen Wangchuk had sat beneath the Head Abbot, here their thrones are of the same height. However, the new king occupies the dominant central position and his throne table, covered with ceremonial scarves, is slightly higher than the abbot's. The civil and ecclesiastical aspects of the state are thus held in balance, but the former now supercedes the latter. The British, who played a key role in the rise of the monarchy, are accorded a place of honour but the status of their represen-tative merits a lower position that leaves the supremacy of the Bhutanese state undimin-ished. (Photo: H. Hyslop, private collection).

The sealing by officials of the contractual document (genja or bagen) which instituted hereditary monarchy in Bhutan, Punakha Dzong, 17 December 1907. Hyslop wrote in his diary: "A scribe now got up and read out the oath of allegiance which all the headmen were to take to the new Maharajah; this was written on parchment, and each of the headmen came up and put his seal to the document. The chief Lama, the Tatsang Khempo, who has possession of the Dharma Rajah's seal, produced this from a casket. It is a huge thing some five inches square ... The sealing of the document took over an hour ..."
(Photo: H. Hyslop, private collection)

ཡུག་ས་གཉིས་ བོན་མ་ཁྲིམས་བདག་པོའི་ཆེན་འཉེནས་རུང་དུ།

ཞུ་གསོལ། རང་རྱ་འབྲུག་ཡུལ་ཁབ་འདི་ར་སྟོན་ལ་་་ རེ་སྟེ་ཆེན་པོའི་ཡར་སྐུ་ས་སྟོབ་སྟོང་་ ཕུན་རྒྱ་ས།

...

To the lotus feet of the Precious Judge, the Exalted one of the Dual System [of Religious and Secular Law].

It is submitted that while from former times in our kingdom of Bhutan the Great Regent took office from among any that came forth from the lamas and teachers of the monastic college or from the council of ministers and the regional governors, there was otherwise no hereditary monarch. Now therefore a contract has been drawn up in firm conclusion containing a unanimous agreement, which is not to be altered, on the part of all officers and subjects including the abbot and teachers of the monastic community, the ministers of the council of state and the regional governors. According to the purport of this contract expressing the deliberations and common desire of all those mentioned above and made evident to all gods and men, Sir Ugyen Wangchuk, the leader of Bhutan and Tongsa Pönlop, has been empowered as hereditary monarch in the Palace of Great Bliss at Pungthang (Punakha), the Second Potala, on 17 December 1907, corresponding to the 12th day of the 11th month of our own year of the Earth Monkey, at a time of favourable astrological conjunction. Accordingly we the above-mentioned lamas and officials, subjects and followers, great and small, shall place our loyalty as witness and render service and honour to the king who has been installed on the Golden Throne and to the succession of his royal heirs. If otherwise there should be any kind of accusing talk arising from evily disposed rumour or false gossip, then such persons are to be expelled from the common fold. In unalterable acceptance of this, the common seal of the abbot, teachers and monastic community; [there follow the individual seals of ministers and governors; lesser officials of the capital and provinces ("the juniormost double-rationed ones"); minor functionaries ("those entitled to riding mounts"); and finally the headmen of the "subject citizens" of each district].

The document containing the contract of hereditary monarchy as adopted during Ugyen Wangchuk's enthronement as king in Punakha Dzong, 17 December 1907. The Shabdrung's state seal is applied at the top. (For a translation of the wording, see Aris 1979: 214.) From a copy reproduced in John Claude White, Sikhim and Bhutan: Twenty-one Years on the North-East Frontier, 1887-1908 (London, 1909), facing p. 226. A translation is provided at left.

*Group at Punakha, 19 December 1907.
Standing from left: Captain Henry Hyslop,
Intelligence Department; Kazi Ugyen Dorje,
the Bhutan Agent; Palden Wangchuk, the
Punakha Dzongpön; Major F.W. Rennick,
Intelligence Department; Kunzang Trinley,
the Thimphu Dzongpön; Kunzang Tsering,
the Deb Zimpön. Seated from left: Captain
W.L. Campbell, Assistant Political Officer,
Gangtok; John Claude White, Political
Officer, Gangtok; King Ugyen Wangchuk;
Dawa Penjor, the Paro Pönlop. (Photo: H.
Hyslop, private collection)*

*Punakha, 19 December 1907. Hyslop wrote:
"We have all be in full dress again today, for
the presentation of the Government subsidy,
the Rs. 50,000 which the Indian Government
give annually according to the Treaty of
1866, in which the Bhutanese ceded the
Duars to the Government of India. ...
The Tongsa and council gave us scarves, and
a small offering of salt, and cloths were laid
in front of White, who then formally handed
over the treasure to the Tongsa. One box was
opened and a bag of a thousand rupees
counted out." (Photo: H. Hyslop, private
collection)*

Whatever the form of its relationship to the British empire, Bhutan now took the decisive step to establish its own monarchy. In the same year of 1906 Ugyen Dorje addressed a long letter to the council of state made up of senior monks and selected officers of the central government and provinces.[38] He pointed out that in the absence of a clear procedure for appointing the regent it was difficult to protect the realms of either religion or state. There had been an enormous increase of late in foreign relations with Tibet and India, quite different from the way it used to be. The high honour accorded to the Tongsa Pönlop by the most powerful nation on earth is referred to again and again. If he, the Pönlop, were to assume "the name of the king of Bhutan", it would not only benefit him and his family but the whole rule of the Shabdrung. The clear implication is that the institution of the Shabdrung would continue unharmed, and the regency too would not cease to oversee internal administration and the monastic communities. There is no direct suggestion yet in this letter that the monarchy envisaged would have a hereditary character, only that the Tongsa Pönlop should be king "for as long as possible". However, the author continues, what will happen to the present peace of the country after the Pönlop dies? The proposal to appoint him monarch is made only as a suggestion for all to consider, for the greater good of the country.

Clearly Ugyen Dorje wrote these words to test the waters and to see how far the matter could be advanced in negotiations beyond the terms he had proposed. If it is recalled that the officers of state to whom the proposal was submitted were, with the exception of the monks, all the nominees of Ugyen Wangchuk himself, it is little wonder that in the end not only was it accepted unanimously but its terms were extended to provide the monarchy with an unambiguously hereditary character. While the Shabdrung's spiritual place and role were left central to the conception of monarchy, providing ultimate legitimacy to the king's line and the whole state, the practically defunct regency was now allowed to die a quiet death.

Ugyen Wangchuk was installed king, without a whisper of dissent, in the dzong at Punakha on 17 December 1907. Although there is no record of the council's deliberations, the decision to establish monarchy appears to have been genuinely popular not only among those responsible for taking it but also with the public at large. Above all it was intended to bring to an end the constant dissension which had plagued the country since almost the start of the theocracy. The great seal of the founding Shabdrung was imprinted in red on the binding contract that brought in Ugyen Wangchuk and his heirs to rule as hereditary monarchs.The hapless regent was notably absent from the ceremony. It was presided over instead by the head abbot in the presence of the British Political Officer who had again come from Sikkim, and attended by the monks, all senior officers of government from the two capitals and the provinces, and by all headmen of the major districts. The head abbot did not rise from his own thrown as his gifts were presented to the new king, but the late Shabdrung's brother, the incarnate lama of the Tango monastery, having removed his own mitre and outer gown prostrated himself three times. He in turn was followed in this way by the somewhat recalcitrant Paro Pönlop, the king's cousin, in his first formal act of

The Thimphu Zimpön, according to the caption to this photograph by Charles Bell, 1910. An incumbent named Sithub had been a signatory to the contract of monarchy in 1907. However, the dowager queen mother Ashi Püntso Chödrön has identified this person as Domchung (alias Kunzang Norbu), the Wangdü Phodrang Dzongpön who was the son of Tsewang Sithub, the Shongar Dzongpön, himself the illegitimate son of Jigme Namgyel's second son Namdröl, a monk who served as the Kurtö Drung. (Photo: C. Bell, Merseyside County Museums)

public submission, and then by all the others in a long line. Several even of the junior officials were related to him in one way or other. The trusted Ugyen Dorje who had played the role of king-maker appeared among the lesser officers since he was at this time still holding only the junior post of administrator of the Ha valley together with the southern agency he had earlier received. He was otherwise much in evidence. The contract of monarchy was read out and then sealed by all present.[39]

Lord Minto, the new viceroy, was careful to ensure the government of India did not go so far as to "guarantee" Ugyen Wangchuk's elevation to the throne. However, the very presence of a British mission as formal witness to the ceremony must have served something close to that purpose. The Political Officer now advocated an increase in the subsidy and much closer official relations to counter the strong danger, as he saw it, of the Chinese meddling in Bhutanese affairs. The Chinese were in fact claiming suzerain rights over Bhutan. In 1907 the amban in Lhasa was reported as having said: "Tibet, Nepal and Bhutan are side by side like the molar teeth in a man's mouth, and the subjects of all three are those of one kingdom". In the same metaphorical vein he asserted: "China, Nepal, Tibet, Bhutan and Sikkim might be compared to the five principal colours, viz yellow, red, blue, black and green. A skillful painter may so arrange the colours as to produce a number of beautiful designs or effects. In the same we would cooperate with one another, we may presumably promote the interests of all".[40] When questioned about Bhutanese relations with China and insignia of office that were supposed to have been received, Ugyen Dorje did admit that a search had finally produced "a hat with an imitation coral button (the insignia of an official in the second rank) and a peacock's feather, now half eaten by insects" which had been presented to the regent Sangye Dorje in 1891.[41] The formal submission Bhutan had made to imperial China in 1734 was certainly by now a hollow fiction. Ugyen Dorje hotly denied any Chinese control whatsoever. In 1908 the Amban addressed a letter to the regent as if there were still no king: "The Bhutanese are the subjects of the Emperor of China who is the Lord of Heaven, and are of the same religion as the other parts of the Empire. You, Deb Raja, and the Two Penlops think that you are great, but you cannot continue without paying attention to the orders of your rulers …".[42] In 1908 a junior Chinese official, the paymaster stationed in Phari, arrived in Paro with twenty soldiers. The Paro Pönlop, who met the official, was very cool. The king refused to have anything to do with him.

It was only after John Claude White had been replaced as Political Officer by Charles Bell and with the increase in Chinese activity in the area that a more active policy to strengthen British interests in Bhutan began to be considered in Delhi and London. This finally resulted in London's agreement to double the annual subsidy paid to Bhutan for the annexation of the duars from fifty to one hundred thousand rupees. A hundred rifles and other gifts would be made to the king. Bell was deputed to Bhutan to negotiate a new treaty, the key clause of which was to read: "The British Government undertakes to exercise no interference in the internal administration of Bhutan. On its part, the Bhutanese Government agrees to be guided by the advice of the British Government in regard to its external relations." Ugyen Dorje was sent ahead to explain the full significance of this to his king, with promises that the salary paid to him by the Government of India as Bhutan Agent would be increased if he were successful in his persuasions.

There seems to have been no opposition either from the king or his councilors to the crucial clause. Indeed, when Bell came for the signing in January 1910, having hurried to outdistance Chinese spies who were also said to be on their way, the king declared himself delighted that Bhutan was now joining the British empire.[43] Just as they refuted all claims at this time to have been part of the Chinese empire, few in Bhutan today would say that Bhutan had ever belonged to the British empire. Yet the key clause by which it ceded management of its external relations to the British has been interpreted by many to mean that Bhutan was henceforth a formal protectorate within the British empire. That same clause was revived in the later treaty of 1949 with independent India, and it is still in force today. It is of course now ignored by both sides as a colonial relic. All the indications of history suggest that whatever formal submissions the Bhutanese authorities may have made to either the Chinese or British empires, this never damaged either their capacity to manage their own affairs or to safeguard their country's ultimate sovereignty. If Bhutan had lain on a major route and if the internal situation had deteriorated at a time when external intervention posed real attractions, then history might have been quite different.

Nevertheless, Bhutan's signing of the treaty of 1910 with Britain provoked very strong reactions from the Chinese authorities in Peking and Lhasa. The Amban sent peremptory commands in letters addressed to the king and the defunct regent. The Chinese foreign office insisted that "...Bhutan is a vassal of China, and from the time of Yung Cheng [1723-6] has paid tribute and frequently received sealed orders from late Emperors".[44] The British responded by insisting on the difference between tributes and presents, and pointed out that Bhutan had signed the treaty of its own free will. However, the rancour was overtaken by the situation in Tibet. The Chinese revolution against the rule of the Manchus was followed by the expulsion of the Chinese presence from Tibet in 1912. The issue of Bhutanese vassalage was referred to vaguely in later times but ceased now to be an issue. They had joined the British camp and were to remain there for the duration of British rule in India.

Charles Bell noted in his diary of the treaty mission that the king had "... consolidated his power to a great extent in Bhutan, though he still has to walk warily in his dealings with the leading chiefs". His cousin the Paro Pönlop was not on the best terms with him, and this came out in the open a little later. Bell was to say afterwards that the king "... is not only a very able Ruler, but he is universally respected both by his subjects and by his foreign friends. Though he has only twice in his life quitted his hermit land, he has all the broad-minded tolerance of one who has lived a cosmopolitan life. His perfect courtesy and quiet sense of humour are the common heritage of the Tibetan nobility".[45] In another work, he pointed out that the king "... had lessened, as far as one man could do, the lawlessness inherent in this hardy but primitive people".[46]

The king made some of his plans known to Bell. The new Shabdrung had been discovered not far from Tawang in territory under Tibetan control and would soon be

Charles Bell, Political Officer, Gangtok, with King Ugyen Wangchuk and his council after concluding the Treaty of Punakha, January 1910. Bell recorded his impressions of the king in his diary for 20 January: "It is clear that he has consolidated his power to a great extent in Bhutan, though he still has to walk warily in his dealings with the leading chiefs ... He is a man for whom one cannot help entertaining a strong regard. In character and intellect he stands above anybody that I have met in Bhutan, Tibet or Sikkim. His acts of kindness and courtesy to my party and myself are too numerous to mention". (Photo: C Bell, Merseyside County Museums).

The ruins of Rinpung Dzong, Paro, with John Claude White and Ugyen Dorje, 1907. Hyslop wrote in his diary: "Rounding a corner we got our first sight of the ruined Jong, for sad to say it was burnt completely out a month ago. The outside walls are still standing, but every bit of wood work has been burnt out, and worst of all everything the Jong contained, with the exception of a few old records, was destroyed. Even in ruins the Jong is most impressive". (Photo: H. Hyslop, private collection)

installed at Punakha. He would appoint Ugyen Dorje his own chamberlain. The Paro Pönlop would not be allowed to resign and so escape his duty of rebuilding the dzong in Paro which had burnt down. Nor would the king allow the former regent Yeshé Ngödrup to be reinstated. As Bell put it, the king was "... in a considerable measure independent of his Chiefs, of his priests and of Tibetan influence".[47]

In fact on his return journey Bell met the regent, who made his aims to have his powers restored very clear. He even tried to woo Ugyen Dorje to his cause by offering him the post of chamberlain if he helped him achieve his goal. (He cannot have known the king intended to give his most trusted follower this post anyway). It must have been to mollify Yeshé Ngödrup that he was made head abbot of the state monks in 1915, and he held the post till his death in 1917. However, the lama had used his position as abbot to gain access to the embalmed corpse of the founding Shabdrung in Punakha. He removed a small part of the body as a talisman for his own use. The gods wreaked their revenge firstly by sending down a big flood in 1915 that carried away the bridges at Punakha, and then in 1918 by causing an epidemic that swept through the country. It is said that the king in his anger at the late abbot came to a decision to forbid the recognition and installment of any future incarnations of the Shabdrung's "verbal principle".[48] The line that had started with the birth of the first incarnation in 1708 therefore came to an end. However, the new incarnation of the "mind" of the founding Shabdrung, the true Dharma Raja, was duly installed. He was Shabdrung Jigme Dorje, born in 1905.

In 1911 the king travelled to Delhi with thirteen of his officials to take part in the great durbar for the King-Emperor George V whom he had met earlier as Prince of Wales in Calcutta. It was the second and last trip he ever paid to India. Among all the Indian princes gathered for this extravagant display of loyalty was his neighbour, the ruler of Sikkim, whom he had also met in Calcutta. Received in audience, he was again decorated, with Charles Bell acting as interpreter. Through him he explained to the King-Emperor that he had travelled for no less than seventeen days in Bhutan before reaching the Indian railhead that took him and his entourage in just two days to Delhi. The one feature of the extravaganza which is said to have greatly stirred him was the mass review of fifty thousand troops: "... all matters connected with the soldiery attracted his close attention".[49] For someone brought up from childhood in the midst of constant fighting, the display was bound to have more than academic interest.

Ugyen Dorje received the title of Raja from the Viceroy as a personal distinction. In the same year he had been promoted to the office of king's chamberlain. The title this carried was *Gongzim*, "Chamberlain to the Ruler", but the earlier version of "The Regent's Chamberlain" (*Deb Zimpön*) was equally used with little sense of anachronism even though the regency had been abolished. The king's letter of appointment,[50] sent with piles of hand-woven textiles and other traditional gifts, had addressed him as the Ha Drungpa. This fiefdom of the Ha valley he continued to hold jointly both with

A formal photograph of the last regent (Druk Desi), Cholé Tulku Yeshé Ngödrup, 25 January 1910. Charles Bell wrote in his diary: " On the road I met the ex-Deb Raja and had an informal chat with him. He was on his way to ask the Maharaja to make him Deb Raja again. He offered Rai Ugyen Kazi Bahadur the post of Deb Zimpön, which carries a seat on the Bhutan Council, on condition that the Kazi should use his influence to secure him the Deb Raja's post. The Maharaja, however, does not intend that any more Deb Rajas shall be appointed in Bhutan, as their work is now done by him". (Photo: C. Bell, Pitt Rivers Museum)

King Ugyen Wangchuk of Bhutan and Chögyel Thutop Namgyel of Sikkim attending the Coronation Durbar of King George V, Delhi, December 1911. Ugyen Wangchuk had earlier met George as Prince of Wales in Calcutta in 1906. Accompanied now by thirteen of his officials, he was accorded a salute of fifteen guns and invested with the title of Knight Commander of the Star of India. Kazi Ugyen Dorje was given the title of Raja as a personal distinction. (Photo: C. Bell, Pitt Rivers Museum)

the post of Bhutan Agent, conferred on him by the British in 1888, and the similar "agency" of southern Bhutan which the king had given him in 1900. That he was compelled to serve two masters simultaneously through nearly all of his official career never seems to have troubled anyone, certainly not his king for whom he had total loyalty. The letter appointing him chamberlain made it clear that the post was intended to be hereditary: "It is my aspiration that from now on the insignia and rank might come down to the lineage of your children".[51]

Though the post carried a seat on the council of state that had charge of internal matters under the king's overall control, Ugyen Dorje's duties still concentrated mainly on external matters. Nevertheless he was the one charged with arranging the final settlement that allowed the supporters of the rebel Alo Dorje to return to their native home at Umtengkha. Alo Dorje himself had died at Chumbi. The border districts of western Bhutan which had been allotted to his supporters came back into the hands of the central government, and those who were left were brought into Ugyen Wangchuk's presence as a gesture of reconciliation.[52] Bhutan's official contacts with Tibet were now formally handled by the British but still a good number of border matters continued to come the way of the chamberlain. It was, however, relations with British India that chiefly preoccupied him.

The old Paro Pönlop continued to make difficulties. He was still powerful enough to make a lot of trouble for the king's chamberlain if he chose to do so. Matters came to a head when some men from Ugyen Dorje's fiefdom in Ha had accidentally set fire to property belonging to subjects of the Pönlop in Paro. The chamberlain appealed to his king for support in this quarrel, indicating his wish to retire if it were not resolved. Ugyen Wangchuk replied that the lazy Pönlop, "sitting comfortably on his fine carpet", had no idea of how much he owed his happiness to the labours of either the king or his chamberlain. The two of them had together braved the rigours of travel on the plains of Tibet and the jungles of the south. The wretched governor had no conception of gratitude. The king, for his part, believed his chamberlain worthy even of being made regent.[53]

Ugyen Dorje continued to be based at his home in Kalimpong outside Bhutanese territory where he maintained considerable business interests. It was there that he put particular effort into one of the projects he and his king were especially keen to develop, namely the modern education of selected boys from their country. In 1914 forty-six boys from Bhutan were put into the Scottish mission school in Kalimpong known after its founder as Dr. Graham's Homes.[54] All or much of the expense of this was borne privately by Ugyen Dorje from his own resources. In the same year a school was started in Ha, and in 1915 one was founded at the king's palace in Bumthang specially for his heir and a few other boys. Lack of funds prevented many other projects from getting off the ground, but twelve of the original students were trained in the 1920s as teachers, sub-assistant surgeons, tanners, forest rangers, mining engineers, lac cultivators and vets. The modern development of Bhutan thus got off to something of a start, but it was wholly hampered by the fundamental resistance on the part of British India to underwrite its cost. Moreover, half of the annual subsidy still had to go to support the state monks and the provincial officers, leaving very little in the hands

The commercial agent of the Bhutanese government at Phari in Tibet, seen here with his two wives. His daughter, who stands on the right, is dressed as a man. Although himself a Tibetan, the agent is wearing a Bhutanese robe. He is almost certainly the "Bhutan Agent" mentioned in Charles Bell's Annual Report of 1912 who tried to intervene in the flogging by the Chinese authorities of a Bhutanese subject. The Chinese ordered that Bhutanese of any rank found carrying knives or firearms in Phari would be summarily flogged and their weapons confiscated. (Photo: David Macdonald, Bell Collection, Pitt Rivers Museum)

The tented camp of John Claude White and party, pitched at high altitude during his first mission to Bhutan in 1905. The place is not identified. Minor officials are supervising a meal served to attendants and porters lined up in two pairs of facing rows. The heavy yak-hair tents contrast with the white cotton tent in the centre whose upper awning is finely decorated with the famous kushütara *weave. (Photo: J.C. White, private collection)*

of the central government. In any case, the king had told White in the early years of the century that he wanted to proceed slowly. The cost of further education for some at least of the students was made possible by the visit of the governor of Bengal, Lord Ronaldshay (later Marquess of Zetland) in 1921, who had made strong recommendations to the viceroy on the subject. The Political Officers who continued to make tours to Bhutan usually did their best to secure a greater commitment for development assistance, but their appeals invariably fell on deaf ears in Delhi and London.

The principle interest of most of the very few foreign visitors, then as now, lay in the genuinely exotic. The reactions of Lord Ronaldshay to what he saw on his trip to Paro in 1921 are typical: "For just as Alice, when she walked through the looking-glass, found herself in a new and whimsical world, so we, when we crossed over the Pa-chu, found ourselves, as though caught up on some magic time machine fitted fantastically with a reverse, flung back across the centuries into the feudalism of a mediaeval age ... [I]t was our entry into Paro that finally brought home to us the era into which we had unwittingly stumbled. So far as we could judge it corresponded with extraordinary faithfulness to that of feudal England, or at any rate of feudal England as it had been pictured for us by the pen of Sir Walter Scott". William Gourlay, ADC to the governor, dutifully picked up the same theme in his own diary: "All afternoon one had a feeling akin to that of the Yankee at the Court of King Arthur. As H.E. remarked, the scenes and incidents might have taken place in England in the days of Ivanhoe. The great baronial castle on its rocks above us commanded the valley. At the foot of the rock were the houses of the cultivators of the plain living under the baron's protection." He described a monk as "a very coarse fat old Friar Tuck", and spoke of "a numerous array of retainers, each one a picture of Gurth in Ivanhoe". It was "a scene from fairyland".[55]

In 1916 the chamberlain Ugyen Dorje died in Kalimpong. Faithful to his word, the king appointed his son Sonam Topgye to succeed him in all his posts, inheriting all his titles and duties. The British too gave him the post of Bhutan Agent which his father had held from them, and he inherited the British-Indian title of Raja. The king was indeed fortunate that his old confidant and key supporter had produced a son of the calibre of Sonam Topgye. Educated at St. Paul's School, Darjeeling, he had assisted his father in all his many duties and so was well prepared. When in 1918 he married the princess of Sikkim, Chöying Wangmo, the king was delighted and sent him gifts and congratulations. In other letters the king begged his new chamberlain to take care of his health on his long southern journeys, where the dangers of malaria and other diseases were very real. He had many religious rituals performed for his safety.[56]

In 1918 the king made another key appointment. The old Paro Pönlop, his cousin Dawa Penjor, who had given him a fair amount of trouble over the years, finally died. He was now succeeded by the king's grandson, Tsering Penjor, born to his daughter Pedrön who had married (in another typical cousin marriage) the king's nephew Dorje Rabden. It will be recalled that when none of the three sons born to Ugyen Wangchuk's first wife survived their infancy, there had been an understanding that he would nominate his nephew Dorje Rabden as his heir. However, that had been overtaken by the birth of sons to his second wife. The eldest of these sons, Jigme Wangchuk, was destined to inherit the throne. Nevertheless, Dorje Rabden, who had been the king's Drönyer or senior household official, still harboured unfilled hopes. It was perhaps to placate him that his son was now given the highly prestigious governorship of the Paro province. It was perhaps also at this time that the Raven Crown itself came into Tsering Penjor's possession, not as a token that he would succeed the first king but rather as a personal gift. Or perhaps he had it from his father who had in turn received it from the king before he changed his mind about the succession. The circumstances are not clear at all. At all events, the new Paro Pönlop was later to wear the crown with great aplomb in the presence of foreign guests.

By this time the king was beginning to feel his age, even if by 1918 he was still only forty-six. His life in Bumthang was taken up more and more with matters of religion. Certainly he put as much if not more effort into the training of a new generation of senior monk-scholars as he did into the further education of students in India. He arranged for seventeen monks from Punakha and Tongsa to undertake a long period of advanced training at the great Gelukpa university of Drepung near Lhasa. He sent others to the Nyingmapa monastery of Dzokchen in eastern Tibet. Other important communities he patronized in eastern Tibet were Pelpung, Surmang and Dzigar. The community at his own seat at Tongsa in particular gained fame as a centre for the study of philosophical logic as a result of his determination to improve standards. His name appears as a patron of the edition prepared by the Karmapa lama of the multi-volume

Tsering Penjor, the Paro Pönlop, wearing the Raven Crown of the Bhutanese monarch to which he was not formally entitled, Paro, 1931. This grandson of King Ugyen Wangchuk had inherited from his father, Dorje Rabden, the king's son-in-law, the hope of succeeding to the throne. Even though Ugyen Wangchuk eventually produced a direct male heir by his second queen, the Pönlop apparently still regarded himself as a legitimate contender. However, he does not seem to have maintained these hopes for many years after the enthronement of King Jigme Wangchuk in 1928. (Photo: J.L.R. Weir, private collection)

King Ugyen Wangchuk enthroned at Kujé Lhakhang, Bumthang, for the investiture of the Grand Cross of the Indian Empire, 28 July 1922. F.M. Bailey reported: "Bhutanese officials entered in order according to their rank, each one bowed down three times to the ground and took out a scarf with a great flourish, presented it to the Maharaja, while huge bundles of silks and other materials were banged on the floor and rolled out as each man presented his gifts. There were also gifts of money, leopard and tiger skins, tea etc. Monks gave presents of idols". (Photo: H.R.C. Meade, Royal Geographical Society)

collection of Nyingmapa "treasure-texts" known as the *Rinchen Terdzö*. He also provided much of the cost of the restoration of the Swayambhunath stupa in Nepal that was overseen by the Tibetan scholar and yogin Shakyashri. Twice a month he arranged for a thousand butter lamps to be lit at the great "cathedral" of the Jokhang in Lhasa. In addition to his major construction at Kujé, his other works of building and restoration are still to be seen in Bumthang and elsewhere. The great rituals he endowed in perpetuity at Punakha are still performed there by the state monks.[57]

Colonel F.M. ("Eric") Bailey held the post of Political Officer in Sikkim for nine years from 1921. A man with wide experience of life in Tibet and the Himalayas, he had served as an undercover agent in central Asia and had conducted pioneering surveys in the region east of Bhutan. He was therefore well suited to lead a mission in 1921 to present yet another decoration to the king, the Grand Cross of the Indian Empire. The king had just suffered the death of his queen Lemo but took part in the occasion with great dignity. The insignia were presented to him enthroned at the great shrine dedicated to the divine guru Padmasambhava at Kujé in Bumthang. Bailey was able to meet the king's whole family, including the heir apparent Jigme Wangchuk aged seventeen, his younger sons Dorje and Nakhu aged eleven and four, and his single daughter Wangmo aged eight. In 1924 Bailey travelled to Bhutan again, this time to Punakha to take part in in the installation of the chamberlain's son, Jigme Dorje, as the Ha Drungpa. The king was keeping his word that this office and others he had given to the chamberlain's father might pass down in his family. In the shaky film which Bailey took, the eight-year-old Jigme Dorje is seen barefoot in the couryard of Punakha Dzong, swathed in ceremonial scarves and surrounded by his father's attendants.[58]

King Ugyen Wangchuk wearing the insignia of the Grand Cross of the Indian Empire, Kujé Lhakhang, Bumthang, 28 July 1922. The honour came to him at a time of great personal sadness, as Bailey noted in his report: "The death of Her Highness [Ashi Lemo], last April, had cast a gloom over the Maharaja who was living in a small house with the body of his wife which, owing to the death of His Highness' favourite lama in Kham in East Tibet, has not yet been disposed of. We were not able to visit him here, but he received us in the house where his daughters live, called La-me Gompa, about a quarter of a mile from our camp". (Photo: F.M. Bailey, Royal Geographical Society)

Far more is known about the first king's interest in religion than his temporal policies and administration. The country as a whole was governed as it always had been by provincial officers. Although under little direct supervision from the centre, they now took their orders from a single source of authority. It is clear that the king undertook no major review of either law or administration during his reign of nearly twenty years. Taxes and labour services are said to have been reduced by him, but the details are all lacking. The whole structure of government remained the same and much of its purpose too. Crucially, the centre of power had shifted from the old winter

Group in Bumthang, July 1922. Seated from left: Captain H.R.C. Meade, Survey of India; Major F.M. Bailey, Political Officer, Sikkim; King Ugyen Wangchuk; the Hon. Mrs Irma Bailey; Dasho Dorje; Lady Cozens-Hardy. Seated on ground in front, from left: Ashi Wangmo, Dasho Nakhu, Dasho Püntso Wangdü. Standing, from left: Rai Sahib Norbhu Dhondup, Confidential Clerk, Sikkim Agency; Tsering Penjor, the Paro Pönlop; Bansi Ram, Survey of India; Sonam Topgye Dorje, the Bhutan Agent. Back row: Sikkimese attendants of the Political Officer. (Photo: H.R.C. Meade, Royal Geographical Society)

capitals in Punakha and Thimphu to the king's palace in Bumthang. This served to bring areas on the eastern fringe under a greater degree of control than had formerly been the case, but otherwise things continued much as they had done under the theocracy. It is as the triumphant and reunifying monarch that Ugyen Wangchuk will always be remembered, not as the promulgator of new laws and policies.

He is also remembered by everyone as a man of peace and wisdom. In his final years after the death of his much-loved queen he went into retreat, living very humbly in a small residence he had made for himself by the side of his daughter's mansion at Lamé Gönpa. There he would receive no one at all during the morning while he occupied himself with his devotions. It was only in the afternoon that visitors would come from far and near and he would attend to matters of govenment. He also built another small house next to the most ancient temple of Jampai Lhakhang. In the 1970s at least one person remembered the time when as a young boy he used to sleep in the same room as the old king, who would spend the whole night telling his rosary beads.[59] He greatly regretted the acts of violence he had committed in his youth, but the unprecedented peace of his long reign must surely have given him a measure of happiness. His subjects regarded him not only as king but also practically as a lama.

In 1926 at the age of sixty-four he succumbed to what the physicians diagnosed as an affliction of the bile. He sent a letter to the state monks in Punakha asking them to pray for him. Should he not recover he said they were instead to use the funds he was sending for his funeral. But he wished to be cremated at the temple of Kujé and nowhere else. He also sent a runner to Kalimpong to summon his chamberlain. To the end he kept asking if he had yet arrived. The king finally expired with his head resting in the lap of his son and heir.

Rani Chöying Wangmo, the Sikkimese princess who married Raja Sonam Topgye Dorje, in Bhutan House, Kalimpong, circa 1935, with her oldest son Jigme Dorje, the future prime minister, and her elder daughter Tashi Dorje. The youngest child in the photograph has not been identified. (Photo: F.M. Bailey, The British Library)

Two of the five Buddhist stupas built facing the dzong in the Paro valley in memory of the first king, Ugyen Wangchuk, after his death in 1926. The photograph was taken five years later in 1931. (Photo: J.L.R. Weir, Royal Geographical Society)

Notes: Chapter Four

1. Except where the citations indicate otherwise, I base the following summary of Ugyen Wangchuk's life wholly on the evidence contained in SMLJ 63-74; BRDK 188-203; BRTU 287-90; BRGI 513-62.
2. Where the sources provide only the age and not the year I have subtracted one year to compensate for the fact that the Bhutanese (and Tibetans) always reckon a person to be aged one at the time of birth.
3. Ashley Eden observed that in 1864 the council of state, which he terms the "Amlah", was largely made up of "young ignorant boys": *Papers Relating to Bhutan* 219.
4. It is not clear how this ties in with the account given by the agent "R.N.". Following his secret survey in Bhutan for the British in 1885-6 he reported that when an earlier Daga Pönlop was murdered his seven sons took refuge at Tongsa, and many years later on attaining manhood they came back and ousted their father's successor. See *Report on the Explorations of ... Explorer RN 1885-86*, 43; BRGI 515.
5. Despite the later death of his usurper, Dungkar Gyeltsen never seems to have made a comeback. All we know of him thereafter derives from SMLJ 65 where it is said his defeat at this time compelled him to move annually between summer and winter residences at Doshong Gönpa and Tekha.
6. The details vary according to the source, but all seem to agree on the general pattern depicted here. The fullest account is in SMLJ, which almost certainly derives from the testimonies of some of those who took part.
7. This matrimonial tactic, frequently used in Himalayan societies to reinforce family interests, was to be employed by the royal family again in the next generation. Ugyen Wangchuk's official second marriage to Lemo was also of this type (see below).
8. Labh 1974: 119; Kohli 1982: 128; Singh 1988a: 332.
9. The implication behind the oath is that whoever loses would have his head, hands and heart removed from his corpse and offered to the guardian deities.
10. The abundant details supplied in BRGI 521-7, only summarized here, mainly derive from an oral account given to Lobpön Pemala by his grandfather Pema Tendzin who was present throughout the campaign.
11. See BRTU 355-63; Aris 1988: 22.
12. Besides Alo Dorje the Thimphu Dzongpön, the group was made up of the Gongzim Tamdrin Ngödrup, Damchö Rinchen, Pusola the Gasa Dzongpön and Kawang Dorje. For a poem on the subject of the conflict by Shabdrung Jigme Chögyel, see BRGI 525.
13. This ritual humiliation of the enemy is called a *gi-dbang* (pronounced "giwang"): BRGI 526. I take this to be the Bhutanese version of a term which in standard Tibetan would be *gri-dbang*, signifying "initiation by the sword".
14. For contemporary British reactions to the civil war, see especially Labh 1974: 119-20; Singh 1988a: 332.
15. He had in fact applied unsuccessfully to the British for arms but was turned down: Labh 1974: 120. It may be assumed that he had done so under compulsion.
16. See Singh 1988a: 333.
17. *Ibid.*; Labh 1974: 119; Kohli 1982: 134-9.
18. "Annual Report on the Relations between the British Government and the Bhutan Durbar for the Year 1911-12", p. 1: Public Record Office, London (hereafter PRO), FO 371/1330 (75984). The fact that Ugyen Wangchuk had sons by his first wife, as he clearly told Charles Bell in 1911, does not seem to be remembered in Bhutan.

19. See BRGI 563.

20. It is not clear to me yet how Ugyen Dorje's efforts to obtain the return of the exiles ties in with the earlier conference held at Phari that is meant to have failed. The negotiations he was involved in also entailed a final meeting in the Chumbi valley, probably in Phari.

21. For the reaction in verse of a Bhutanese yogi to this first British invasion of Tibet, see BRGI 533-4.

22. BRGI 531-2. The document is cited in full together with several others in the Dorje family archives to which the author had unrestricted access.

23. The best popular account of the famous Younghusband mission is still Fleming 1961. The Bhutanese involvement is explained in Labh 1974: 127-48; Kohli 1982: 147-65; Collister 1987: 138-9; Singh 1988a: 333-48.

24. Quoted in Singh 1988a: 341.

25. See *Ibid*: 341.

26. See Aris 1994.

27. Fleming 1961: 200.

28. *Ibid.* 200. Perceval Landon, the *Times* correspondent travelling with the mission, had a less flattering view of the Pönlop. He described him rather pompously as "a small man with a powerful but plebeian countenance, and his habit of perpetually wearing a grey uncloven Homberg hat pressed down all round his head to his eyebrows, instead of his official crown, does not increase his dignity ... a cheerful but not particularly distinguished adjunct to the Mission": quoted *ibid*.

29. *Ibid.* 229.

30. Quoted in Kohli 1982: 164.

31. Fleming 1961: 261.

32. Reproduced in BRGI 535-6.

33. It is attributed to one Jami Tsewang Pedrön but has never been committed to writing.

34. Kohli 1982: 166, citing the Curzon Papers.

35. Quoted in Labh 1974: 156.

36. See White 1907, 1909a, 1909b, 1914.

37. Quoted *ibid.* 154.

38. Reproduced in BRGI 543-6.

39. Besides the various published accounts of White, descriptions of the enthronement were also recorded by Captains Campbell and Hyslop, who were present in the mission. For details, see Appendix 2 below.

40. Quoted in Kohli 1982: 172.

41. See Collister 1987: 156.

42. Quoted in Kohli 1982: 176.

43. Charles Bell, "Diary of my Mission to Bhutan for the Months of December 1909 and January 1910": Oriental and India Office Collections, British Library (hereafter OIOC), L/P&S/10/221, p. 6.

44. Quoted in Singh 1988a: 356-7.

45. Bell 1924: 104. Ugyen Wangchuk would not have been pleased to be referred to as a Tibetan!

46. Bell 1928: 56-7. The context of the remark was provided by the story of how Bell's Lepcha orderly had refused the enticements of a Bhutanese official to bring people from Sikkim to settle in his province, telling him "You have no law in your land, I prefer to remain in Sikkim".

47. OIOC, L/P&S/10/221, p. 6; "Annual Report ... for the Year 1911-12", p. 1.

48. SMLJ 72.

49. Bell 1924: 104; "Annual Report ... for the Year 1911-12", p. 1.
50. Reproduced in BRGI 548-9.
51. *Ibid.* 549.
52. The date of this is not certain. See BRGI 551.
53. *Ibid.* 552-3. Again the date is not known.
54. Labh 1974: 190. BRGI 550 has the figure at thirty-four: seventeen from Ha and seventeen from the east of the country.
55. See Appendix 2 under Ronaldshay for reference to Gourlay's diary. My copy was made from one in the hands of the late Parasmani Pradhan of Kalimpong, but I have not seen it deposited elsewhere.
56. *Ibid.* 553.
57. For Ugyen Wangchuk's religious works, see especially SMLJ 71-2; BRGI 550-1, 555-7.
58. It is claimed in BRGI 557-8 that the installation took place in the interval between Ugyen Wangchuk's death in 1926 and the enthronement of his son in 1927. However, the date of 1924 is confirmed in the British records. For details of the film, see Appendix 2 below.
59. The late Lyonpo Sangye Penjor's father, Dasho Trinley Namgyel, told me this when I visited him at Pangtey Gompa in Bumthang.

Five
The Second King

Throughout its long history the Bhutanese theocracy had been bedeviled by problems of succession. These can all be traced back to their source in the failure of the founding Shabdrung to produce an acceptable heir. There developed no universally accepted method of discovering his incarnations, nor of appointing their regents. The absence of constitutional provisions for orderly succession encouraged a fluid, constantly changing situation that promoted cycles of dissension and fragmentation. Now with the establishment of monarchy the way ahead was clear.

The birth and survival of Jigme Wangchuk in 1905 had been particularly welcomed. Three sons born to his father Ugyen Wangchuk's first official consort had all died in their infancy, and the king had himself suffered serious illness.[1] With hindsight the king's second marriage took on special significance because of the sacred life-sustaining pill his new consort had presented to him when she came as his bride. The monk Geshé Mindruk who had introduced her to the king had said he should cease to be sad because soon a son would be born that would survive. The monk died soon after, and when Jigme Wangchuk was born to Ashi Lemo in 1905 some said it was this favoured chaplain who had chosen to be re-embodied in this way. He had attained mastery over the circumstances of both his death and rebirth.[2]

The recorded details of Jigme Wangchuk's youth are even more sparse than those of his father. His attendance at the palace school set up for him in Bumthang resulted in his acquiring the local literary skills and some proficiency both in English and Hindi. Like his father before him he was brought up in the tradition of household service, working with the other attendants who waited on the person of the ruler. At the age of thirteen in 1918 he was appointed the Drönyer or chief household officer to his father in his capacity as Tongsa Pönlop, a post the king retained in addition to the throne. In 1923 when he was eighteen he was elevated by his father to the Tongsa governorship itself as a preparation for future succession. Nothing is recorded about his tenure of this office since it was more in the nature of an honorary sinecure like that of the Prince of Wales. Throughout this period he continued to wait on his father, and when his mother died he bore the responsibility of overseeing many of her funeral rituals.

In the same year that Jigme Wangchuk was made Tongsa Pönlop he married his first cousin once removed. Ashi Püntso Chödrön, who is still alive today as the Dowager Queen, is the daughter of King Ugyen Wangchuk's sister's daughter, Ashi Demcho. Her marriage to the future king in 1923 was an arrangement typical of the region as a whole and particularly favoured by the family in this period. Like Ugyen

King Jigme Wangchuk wearing the Raven Crown, Bumthang, 26 July 1933. Peggy Williamson, who was present on the occasion, recorded in her memoirs: "His Highness looked splendid in all his medals and a round hat topped with a small peacock's head [in fact the raven]. They all came back to dinner and after more games we finished up singing 'Auld Lang Syne' together". (Photo: G. Sherriff, Museum of Mankind)

115

Wangchuk's second marriage it served not only to reinforce the ties of kinship and property but it also linked the royal family to an important branch of the local nobility. Ashi Püntso Chödrön's father, Dasho Jamyang, was the hereditary lord (*Dung* or *Shengo*) of the Chumé valley which adjoined the Chökhor valley that had the palace at its centre.[3] His line went back along yet another branch of Pemalingpa's descendants to the saint's son Dawa, known as the "Heart-Son" (*Thuksé*), born in 1499 in the twenty-sixth generation of the Nyö clan. It was Dawa's grandson Tenpai Nyima who had founded the ancestral temple of Trakhar (or Prai) that became the seat of his descendants.[4] Substantial landowners, they maintained also a wide network of religious affiliations throughout the region and beyond. It was six years after Jigme Wangchuk's marriage to Püntso Chödrön, in 1928, that she bore him a child, his heir Jigme Dorje Wangchuk. She had no other children, but the marriage then developed in an interesting way we shall consider later.

King Ugyen Wangchuk died when his heir was twenty-one in 1926. Before his death he had made his worries about the succession known to the Political Officer in Sikkim, Colonel F.M. Bailey. His nephew Dorje Rabden, whom he had once designated his heir before the birth of Jigme Wangchuk, was expected to make trouble. He had amassed considerable wealth by trading and might win a following by distributing largesse.[5] However, it was not now Dorje Rabden himself who might contest the throne but rather his son Tsering Penjor, the Paro Pönlop, who had in his own possession the king's Raven Crown.[6] As early as 1922 the king had considered abdicating to allow for the true heir to succeed without difficulty.[7] It was for this reason that upon the death of Ugyen Wangchuk it seemed essential for his son to accede to the throne with some speed.[8]

Six months after his father died Jigme Wangchuk travelled to Punakha while the funeral rites for his father were still continuing. The remains had not even been cremated. On 14 March 1927 he was installed in Punakha as king in the presence of the reigning Shabdrung, the twenty-two-year-old Jigme Dorje, and the head abbot of the state monks. Colonel Bailey attended to represent the Government of India and to present the insignia of Companion of the Indian Empire. Conspicuously absent was Dorje Rabden, who pleaded the excuse of his mother's illness. However, his son the Paro Pönlop made the required gesture of formal acquiescence, prostrating on the ground three times. It was suspected at the time that he probably did this with the same reluctance as his predecessor on the occasion of Ugyen Wangchuk's enthronement in 1907. Bailey commented: "The fact that the Paro Pönlop's father did not attend the ceremony of installation points, I think, to his dislike of the present position and it is always possible that he himself or the Paro Pönlop under his instigation may give trouble. One of the chief factors likely to prevent this is the fact that they have very few arms".[9] The king had five hundred modern rifles, the Pönlop only fifty. The late king had confided in Bailey his wish to curtail the power and position of the Pönlop but he had died before doing this. As Bailey put it: "The Paro Penlop is to a great extent independent. He collects revenue from a large area of which a small amount goes to the monasteries of Punakha and Trashichodzong, but none actually to the Maharaja

Coronation photograph of the second king, Jigme Wangchuk, wearing the Raven Crown and seen here with his younger brother Nakhu and ceremonial bodyguard, in the main courtyard of Punakha Dzong, 1927. (Photo: F.M. Bailey, The British Library)

King Jigme Wangchuk, centre, wearing the Raven Crown, a year after his accession to the throne, at Dewangiri in southeast Bhutan, 1928, with his younger brother Nakhu, Raja Sonam Topgye Dorje, his elder brother Dorje, and Rani Chöying Wangmo in Tibetan dress. The brothers of the king wear the white kabné *shawl of ordinary laymen. Ceremonial dancers and bodyguards stand behind. Ritual lap-covers (*chasipang- kheb*) line the walls of the tent and the seats. (Photo: F.M. Bailey, The British Library)*

for expenses of the central administration. This position is most unsatisfactory. The power and independence of these local chiefs has previously been the cause of trouble in Bhutan".[10]

The enthronement took place without obstacle. The new king took particular care to make lavish gifts to the state monks, including a full set of volumes containing the Buddhist canon and its commentaries, thirty-five dance robes and nine ceremonial capes of the finest Chinese silk brocade and some of the prized cattle from eastern Bhutan known as *mithun*. He ordered a new golden finial for the roof of Punakha Dzong in memory of his father and supplied a quantity of gold for regilding the faces of the Buddhist deities in all the chapels of the dzongs.

On returning to Bumthang the king was able to devote himself to his father's final rites. These were performed according to the will of the late king at the temple of Kujé and supervised by two grand abbots from the eastern Tibetan monasteries of Dzokchen and Benchen. In the following year he travelled to Dewathang (Dewangiri) in the south for a meeting with the Political Officer. Present too were the king's chamberlain Sonam Topgye and his wife.

After the birth of his heir in the same year, 1928, the king built himself a fine new palace in Mangdelung called Kunga Rabden. He had inherited or acquired the place at Tekha where his paternal uncle Dungkar Gyeltsen had settled after losing his office of Tongsa Pönlop. With its warmer, more temperate climate the valley of Mangdelung provided a welcome relief from the harsh winters of Bumthang. Indeed, the king was eventually to build himself no less than three more residences at various points in this long, well cultivated valley, at Samdrup Chöling, Yungdrung Chöling and Beling. He chose to spend his life moving between these great mansions, back and forth according

The palace of Samdrup Chöling, Mangdelung, built during the reign of the second king, Jigme Wangchuk, and demolished in the 1980s. This view was taken in 1970. (Photo: Michael Aris)

Kunga Rabden Palace, one of several summer residences of the royal family located in the Mangdelung district south of Tongsa, 1949. Masked dancers in the foreground are performing "The Drum Dance of Dramitse" to entertain the king's British visitors. (Photo: G. Sherriff, Sherriff Collection)

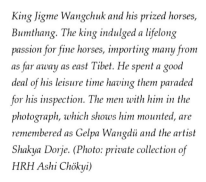

King Jigme Wangchuk and his prized horses, Bumthang. The king indulged a lifelong passion for fine horses, importing many from as far away as east Tibet. He spent a good deal of his leisure time having them paraded for his inspection. The men with him in the photograph, which shows him mounted, are remembered as Gelpa Wangdü and the artist Shakya Dorje. (Photo: private collection of HRH Ashi Chökyi)

to the seasons and following the general pattern of transhumance common to the whole region. Here he could breed the fine horses that were his abiding passion. It was the homeland of all his relatives, he understood all the variants of the local language, and he rarely moved beyond. Wherever he happened to be residing, there lay the centre of his government. In 1931 the Political Officer travelled with his family to the king's primary home in Bumthang to invest him with the KCIE.

When trouble arrived it came from the most critical source imaginable. The dangers to him presented by the Paro Pönlop and his father at the time of the succession never in fact materialized, perhaps because they had always been more of an imaginary kind.

119

Indeed, how many plots of the past had taken concrete form only when a counter-plot to their imagined threat had first taken hold? It was to the king's credit that, emulating his father, he had not used heavy methods to suppress these relatives who were widely thought to be planning revolt. But now there appeared strong evidence of real opposition in a form potentially far more serious than a mere fifty rifles.

The Shabdrung had been born in 1903 close to the Gelukpa stronghold of Tawang across the Bhutanese border in territory that fell under Tibetan control. The Tibetan government was later to claim him as a subject. So too did the Bhutanese, who maintained that the family had originally come to that area from Bhutan and had not lost their citizenship. The truth may lie somewhere in between, for even today there are pastoral communities in that area for whom the international frontier means very little, with frequent comings and goings between the settled communities on both sides. Sharing the same group of interrelated dialects and with their own distinctive dress styles, the Brokpa, Mönpa and Dakpa peoples of the region present variations of life style and local culture that together give the area a specificity all its own, quite separate from the much larger groups to the north and west, but of a complex and fragmented kind. It is thought by some that Shabdrung Jigme Dorje came originally from a Dakpa group that has ties on both side of the border, but that is not confirmed.

He had been brought across the border from his birthplace to the traditional seats of the Shabdrungs at the monastery of Talo in the Punakha valley. He had received his education at the hands of some of the senior state monks and had also been to Tibet for more studies. His mother and an elder brother had accompanied him to Talo. The first sign of trouble was seen when it transpired that he had issued an edict in his own name awarding the community of his birth across the border grazing rights within Bhutanese territory. The king was deeply incensed. It was an infringement of the whole convention whereby the Shabdrung attended only to spiritual matters, leaving temporal affairs to the secular ruler. The young lama was said to be under the influence of his mother who, it is presumed, caused him to make the award. There was a long history of grazing disputes in that area and the Shabdrung had absolutely no right to intervene in favour of Tibetan subjects in this unlawful and high-handed way. The king requested Colonel Bailey to admonish the Shabdrung, but Bailey pointed out that this lay well beyond his own political brief.[11] The scene was thus set for a play that has superficial resemblance to the story of Henry II and Thomas Becket.

The king was to later claim that from the year 1930 "... the Shabdung Rimpoche had been performing ceremonies calculated to do me harm, and had been invoking deadly maledictions upon me. In addition, he had been needlessly giving great trouble to the people ... It was not customary in the past for the Shabdungs to co-habit with women ... The present Shabdung lost his celibacy with his eyes open. This was most unbecoming, but I said nothing against his action".[12] Gongzim Sonam Topgye wrote to his friend Colonel Bailey: "His [the Shabdrung's] main grievances are that 'He has no power whatsoever' or any large tract of land in Bhutan to call his own. The Chiefs including the Maharaja are not treating him in a manner he [they] should be considering his high position".[13] To the charges of black magic and lechery there was now to

King Jigme Wangchuk wearing the insignia of Knight Commander of the Indian Empire which had just been presented to him by Lieutenant-Colonel J.L.R. Weir, who stands to his right in the dress uniform of Political Officer, at Kujé Lhakhang in Bumthang, 1931. At this time the king possessed 520 modern rifles presented to him and his father over the years by the British. The bodyguards who attended him formed the core of the fledgeling Bhutan army, which only developed its present structure after the accession of the third king in 1952. (Photo: J.L.R. Weir, private collection)

be added that of high treason.

In the spring of 1931 the Shabdrung sent his brother Chökyi Gyeltsen and an escort to seek a meeting with Mahatma Gandhi in India where he was leading the nonviolent movement for independence. They took with them "eleven different kinds of cloth, two pan pots, two lime pots and one Pangkheb (apron) made out of silk thread. The Shabdung instructed them to give Gandhi the presents and to inform him that he (Shabdung) himself would later on meet him and make friendship with him. [Chökyi Gyeltsen] was instructed to tell Gandhi that in days gone by Bhutan used to be ruled by the Shabdungs, but the present Shabdung had no power of any kind and asked him to render necessary help for the restoration of his powers".[14] It is difficult to think of a person more unsuited to joining a plot of this kind than Gandhi. The brother and the two servants who accompanied him crossed India and finally met him at Borsad. They failed to recruit the Mahatma, but a brief report appeared in the Indian press which came to the notice of Gongzim Sonam Topgye who forwarded it to the king. On being questioned about the trip, the brother "... out of impertinence, would not tell me the truth. While I was thinking of sending another man to talk over the matter, Shabdung, for no reason at all, arrested one of my Zimgaps (body guards) and had him beaten to death".[15] It seems it was at this point or earlier that the Shabdrung made plans to leave for China by way of India, sending his baggage on ahead. It was taken as far south as the border settlement of Pasakha before being recovered by a party of state monks who brought it back to Talo.[16]

With the southern route blocked the Shabdrung now made plans to go to Tibet and from there if necessary to China. The Panchen Lama Chökyi Nyima was at that time expected by some to return from long exile with the support of a strong contingent of Chinese troops, and the Shabdrung hoped now to obtain their help in wresting power from the king. The Dalai Lama was also believed to be keen to lend his support. In fact the plan seems to have been just as fanciful and ill-conceived as the earlier one to win help from India. When the king heard of it, he asked the state monks to intervene and persuade the Shabdrung to remain in the country. But he refused to listen and so "... the good accord between priest and patron grew worse and worse".[17] A relative of the head abbot then spread a rumour that the Shabdrung had indeed fled to Tibet. When it reached the ears of the Paro Pönlop, who was entirely on the king's side whatever his position may have been at the start of the reign, he despatched his own troops in pursuit. Crossing the frontier they penetrated Tibet as far as Khangmar and Samada in the Tsang province. They "... openly announced that their orders were to arrest or kill the Shabdung Rimpoche and his party".[18] As it turned out, the report of the Shabdrung's flight proved entirely false. He had never left Talo at all.

However, the king was now determined to find out the truth of what lay behind the Shabdrung's intentions and so he sent a delegation of trusted followers to Talo.[19] Fearing serious trouble the state monks sent their own peace mission of forty of their community headed by the senior teachers of tantra and chanting, but with little effect. The family and followers of the Shabdrung were all arrested and sent under guard to Tongsa to be interrogated by the king. The Shabdrung himself was allowed to remain at Talo under strict surveillance.

On 12 November 1931 the Shabdrung died. The king explained in a letter to Colonel Weir, "The fact of his passing was not even noticed by the monks who were sleeping in the same room ...".[20] The only Bhutanese chronicle which deals with the matter says: "Saddened by the deeds he had committed from listening to the plots of these evil persons the Shabdrung died on the 1st day of the 10th month".[21] Colonel Weir reported to Delhi three weeks after the death: "The cause of the Shabdung's death is still a mystery. I have however learnt the significant fact that one of the Shabdung's servants, who had accompanied the Shabdung's brother on his visit to Gandhi and had been

Shabdrung Jigme Dorje (1905-31), the sixth and last officially recognized "Dharma Raja" of Bhutan, photographed in his apartment in Punakha Dzong, 1927, shortly after the enthronement of the second king, Jigme Wangchuk, and four years before the alleged assassination of the lama took place in 1931. He wears a crown with false braids and ordinary monastic robes(right) and the ritual robes of the Black Hat dance (below). (Photo: F.M. Bailey, The British Library)

summoned to the Maharaja's presence to give an account of his actions, was found dead outside the walls of Talo monastery (the residence of the Shabdung) in circumstances which indicated suicide by poisoning. It does not seem improbable that the Shabdung has sought a similar way out of the difficulties into which his recent imprudent actions have led him ... By the death of the Shabdung Rimpoche a chapter of Bhutanese history, fraught with potential danger to the existing rule, may be considered closed".[22] The suicide theory was regarded with strong scepticism in Delhi, and the possibility of it being a case of "Who will rid me of this turbulent priest?" remains present in many minds. Stories told in Bhutan still speak of the use of a silken scarf in the dead of night. The truth of the matter has never been formally established and perhaps will never come to light.

On 15 April the Tibetan cabinet wrote to the king pointing out that the Shabdrung had been a Tibetan national who was "entitled to rank and position in the Tibetan government". They demanded a full explanation of his death and called on the king to hand over the lama's relatives to the Tibetan authorities.[23] The tone of the letter was that of a suzerain to a subject country and caused deep offense. For a time wild rumours circulated that the Tibetans were planning an invasion. On the request of the king the British then intervened with evidence supplied by the king that the Shabdrung had been a Bhutanese national and the matter was therefore internal to Bhutan. The Dalai Lama accepted this position, but pointed out that the Bhutanese had sent troops into Tibetan territory without permission.

Eventually all was smoothed over. The family of the Shabdrung were released from confinement and the king made them generous gifts, so that "they prospered more even than during the Shabdrung's lifetime".[24] Despite the extraordinary reverence in which all Shabdrungs, even those among them who broke their vows, are held by the Bhutanese at large, nobody seems to have taken up the cause of the one who died at Talo. The matter was for the time closed. However, it reappeared later with the birth of two or more children in eastern Bhutan who were claimed to be true embodiments. At least one, perhaps two, of these are also said to have been murdered.[25] During the Chinese invasion of India in 1962 the Indian authorities brought down another claimant from Tawang to safety lest he fell into Chinese hands and became their puppet.[26] Today with the close linking by marriage of the present king to the family of Shabdrung Jigme Dorje it is widely felt that, whatever blame may have attached to his grandfather in the matter, proper amends have been made in the sight of all.[27] The figure of the founding Shabdrung presides over the monarchy and nation as the ultimate source of all spiritual value, power and legitimacy. As patron saint and supreme architect of the country he overshadows the human failings of all his later embodiments. There is no incarnation recognized and installed, but his spirit is everywhere present.

The importance of the events of 1931 cannot be exaggerated; they were perceived at the time as posing a very serious threat to the whole institution of monarchy. It was the only real challenge to the king's authority he had to face in the course of a long reign. Thereafter life at court took on a settled and domestic character that it never lost. To

The relatives of Shabdrung Jigme Dorje (1905-31) The younger lady to the right is his elder sister Dorje Wangmo, wife of Sangye Tendzin (centre), the son of Ngödrup (to his right). Ngödrup was the neice of Cholé Tulku Yeshé Ngödrup (1851-1917), the last in the line of regents. The marriage of Sangye Tendzin and Dorje Wangmo thus brought together the families of the last officially recognized incarnations of the Shabdrung's verbal and physical elements. The boy seated on the far right is their son Ugyen Dorje, father of the present queens of Bhutan. The founding Shabdrung is depicted in the thangka hanging in the centre behind the group. (Undated photograph, private collection.)

gain a general view it seems best to look at three of the king's abiding preoccupations, namely family and religious matters, reform and development, and the issue of Bhutan's international status.

In 1932 the king took a second consort. Ashi Pema Dechen was his queen Ashi Püntso Chödrön's only sister, and before her marriage to the king she was a fully ordained nun. She had taken to a religious life but she also stood to inherit the family estate of Wangdü Chöling from her aunt, Ashi Yeshé Chödrön, who was King Ugyen Wangchuk's sister. The natural dignity and genuine spirituality of the young nun was lightened by great charm, beauty and gentle humour. It was certainly with the positive encouragement of her aunt that she now joined her elder sister as royal consort. The arrangement was intended to serve two purposes, aided by the strong matrilineal element in the local inheritance customs of this part of the country. First, it would help to mend the strained relations that had developed between the king and the aunt's son Dorje Rabden, who had once been thought to be a contender for the throne. Second, if Ashi Pema Dechen were to marry her cousin and produce heirs, they would inherit the estate and keep all its wealth within the royal family.[28] The family tended to produce daughters in abundance, and the property would very likely continue to pass down through their line. The fact that the king had already produced a male heir destined for the throne by one sister would not prevent any children he might have by the other sister from inheriting the estate. Moreover, there were many cases of a husband taking two wives if the economics of the family allowed.

The union was planned in this way for political and economic reasons, but it succeeded because of genuine affection. In 1943 Ashi Pema Dechen gave the king a son, Namgyel Wangchuk, and three daughters appeared at regular intervals: Chökyi in 1937, Deki Yangdzom in 1944, and Pema Chödrön in 1949. In the year that his first daughter was born, the king built a new palace at Domkhar in the Chumé valley for his elder consort. As in the case of all his palaces, a community of serfs (*drap*) was attached to the new residence for its maintenance. Separate provisions were usually

Three royal ladies in Bumthang, 1949. This style of crown (pesha) *and brooch* (ting-khab) *are no longer in vogue, but the Tibetan-style striped woollen apron* (dong-kheb) *is still worn by women in Bumthang. Above, Ashi Pedrön, eldest daughter of King Ugyen Wangchuk by his first queen, Rinchen. Top left, Ashi Püntso Chödrön, senior consort of King Jigme Wangchuk. Left, Ashi Wangmo, the unmarried older sister of King Jigme Wangchuk and a disciple of the Karmapa Lama. (Photos: G. Sherriff, Museum of Mankind)*

King Jigme Wangchuk and Queen Püntso Chödrön, the present Dowager Queen Mother, at their palace of Kunga Rabden, Mangdelung, 1949. George Sherriff noted in his diary for 2 April that the king "... has aged greatly. But he is still the pleasant thoughtful man he always was to meet. He remembers all the old Political Officers and asked after all by name, Bailey particularly". The king was destined to die in this palace three years later. (Photo: G. Sherriff, Royal Botanic Gardens, Edinburgh)

made for the two halves of the family, the senior consort with the heir apparent on the one side, and the junior consort with the king's later children on the other.

The close accord of the two sisters throughout their lives and their total lack of rivalry meant that much continued to be shared in common. Together they devoted their energies to religious activities on behalf of the king. Ashi Pema Dechen never really lost her vocation despite her marriage and after the death of the king she conducted her life very much as though she were once again under religious vows. The king's sister Ashi Wangmo was also a nun for much of her life, never marrying. She was the disciple of several noted lamas, in particular of the Karmapa incarnation who stood at the head of all the Kagyüpa schools.

The family was responsible for establishing two important new Nyingmapa communities in Bumthang outside the aegis of the state monasteries; with their own funds they endowed these "colleges of study" (*shedra*), one attached to the ancient monastery of Tharpaling and the other at Nyimalung on land from the estate of the queens' father. For the post of abbots of these communities they secured the services of Geshé Tenpa Rinchen for the former and Doring Tulku and Geshé Pema for the latter, all eminent teachers. The king himself would attend the rituals performed in these communities and arranged for regular trips of inspection to ensure there was no laxity of standards. A number of distinguished lamas were invited down from Tibet to give teachings. Indeed the whole frontier with Tibet remained as open as it had always been, allowing for many forms of cultural contact. Some of the monks who later came to renown in the country ran away secretly in this period to Tibet to continue their studies there, incurring the king's anger. Others were sent officially by the king in

The future third king Jigme Dorje Wangchuk at the age of five in Bumthang, 1933. From the age of seven he was educated by private tutors in English, Hindi and Tibetan. From the age of fourteen he was in attendance on his father. (Photo: G. Sherriff, Museum of Mankind)

Opposite:
King Jigme Wangchuk with his two sister-queens Püntso Chödrön (left) and Pema Dechen (right) and Betty Sherriff at the palace of Kunga Rabden, 1949. Two of the king's children by his junior queen Pema Dechen stand barefoot next to him: on the left the princess Chökyi dressed in boy's clothes and on the right the prince Namgyel Wangchuk. (Photo: G. Sherriff, Sherriff Collection)

Opposite:
A young lama arrives in Bumthang to be greeted by local monks. He can probably be identified with Pema Ösel Gyurmé Dorje (1930-55), the tenth incarnation of the "verbal principle" of Pemalingpa (1450-1521). It is known from the biography of this Tibetan lama by Dünjom Rinpoche that at the age of fifteen, in 1944, he interrupted his studies at Lhalung to accept the invitation of King Jigme Wangchuk to visit him at his palace of Wangdü Chöling in Bumthang. He visited the royal family again at the age of twenty-three, in 1952, when he performed the funeral rites of King Jigme Wangchuk and his aunt Yeshé Chödrön. This gifted young lama himself died at the age of twenty-five in Tibet. (Photo: private collection of Ashi Chökyi)

pursuit of the kind of curricula and standards he and his family wanted to introduce to Bhutan. Following the tradition set by his father, he arranged for monks of the state community in Tongsa to study at the distant Kagyüpa monastery of Surmang in east Tibet. The long-term effect of this effort was that when the northern border was closed following the Chinese take-over of Tibet in the 1950s, Bhutan was left with an elite of highly trained monks and scholars who had received the best training Tibet could offer. They were well prepared then to help in the task of making Bhutan's religious institutions stand firmly on their own feet. They could also later tap into some of the great reserves of learning among the Tibetan refugees settled in the subcontinent.

The king's male relatives were expected to serve him in any capacity he chose to give them. His younger brothers Dasho Gyurmé Dorje and Dasho Nakhu (Karma Trinley Lhundrub) were in constant attendance, the latter acting as his head of household, Drönyer, for much of his life. It seems both were actively discouraged from marrying since this might produce future complications of inheritance and succession. Both died young of illness, Gyurmé Dorje in 1933 and Nakhu in 1949.

The king's cousin Tsering Penjor continued as Paro Pönlop until he died in 1949 having held the office continuously for thirty-one years. He never gave the trouble expected of him early in the king's reign. Indeed, he had taken a more than active role in countering the danger posed to the king at the time of the Shabdrung's planned rebellion. He too never married, officially that is, but had liaisons with a variety of women and produced an indefinite number of children. He was described by the Political Officer in 1938 as "a stout and inactive batchelor".[29] He "reminded me of a friend who, on attaining to the dignity of knighthood, thought of asking to be dubbed Sir Cumference".[30] The Paro district, which incorporated many outlying areas to the north and south, remained his personal fief. Nothing is recorded of any innovations or reforms he may have brought in. Unlike his predecessor Dawa Penjor, he maintained good relations with the family of the king's hereditary chamberlain in Kalimpong, cooperating with Sonam Topgye in the reception of a steady flow of British guests. These all found him highly diverting and eccentric, an essential part of the local colour. The palace of Ugyen Pelri which he built himself on the flat ground below the great dzong remains a miniature masterpiece of design and decoration. The Pönlop gave it the form of the heavenly palace of the great guru Padmasambhava because, it is said, he saw himself as one of that saint's emanations or embodiments. He had a talent too for directing the panoply of processions and dances with which guests were invariably received, easily adjusting their originally divine or military purpose into that of secular display. For the British everything conformed exactly to what they had hoped to find in Bhutan, an unchanging medieval world where they could take comfort from the high place accorded them. For the lord of Paro, the honour done to him by receiving important guests in the sight of his subjects was probably sufficient reward. Thus one

Tsering Penjor, the Paro Pönlop, in the centre with his guests, from the left: Frank Ludlow (botanist), Margaret Williamson, Frederick Williamson (Political Officer, Sikkim), Dr. D. Tennant, George Sherriff (botanist), Sonam Tobgye Dorje (Gongzim and Bhutan Agent), at Paro, 25 June 1933. (Photo: "Taken by a local Nepali", Williamson Collection, Museum of Archaeology and Anthropology, Cambridge)

Ugyen Pelri Palace and its grounds as seen from Rinpung Dzong, and the Paro valley and river, looking north, 1943. (Photo: W. Henderson, private collection)

Lady Linlithgow and the Paro Pönlop, with Prince Thondup Namgyel of Sikkim behind, in Ugyen Pelri Palace, Paro, 1943. Joy Wilson, a member of the party, recorded in her diary: "The Penlop hypnotised me. He has two wives of which one never speaks. They are for some reason not recognised. I feel he must be a Hermaphrodite. There is something so unnatural in his whole appearance". (Photo: W. Henderson, private collection)

Lady Linlithgow, wife of the Viceroy of India (right) *and Sir Basil Gould, Political Officer, Sikkim* (left) *take their leave of the Paro Pönlop at Ugyen Pelri Palace, Paro, on their return to Sikkim and India by way of Tibet, 1943. The other members of the party included Mrs. Joy Wilson* (left) *and the Countess of Hopetoun* (right). *Partly obscured are Colonel Henry Elliot and Prince Thondup Namgyel of Sikkim. (Photo: W. Henderson, private collection)*

provincial elite helped to sustain the other with the available rituals and symbols of power. Matters of politics were rarely on the agenda. The ceremony was the thing.

As in the previous reign, the formulation of policy lay in the hands of the king, but closely advised by a few confidants including his chamberlain. Sir Basil Gould noted of the king that he had "the gift, as had his father, of picking out good men and sticking to them and their families ... He treats them in a manner which gives them confidence and inspires loyalty ... He talks freely with men and women of every class ...".[31]

Ugyen Pelri Palace and its grounds as seen from Rinpung Dzong, and the Paro valley and river, looking north, 1943. The palace was built by Tsering Penjor, the Paro Pönlop, on the model of the divine palace of Guru Padmasambhava known as the Glorious Copper-Coloured Mountain. The Pönlop, who regarded himself as an incarnation of the guru, is still remembered for the way he caused the building to be demolished several times before he was satisfied. (Photo: W. Henderson, private collection)

Foremost among his councilors stood "Raja" Sonam Topgye, who inherited the role of his father, particularly on all questions of contact with British India. It was he who arranged the only Indian trips which the king ever made, once very briefly to Gauhati in Assam and once to Calcutta and Kalimpong. Hugh Richardson's warm memories of Sonam Topgye and his wife, the Princess of Sikkim, must reflect the views of the many British with whom they maintained contact at the official and private level:[32]

I met Raja Sonam Tobgye Dorje on my visits to Gangtok where he often came to discuss Bhutan affairs with Sir Basil Gould. In my brief tenure of office as Political Officer, Sikkim, I also met him and we talked about his concern at the growing number of Nepalese in southern Bhutan. I met him also in Kalimpong where he and Rani Chuni [Chöying Wangmo] entertained me at Bhutan House, and in Darjeeling and Calcutta where he was a well known and tremendously popular figure on the race-courses, well in with all the owners and jockeys. Best of all I was entertained by him and Rani Chuni on my two visits to Bhutan where we enjoyed all sorts of

Formal studio portrait of King Jigme Wangchuk and Queen Püntso Chödrön, Calcutta, 1935. Signed by the king in roman and by the queen in Bhutanese cursive, and presented to Colonel and Mrs F.M. Bailey. Many copies of this photograph were later distributed in Bhutan. (Photo: Merseyside County Museums)

activities. Tobgye was always easy to get on with, open, genial, generous and full of fun, but deeply serious about Bhutan affairs. Rani Chuni was as you know small, erect, dignified, reserved and always beautifully dressed. She was not a person with whom one could take liberties but she had a quiet sense of humour. She appeared to be strict with her family. She could expand at times and I remember her talking about her great debt to Sir Charles Bell for getting her out of the stifling atmosphere of the Sikkim court when she was a girl and helping to get her a proper education. Behind the appearance of stiffness there was always a gleam of amusement and a genuine though not effusive kindness.

"The Bhutan Party at 42 Chowringhee, Calcutta, 2 January 1935". Second row, seated from left to right: Rani Chöying Wangmo (with her elder son Jigme Dorje, future Prime Minister, standing behind her, and next to him her second son Ugyen Dorje, the Phodrang Rinpoche, in the arms of a servant), Frederick Williamson (Political Officer, Sikkim), Queen Püntso Chödrön, King Jigme Wangchuk, Margaret Williamson, Raja Sonam Topgye Dorje (with eldest daughter Tashi Dorje standing next to him). The children seated on the ground in front of the king and queen are Jigme Dorje Wangchuk and Kesang Chödrön Dorje, the future third king and queen. The man in the fourth row directly above Margaret Williamson is Dasho Jamyang, father of the queens Püntso Chödrön and Pema Dechen. Some of the royal attendants who accompanied the party were in fact state monks of Punakha, selected for their knowledge of court discipline and dressed as laymen for this trip. (Photo: Williamson Collection, Museum of Archaeology and Anthropology, Cambridge)

The 1935 Indian trip concluded with a visit to Sikkim's capital at Gangtok where the king was received by the ruler of this neighbouring British protectorate, the Chögyal Tashi Namgyel, his chamberlain's brother-in-law. They had earlier met in Calcutta. The return journey took the king's party back to his kingdom by way of the Chumbi valley of Tibet and so through all the valleys east to Bumthang. In the company of Sonam Topgye on this trip he is said to have begun a systematic review of social conditions, administrative practices and judicial proceedings. There followed a number of important reforms.[33]

It was, for instance, discovered that the tax obligations of many estates rendered vacant by the dying out of whole families continued to be imposed upon the communities where these estates had been located. The population of the country appeared to have dropped as a result of disease, but the tax registers in the hands of the administration had not been altered. The burden upon most of these shrinking communities was therefore very heavy, and there was little incentive for local administrators to improve the situation. On the other hand it was also discovered there existed a whole class of indigent, untaxed and landless citizens called *zurpa*, literally "those who live on the side". The obvious decision – to fill up the vacant tax estates with these landless subjects – was duly taken. No increase of much needed revenue was yielded by this measure but it did much to alleviate two major sources of grievance.

Wherever possible it was also decided to reduce the taxes themselves, both those paid in kind and those rendered in the form of labour services. The government tax

Gongzim Sonam Topgye Dorje on the right, with an unidentified attendant; his wife Rani Chöying Wangmo and daughter Ashi Tashi are on the left; between them is Daw Khin Kyi, widow of General Aung San of Burma; India, late 1940s or early 1950s. (Photo: private collection of Aung San Suu Kyi)

records were revised to reduce the obligations of those who incurred particularly heavy obligations. Previously it seems every household had to supply firewood and hay to the dzong along with various other commodities that varied from district to district. For instance, in eastern Bhutan "tax cloth" had to be woven. Practically all of this type of tax was abolished. The need to supply free transport services to government was also adjusted, and for the first time these began to be paid for. Those households which had an insufficient number of members to provide porterage were provided with a horse or mule to assist them. The law that every male foal born to a taxpayer's mare had to be delivered to the government was abolished.

For centuries the law had demanded that if a murderer were caught red-handed he should be bound to the corpse of his victim and then executed by the drowning method.[34] In cases where manslaughter fines were imposed, these were calculated to reduce the guilty person to total penury. All manner of senior and junior officials both of the central and provincial governments had to be paid fees for handling the case at every stage. For instance, when a particular officer received a verbal or written report on the case, he was entitled to a gift which he retained as a perquisite of office. Similarly, any government messenger involved in the case was entitled to his due. All this was now revised to provide for a single fine to be paid to the central government alone. The traditional method of execution described above was abolished. One might wonder whether in fact it had been used in the twentieth century at all.

King Jigme Wangchuk made repeated requests for British aid through the Political Officers in Sikkim. The country's own paltry revenue was barely sufficient for the needs of her own traditional administration and the support of the state monasteries. External finance was limited to the old British subsidy of one hundred thousand

King Jigme Wangchuk of Bhutan and Chögyal Tashi Namgyel of Sikkim, at the Calcutta Races, 1935. The first two kings of Bhutan only visited Calcutta, the nearest Indian city to Bhutan, once in their lifetimes. (Photo: Williamson Collection, Museum of Archaeology and Anthropology, Cambridge)

rupees per year, and a similar sum was raised from the British in return for removing liquor shops from within ten miles of the southern frontier. This was totally insufficient for anything except maintaining the very slight momentum for development that had begun in the preceding reign and building upon it in a modest way. The schools in Ha and Bumthang were maintained, and a few students who had received their education in Kalimpong continued to proceed to further studies in India. The pressing need for inoculations was met in a sporadic way by a few visiting doctors. The ravages of venereal disease were treated similarly. In 1942 Sir Basil Gould eventually succeeded, after much argument, in having the British subsidy doubled for the duration of the war, but with no further commitment. Among the projects he and the king were advocating were "conservation of forests, improvement of communications, 'suppression of the more extravagant forms' of feudalism, and adoption of a system of taxation that would provide revenue for reforms including a system of education".[36] The increase in the subsidy meant that a few halting steps could be taken towards realizing these hopes. However, British policy on development issues was wholly conditioned by the heavy weight of official inertia in Delhi. There was a strong and traditional suspicion there for Political Officers who championed the cause of local reform. Their efforts, it was thought, would not only entangle the government in complex matters of no concern to them but would carry heavy bills for which there was no budget. The question of raising extra funds from London never seems to have been raised. There was no precedent. It was therefore with genuine cause and feeling that many years later the king's heir could say: "I am prepared to recount how hard we tried for British aid and how reluctant they were to grant that aid ...".[36]

In military matters, however, there was progress. The five hundred rifles in the hands of the king when he succeeded to the throne rose to about two thousand during his reign. After the Shabdrung's unsuccessful revolt in 1931 the government of India agreed to provide training to fifteen Bhutanese soldiers in Shillong. By the early 1940s the number of trainees had steadily increased. The British officer of the Gurkha regiment where the largest batch of these was attached wrote that they were "without exception the finest party of recruits" he had ever seen.[37] On returning to Bhutan they formed a regular platoon of bodyguards. Together with a reserve of 1,900 rifles this became the nucleus of what later emerged, with the help of independent India, as a standing army.

As Indian independence drew nearer worries in Bhutan about how its status would be affected increased. What was the legal definition of Bhutan's place within the British empire, assuming it had one at all? Would it now be absorbed in the new republic? Could it use the transfer of power in the subcontinent to bolster its own independence? Were there some immediate practical gains to be won? What kind of relationship would develop with India's new rulers?

Even before the king had succeeded to the throne, it had been officially decided in Delhi that Bhutan was a state under the suzerainty of the British government. Moreover, it was also an Indian state under the suzerainty of the King Emperor. However, since it had been left alone to exercise its own internal sovereignty, which was in any case guaranteed by treaty, there was a "convenient ambiguity" over its status.[38] In the early 1930s it was thought advisable to make provisions that would allow Bhutan to be admitted in future to an Indian federal structure, but only if it so desired. By 1940 it was decided that federation after all provided no solution to Bhutan's status since it was "a Protectorate in close treaty relations with HMG".[39]

In 1946 the Cabinet Mission appointed to draw up plans for Indian independence turned down a request from King Jigme Wangchuk to make his case. He wished to point out that Bhutan was not an Indian state and never had been. On the contrary, Bhutan had in the past acknowledged Tibetan suzerainty. Moreover, there was a

King Jigme Wangchuk and Gongzim Sonam Togye Dorje in the valley of Ha during the last official British mission to Bhutan before Indian independence, led by Arthur Hopkinson, Political Officer, Sikkim, in 1947. The king wears the insignia of Knight Commander of the Star of India which he had just received. Soldiers of the Bhutan army on parade to the right contrast with the traditional bodyguard to the left. (Photo: A. Hopkinson, private collection)

The future third king of Bhutan, Jigme Dorje Wangchuk (centre), with the princes of Sikkim, George (right) and Thondup (left), in the Ha valley, 1947. Thondup, the younger brother, succeeded his father Tashi Namgyel as Chögyal of Sikkim following the death of George in a plane crash. (Photo: A. Hopkinson, private collection)

danger now that her treaty agreements with Britain would be adversely affected. When the Mission refused to receive the king's deputation, merely giving an assurance that Bhutan's position would be carefully looked at in due course, the king's fears that Bhutan was to be left in a weak and potentially dangerous situation began to be openly shared by the Political Officer in Sikkim, Arthur Hopkinson. He supported Bhutan's desire to remain in the British Commonwealth, to have some pockets of the duars returned to it, and a new tripartite agreement drawn up with Britain and India as co-signatories with Bhutan. It later became the official position in Bhutan that India should return all those forested areas of the duars that were not under tea cultivation. Failing that, the annual subsidy should be hiked in a way that reflected the true value of all this "stolen" land.[40] The Cabinet Mission in the end decided that the British government should not enter into any new treaty relationship with the frontier states and the most they could do for Bhutan was provide help in negotiating a fresh treaty with the new government of India.

It was nearly two years after the formal transfer of power in 1947 that negotiations began for a new treaty. This resulted in a document signed on 8 August 1949 that did little else except reaffirm the provisions of the old 1910 treaty. Bhutan's independence was recognized, her internal administration was left in its own hands, but the Bhutan government still agreed "to be guided by the advice of the Government of India in regard to its external relations". Thirty-two square miles of territory at Dewangiri (Dewathang) were returned to Bhutan. Most important of all, no formal protectorate was claimed by India over Bhutan. The door was thus left open to the future strengthening of Bhutan's position under international law. The king's worst apprehensions, namely that Bhutan would become another Indian state, had not been realized. Nevertheless, residual fears of Indian or even Chinese absorption were still felt. It was natural therefore that Bhutan at this time began to look to membership of the United Nations as the final guarantor of its sovereignty.[41] It was to be a further twenty-two years before that hope was realized.

While the king had been taking steps to ensure that he bequeathed an independent Bhutan to future generations he was at the same making provisions for the eventual succession of the heir apparent. His son Jigme Dorje Wangchuk had been educated like himself by tutors at the palace school in Bumthang. In due course the king had appointed him chief household officer, or Drönyer. The need was felt, however, to break with precedent and to arrange for the heir to experience something of the world beyond the borders of Bhutan. He spent time therefore in further private studies in Kalimpong before travelling to the United Kingdom to spend six months with the family of the king's friend, the well-known botanist George Sherriff. He was accompanied there by Jigme Palden Dorje, eldest son of his chamberlain, who was being similarly groomed for high office. It was clearly intended that the two young men would later give each other close support, forming a pair in the same way as their fathers and grandfathers had done. Indeed, Jigme Dorje had already taken

Jigme Dorje, the Ha Drung, in the Ha valley, 1947. Upon the death of his father Sonam Topgye Dorje in 1952 he inherited the post of Gongzim (chamberlain to the monarch) and served the third king Jigme Dorje Wangchuk as Prime Minister (Lönchen) until his assassination in 1964. (Photo: A. Hopkinson, private collection)

over many of the duties of his father and was destined eventually to succeed him as chamberlain (Gongzim) with the rank of prime minister. Upon their return in 1950 the king appointed his son to fill the office of Paro Pönlop left vacant by the death of his cousin in the previous year. The key post thus came back into the hands of the immediate royal family for the first time since Ugyen Wangchuk had held it before he rose to the governorship of Tongsa and thence to the throne.

It was there in Paro a year later that the crown prince married Ashi Kesang, younger daughter of the king's chamberlain and sister of the future prime minister. The long relationship of trust and service which had linked the two families so intimately over the preceding two generations was thus finally cemented in marriage. The royal couple were destined to spend the years of their early marriage together in Paro and Thimphu. As a result the centre of government shifted back from Bumthang to the old summer capital in Thimphu where it is now permanently established. It was from there that all the coming changes, so fundamental to present life, were to be introduced by the new king and his prime minister. The firm foundations they laid together at that time outlived the tragic assassination of the prime minister in 1964.

But all this is to anticipate a continuing story that lies beyond the present purpose. Here the story comes to a close with the death of the second king at his palace of Kunga Rabden in 1952. By that time the immediate survival of both the kingdom and the dynasty was no longer in doubt. If the primary duty of a hereditary ruler is to bequeath to his heirs a stable throne in a kingdom whose sovereignty is assured, it may be said this king did so in full measure.

The king's death had been long expected. Unheard of animals had appeared in the river below the palace, and the river itself had changed colour. A strange star was seen on the horn of the moon in daytime. The pole of the king's archery tent broke and so did the pole of the tall prayer flag at his main palace. Blood was seen to flow from an image of the Lord Buddha in the old winter capital. With all these omens it was sure that the "sun of happiness was setting". [42]

The future king Jigme Dorje Wangchuk, aged twenty-one, in office as Tongsa Drönyer (Guestmaster of Tongsa) at Kunga Rabden in 1949, in barefoot attendance on his father, who retained the position of Tongsa Pönlop in addition to occupying the throne. A year later, after returning from six months spent with the Sherriff family in Scotland, the prince was appointed Paro Pönlop. (Photo: G. Sherriff, Royal Botanic Gardens, Edinburgh)

Notes: Chapter Five

1. A fourth son who died in infancy, born to the second consort Lemo, is also mentioned in Charles Bell's report for 1911-12:PRO, FO 371/1330 (75984), p.1.
2. BRGI 563-4. Geshé Mindruk was of the noble family of the Durwai Dung in Bumthang. The Bhutanese sources for the life of King Jigme Wangchuk are BRGI 563-79; BRDK 203-6; SMLJ 73-9; BRTU 290-2. For a summary of contacts during his reign with the British authorities in India and later with the government of independent India, see Labh 1974: 197-210; Collister 1987: 177-200; Singh 1988a: 361-71. See also especially Gould 1957; Fletcher 1975; Williamson 1987.
3. See Tables 1 and 2.
4. According to BRTU 242-3, Tenpai Nyima was born in 1569 and his elder brother Pema Trinley in 1564, that is when their father was aged sixty-five and seventy respectively. This seems a bit unlikely.
5. See Labh 1974: 197.
6. See photograph, p. 106
7. Bailey's confidential memorandum on "Bhutan Affairs", 28 April 1928: OIOC, L/P&S/12/2229. Among other matters Bailey noted: "A possible source of difficulty for Bhutan, and one to which His Highness [Jigme Wangchuk] is quite alive, is the settlement of a large number of Nepalese in the lower valleys".
8. There is an account in BRGI 565-6 of how a dismissed Tongsa Drönyer, one Ugyen Dorje, was also causing difficulties at this time. He had acquired power and influence while taking charge of the funeral arrangements of Queen Lemo and this had made good relations with the future king difficult. I cannot trace mention of this person in other sources. Perhaps his name is an alias for Dorje Rabden.
9. Bailey, "Bhutan Affairs", 1928, para. 4. I can only assume that the Raven Crown worn by the king on the occasion of his enthronement was borrowed from the Paro Pönlop, who still had it in his possession some four years later (see photograph, p. 106). Unless one of these was a replica of Ugyen Wangchuk's crown I see no other explanation.
10. *Ibid.* para. 3.
11. Bailey's letter to the Foreign Secretary to the Government of India, 5 April 1928: OIOR, L/P&S/12/2229. In the course of his investigations Bailey discovered that the Bhutanese had been quietly conducting their own relations with Tibet in contravention of the 1910 treaty, which had placed the conduct of such relations in the hands of the British government.
12. King Jigme Wangchuk to J.L.R. Weir, 18 November 1931, p. 3: OIOC, L/P&S/12/2222.
13. Gongzim Sonam Topgye to F.M. Bailey, 2 October 1931: OIOC, MSS EUR F 157.
14. King Jigme Wangchuk to J.L.R. Weir, 18 November 1931, p. 5.
15. *Ibid.*, p. 4.
16. SMLJ 75-7, esp. 75. This is the only Bhutanese source which treats the matter in some detail, corroborating the British records and adding some detail.
17. *Ibid.*, 76.
18. J.L.R. Weir to Foreign Secretary, 11 Nov. 1932: OIOR, L/P&S/12/2229.
19. The party was made up of Chözim Adap Sangye, Gangteng Tulku Trinley Dorje, Paro Drönyer Tsendong Namgyel and a group of bodyguards (*zingap*): SMLJ 76.
20. King Jigme Wangchuk to J.L.R. Weir, 18 November 1931, p. 6.
21. SMLJ 76-7.

22. Weir later told the Dalai Lama he was personally convinced the death was the result of natural causes rather than suicide. J.L.R. Weir to Foreign Secretary, 3 December 1931, paras. 2-3; 11 November 1932, para. 5: OIOC, L/P&S/12/2229.

23. Tibetan Kashag to King Jigme Wangchuk, 15 April 1932, enclosed in J.L.R. Weir to Foreign Secretary, 29 May 1932: OIOC, L/P&S/12/2229.

24. SMLJ 77.

25. BRDK 129-30.

26. See Nari Rustomji's account of how he took the boy to safety: Rustomji 1971: 282-3. He is still living in India.

27. See Table 2, p.50 above.

28. This is the explanation given in BRGI 568-9.

29. Sir Basil Gould, quoted in Collister 1987: 177.

30. Gould 1957: 188.

31. Quoted in Collister 1987: 193.

32. Letter from Hugh Richardson to the author, 22 May 1994.

33. I base the following on BRGI 575-7.

34. See the law code of 1729 translated in Aris 1986: 160-1.

35. Collister 1987: 192.

36. The words are those of King Jigme Dorje Wangchuk to the National Assembly of Bhutan in 1971, quoted *ibid.* 197.

37. Quoted in Collister 1987: 194.

38. The viceroy Lord Reading's phrase, quoted in Singh 1988a: 367.

39. *Ibid.* 368.

40. BRGI 573.

41. "Raja" Sonam Topgye Dorje wrote to his old friend Colonel Bailey about his fears, seeking his advice. On 17 January 1948 Bailey replied to "Tubby" saying: "If the Govt. here definitely will do nothing I think you could approach the United Nations Organisation and ask that steps be taken to maintain your independence and prevent being absorbed by either India or China. I confess I do not know how this would be done. Could you not come yourself to discuss this or send Jigme?": OIOC, MSS EUR F 157.

42. BRGI 578-9.

Six
The Crown Past and Present

The apparent speed with which Bhutan finally turned from what Lord Curzon had called the "incomprehensible hierarchy" of its old theocracy to a hereditary monarchy must be seen in the context of a Buddhist culture thoroughly imbued with the notion of kingship. Bhutanese literature of all periods is replete with references not only to the Maurya kings, principally Asoka, under whom Buddhism had prospered in ancient India, but also to the ancient "religious kings" of the Tibetan empire who had introduced the faith to the Land of Snows. Legends, folk stories and songs told of the virtues of wise kings who protect the faith and cause it to prosper. Almost all of Bhutan's myths of origin are dominated by a royal element. The Shabdrungs of the Bhutanese past and their regents too had drawn from the traditional Buddhist conception of royalty in defining their roles and developing their institutions. The one-valley, self-styled "kings" who ruled in the east of the country before the unification of the seventeenth century were typical of the whole cultural empire, of which Bhutan forms only a small part, where small and isolated polities could survive intact for long periods. Implicit in the wider Buddhist culture that linked the polities of the past to the almost independent baronies of the theocracy was the idea that a greater, conquering monarch might one day bring them all together. It could also be claimed that the manner in which the Bhutanese monarchy was created outwardly conformed to the ideal of the first king of Buddhist legend, King Mahasammata, whose name the Tibetans and Bhutanese commonly translate as "The King Elevated by Many".[1] Although the noun for "king" (gyelpo) derives from the verb to "conquer" (gyelwa), the element of popular consent as a legitimizing factor is also present in the wider conception of kingship. Moreover, in the Mahayana Buddhist world the figure of the bodhisattva who defers nirvana to alleviate the sufferings of the world lies close to hand as a further model for kings.

All these elements of belief and attitude conspired with the circumstances of history and Ugyen Wangchuk's own personality to offer him a direct path to the throne. The same path, drenched in the blood of the enemies of the faith, stretched back to his forebears through a divine pedigree descending from the Gods of Clear Light. It could be argued that if he had not already possessed such a lineage one would have had to be invented for him. But in his case the need genuinely did not arise. The chronicler can point with truth to his ancestors in the line of the Dungkar Chöjé going back to Pemalingpa. The famous saint was known to descend from the gods and to be in closest relationship with the divine guru Padmasambhava. Genealogy could thus be used to reinforce the primary character of a Buddhist king as supporter of the *dharma* and the *sangha*. The long era of peace which followed the enthronement of the first king was but the natural and expected gift of a bodhisattva.

Moreover, kingship meant much more to the world in the early twentieth century than it does now at its end. Some of the princely families of India then retained a semblance of power and much privilege. The King-Emperor ruled by means of a carefully orchestrated fiction. Nepal had its king, and so did Sikkim. For the first fifty years or so of the Bhutanese monarchy the kings were fitted into the regional order; they were known to the world by the Anglo-Indian styling of "His Highness the Maharaja of Bhutan". It was only after Indian independence and with the first moves to have Bhutan's sovereignty recognized by the world community that the modern form "His Majesty the King of Bhutan" was adopted.

To the Bhutanese he was and remains "The Precious Master of Power, the King of Drukyul".[2] More intimately he is referred to as "the chief",[3] and addressed formally by the honorific word for "foot".[4] The seat he occupies is the same "golden throne" reserved for high lamas, and his yellow shawl is in origin the outer garment worn by high monks, pleated in a special way. Just as the ruling lamas of old were conflated with kings, so the kings of the present are treated in much the same way as supreme lamas. The other fundamental symbol of royalty, the Raven Crown, was first modified and domesticated by Ugyen Wangchuk from the one he inherited from his father, for whom it was originally designed by a lama. The etiquette of court behaviour is entirely modelled on monastic tradition,[5] and there is no honorific language used in speaking to or about the king which cannot also be used for a lama.

The moment of actual empowerment is not in fact the formal investiture of public enthronement, which takes place later. Instead, the real assumption happens when the new king presents a ceremonial white scarf, symbolizing the purity of his intentions, to a scroll-painting of the protective deity of the realm. This short ritual is held in the presence of the embalmed remains of the founding Shabdrung, enshrined to this day in the dzong at Punakha where he died. An omen of fortune for the king and his kingdom is found in the way the scarf is seen to fall upon the painting. In return the king receives a scarf of office as if from the very hands of the country's first unifier.

Alongside these customs and symbols inherited from the theocracy, which serve to underline the sacred nature of kingship and its remote position high above the world of ordinary mortals, there survives a complementary tradition which requires the king to be wholly accessible to his people. Any subject, however low, has the right to present a grievance. In cases of serious loss or affliction, welfare can always be requested.[6] A petitioner must, however, have good cause or be prepared to face serious trouble. The king further keeps in touch with popular need and sentiment through his friends and confidants, usually out of office, who are termed "kadröp", literally "those who fulfill the command".[7]

The rural setting of the Bhutanese monarchy, in contrast to the urban background of most others, can only but promote the contact of the king with his people. Compared with many other monarchies there is a relative absence of hidebound ritual. Thus when the king presides over a libation ritual called *Marchang* he does so in much the same way as any villager at an archery contest. Moreover, the only priest whose office is permanently tied to the throne is a relatively junior state monk still called "the regent's ritual protector",[8] as if the old theocracy were still frozen in place. Far from being in daily attendance on the king, this chaplain is rarely if ever seen in the palace. The officers of the royal household are still limited to a "guestmaster" (*drönyer*), "chamberlain" (*zimpön*) and "food-master" (*sölpön*), though one or more of these posts are often vacant. The present monarch, like his late father before him, chooses to live very simply with only a minimum of ceremony, far more concerned as he is with the practical welfare of his people than with court ritual. Yet, paradoxically, recent years have also witnessed the formal codification of that ritual and its imposition on the country at large, a reflection of growing nationalism and the search for national identity.

Traditions can be maintained, revived or recast, others invented. In the end it is the king alone who decides to what degree he retreats into ceremony and obfuscation or emerges into the light of day. Ritual and reality have to be balanced in new and meaningful ways. The king has to sense the mood of his subjects, and win their trust to express their will clearly and with no reserve.

Notes: Chapter Six

1. *Mang-pos bkur-ba'i rgyal-po* (pronounced "mangpö kurwai gyelpo").
2. *Brug rgyal-po mnga'-bdag rin-po-che* (pronounced "Druk gyelpo ngadak rinpoché").
3. *dPon* (pronouned "Pön" in Dzongkha and "Pon" in the language of Bumthang and adjoining regions)
4. This is the same *Zhabs* (pronounced "Shab") as in *Zhabs-drung* ("Shabdrung"), a religious title found in many parts of the northern Buddhist world meaning literally "In Front of the Feet".
5. The term used for court ritual and behaviour is *sgrig rnam-gzhag* (pronounced "Drik namzhak"), literally "the fundamentals of [monastic] order". It now covers every aspect of formal behaviour observed not only in the presence of the king but on every occasion of ceremony. Courses in this are obligatory for all government servants and schoolchildren.
6. The word for welfare, *skyid-sdug* (pronounced "kyiduk") is made up of the words for "happiness" and "suffering".
7. *bKa'-sgrub-pa.*
8. *sDe-pa'i srung-'khor-pa* (pronounced "Depai sungkhorp").

Appendix 1

The Rulers of Bhutan, 1822-1972

Note: The first section below includes those regents (Druk Desi or "Deb Rajas") who reigned in the closing period of the Bhutanese theocracy during the lifetime of Jigme Namgyel (1825-81), father of the first king (Druk Gyelpo) Ugyen Wangchuk and during the latter's youth before he won the throne. The dates of accession on the left are those supplied according to the Western calendar in BRGI (see Bibliographies) and supercede those in Aris 1979: 272-3. Because of a discrepancy between the lunar system of the Bhutanese calendar and the Western year, the conversion may sometimes have produced a date that is wrong by one year. The enumeration of rulers also follows that of BRGI. State monks and recognized reincarnations who came to the throne are identified as such with the delta symbol Δ in front of their names. A dagger † after a ruler's name indicates that he met a violent death by sword, poison or, it is claimed, by magic. An asterisk * indicates the ruler was forcibly deposed.

The final regents of the Bhutanese theocracy

1822	Δ Purgyel alias Chökyi Gyeltsen* (1774-?), 32nd Druk Desi
1831	Dorje Namgyel † (1779-1833), 33rd Druk Desi
1833	Trinley (?-1835), 34th Druk Desi
1835	Δ Phurgyel alias Chökyi Gyeltsen* (again), 35th Druk Desi
1838	Dorje Norbu (1800-48) and Tashi Dorje (1782-1850), jointly 36th Druk Desi
1847	Tashi Dorje (1782-1850), 37th Druk Desi
1850	Δ Wangchuk Gyelpo † (1800-1850), 38th Druk Desi
1850	Δ Shabdrung Jigme Norbu (1831-61), 39th Druk Desi
1851	Chakpa Sangye † (?-1851), 40th Druk Desi

1852	Δ Damchö Lhundrup alias Barchung, 41st Druk Desi
1854	Δ Jamtrül Jamyang Tendzin (1831-55), 42nd Druk Desi (with Damchö Lhundrup)
1855	Kunga Pelden alias Sonam Topgye (?-1860), 43rd Druk Desi in Punakha
1855	Umadewa alias Sherab Tharchin † (?-1857), 44th Druk Desi in Thimphu
1861	Nadzi Pasang alias Döndrup alias Püntso Namgyel*, 45th Druk Desi
1863	Tsewang Sithub*, 46th Druk Desi jointly with:
1863	Δ Tsultrim Yönten †, 47th Druk Desi
1864	Δ Kargyü Wangchuk (?-1864), 48th Druk Desi
1864	Δ Tsöndrü Pekar (?-1864), 49th Druk Desi
1864	Tsewang Sithub (again), 50th Druk Desi
1870	Jigme Namgyel (1825-81), 51st Druk Desi
1873	Dorje Namgyel † (?-1873), 52nd Druk Desi
1879	Chögyel Zangpo (?-1881), 53rd Druk Desi
1882	Lama Tsewang alias Sonam Gyeltsen (?-1884), 54th Druk Desi
1884	Δ Gawa Zangpo* (?-1885), 55th Druk Desi
1886	Δ Sangye Dorje (1839-1903), 56th Druk Desi
1903	Δ Cholé Tulku Yeshe Ngödrup* (1851-1917), 57th Druk Desi

The kings of Bhutan of the Wangchuk dynasty

1907	Ugyen Wangchuk (1862-1926), 1st Druk Gyelpo
1927	Jigme Wangchuk (1903-52), 2nd Druk Gyelpo
1952	Jigme Dorje Wangchuk (1928-72), 3rd Druk Gyelpo
1972	Jigme Senge Wangchuk (1955-), 4th Druk Gyelpo

Appendix 2
British Photographs and Films of Bhutan, 1864-1949

Abbreviations

MAA	Museum of Archaeology and Anthropology, University of Cambridge
MCM	Merseyside County Museums, Liverpool
MM	Museum of Mankind, London
NFA	National Film Archive, London
NHM	Natural History Museum, London
OIOC	Oriental and India Office Collections, British Library, London
PRM	Pitt Rivers Museum, University of Oxford
RBG	Royal Botanic Gardens, Edinburgh
RGS	Royal Geographical Society, London

EDEN 1864

The Hon. Ashley Eden was deputed on a mission to deal with Bhutanese "outrages" committed on the southern border. He was accompanied by Capt. W.H.J. Lance, Capt. H.H. Godwin-Austin and Dr. B. Simpson. The mission approached Punakha by way of Dalingkha (Dalingcote), Ha, Paro and Thimphu, and returned by the same route. The failure of the mission directly led to the outbreak of the Anglo-Bhutanese War of 1864-5. See Eden, "Report on the State of Bhutan and on the Progress of the Mission of 1863-64", in *Political Missions to Bootan*; H.H. Godwn-Austin, "Bhutan and the Himalayas East of Darjeeling", *Scottish Geographical Magazine*, x (1894), pp. 635-40; D.F. Rennie, *Bhotan and the Story of the Dooar War* (London, 1866; repr. New Delhi, 1970). Two albums preserved at the **RGS**, contain photographs taken during the Eden mission, along with other views of tribal people in the former North-East Frontier Agency (Abors, Mishmis, Nagas etc.) and in the Darjeeling area. The albums are numbered A124 and A125. The first of these is inscribed: "To Agnes from her affectionate husband on the anniversary of her birthday. 26th Feby. 1869 [signature illegible]".

ANON PRE-1868

Plate 43, by an unidentified photographer, in J. Forbes Watson and John William Kaye (eds.), *The People of India: A Series of Photographic Illustrations with Descriptive Letterpress* (London, India Museum, 1868). The caption reads: "Group of Bhotanese chiefly of Tibetan origin. Bhotan." Three Bhutanese are seen in a typically posed attitude of this period, probably taken in Darjeeling.

BELL 1904

During the Younghusband Expedition to Tibet in 1904 Ugyen Wangchuk, the Tongsa Pönlop of Bhutan, sought to act as an intermediary between the Tibetan government and the British authorities. His arrival in the Chumbi valley of Tibet was photographed by C.A. (later Sir Charles) Bell. The **MCM**, Liverpool, preserves Bell's own album of 1904 as C.B. Album 6 ("Photographs" embossed on the cover). The papers of Charles Bell are held at the **OIOC**, MSS Eur F 80.

BAILEY 1904

Another photograph of Ugyen Wangchuk during this same mission of 1904, this one taken in Lhasa by F.M. ('Eric') Bailey, is to be found in the **RGS**, London, catalogue no. 071827.

JOHNSTON & HOFFMAN 1904

Three identical prints of a photograph of Ugyen Wangchuk, taken by the Calcutta firm of Johnston and Hoffman during the same mission of 1904, are found in the Curzon Collection at the **OIOC**, London (Photo [album] 430/53(84)), in the **MCM**, Liverpool (C.B. Album 1 [50.31.148] inscribed "Chumbi/C.A.Bell/March 1905", towards the end), and in the **RGS**, London (PR/030409). Ugyen Wangchuk is shown standing and wearing the Raven Crown. Also seen are the Bhutan Agent Ugyen Dorje and the Thimphu Dzongpön. There is a further portrait of Ugyen Wangchuk in Lhasa, seated, photographer unknown, in the **OIOC**: Photo [album] 355/6(61).

WHITE 1905

John Claude White was deputed in 1905 on a mission to present the insignia of the K.C.I.E. to Ugyen Wangchuk, who was then Tongsa Pönlop. He was accompanied by A.W. Paul and Major F.W. Rennick. The mission reached Bumthang by way of Ha, Paro, Thimphu, Punakha, Wangdü Phodrang and Tongsa, returning by way of Lingshi. See J.C. White, "Across Unknown Bhutan", *Wide World Magazine,*, xix (1907), pp. 322-7; J.C. White, *Sikhim and Bhutan: Twenty-one Years on the North-East Frontier, 1887-1908* (London, 1909), chs. 13-15; J.C.White, "Castles in the Air: Experiences and Journeys in Unknown Bhutan", *The National Geographic Magazine*, xxv (1914), pp. 365-453. Albums containing photographs taken by White during this mission are preserved in London at the **OIOC** (Photo [album] 20) and the **RGS** (D.4), and in the private collection of Kurt Meyer, Los Angeles. All have captions, those in the **RGS** album being printed rather than in manuscript. The **OIOC** album is inscribed "recd. India Office 22 Nov. 1907", and is otherwise identical to the **RGS** volume. The Meyer album duplicates some of the views, the order is different, and views taken by White during his later trips of 1906-8 may be included. The White negatives have yet to be located if indeed they survive at all. **OIOC**, Photo 613 (purchased at Sotheby's on 28 Oct. 1981 as Lot 144) consists of 43 photographs, formerly mounted in an album, taken by White mainly in Bhutan, but the last ten are of Sikkim and Tibet. The portrait of the last regent in **OIOC** Photo 20 (16) is duplicated in **OIOC** MSS Eur G 38/1(33e).

WHITE 1907-8

John Claude White was deputed to represent the Government of India during the installation of Ugyen Wangchuk as the first hereditary monarch of Bhutan in 1907. He was accompanied by Major F.W. Rennick, Capt. W.L. Campbell and Capt. H. Hyslop (see next entry). The mission entered Bhutan by the Tremo La and proceeded by way of Paro and Thimphu to Punakha. White returned by way of Paro, Lome La and Dogna [Dungna?] Dzong to Jaigaon. Campbell returned by way of Paro and Ha. Renick and Hyslop returned by way of Chapcha and Pasakha (Buxa). White's albums from this mission do not seem to have survived but there are a number of photographs reproduced in his article, "My Journey in Bhutan", *Wide World Magazine*, xxiii (1909), pp. 13-23, 179-85. See also his *Sikhim and Bhutan*, chs. 18-19, and his "Castles in the Air" and "Across Unknown Bhutan" (cited in full above). Capt. Campbell's printed diary of the mission has also survived: "Diary of the Visit of the Political Officer in Sikkim to Bhutan in December 1907" (it is not clear where this is deposited, probably in the **OIOC**).

HYSLOP 1907-8

Capt. Henry Hyslop, who accompanied the above mission, prepared an album of photographs pasted in alongside a printed version of part of his journal entitled "Extracts from My Diary, Written whilst Accompanying the British Mission to Bhutan, 1907-8". The album is now in the private collection of Kurt Meyer, Los Angeles. It consists of 48 pages, some wholly occupied by photographs, but mostly with both text and photographs (108 of the latter, including 15 full plates). An undated letter in Bhutanese addressed to Hyslop by Ugyen Wangchuk is pasted onto p. 44.

BELL 1910

Charles Bell, accompanied by Capt. Robert Kennedy, visited Bhutan in 1911 to conclude a treaty whereby Bhutan agreed to be guided by the advice of the British Government in the conduct of her foreign relations. See C.A. Bell, "Diary of My Mission to Bhutan for the Months of December 1909 and January 1910": **OIOC**, London, L/P&S/10/221; R. Kennedy, Diary of his visit to Bhutan, 1909-10: **OIOC**, MSS. Eur.F.157/224 (Bailey Collection). Nine of Bell's original albums are preserved at the **MCM**, Liverpool. Among these, five contain photographs of Bhutan, of which the three most interesting are: C.B. Album 5 (50.31.142) ["BHUTAN" embossed on cover]; C.B. Album 7 (50.31.154); C.B. Album 9 (50.31.156) ["TIBET" embossed on cover] (See also JOHNSTON & HOFFMAN

1904 above and BELL 1911 below.) A few of the original negatives have been located at the **PRM**, Oxford, but none have yet turned up in the major collection of Bell's negatives at the **OIOC** (photo 6). An album of Bell's Bhutan photographs is kept at the National Archives of India, Delhi (Extl., Sept. 1910, nos. 221-2, pt. B), but it has not been examined. The Bell Collection at the **PRM**, Oxford, contain the following Bhutan views dating from 1910: BL H 34, BL P 10, BL P 11, BL P 248. Other Bhutan views in this collection are of uncertain date, and it is not yet clear if the negatives are in the **PRM** or **OIOC** collections: BL H 33, BL H 320, BL Q 12. Similarly, the negatives of the "Photographs illustrating mountains, rivers and lakes in Bhutan" mentioned in Bell's typescript catalogue, also the "Photographs illustrating life and customs in Bhutan" (see **OIOC**, MSS Eur F 80) have not yet been located.

BELL/MACDONALD 1911

In 1911 Ugyen Wangchuk attended the coronation durbar in Delhi. One print is preserved among Charles Bell's photographs at the **MCM**, Liverpool (C.B. Album 3 (50.31.150) towards end), and five negatives at the **PRM**, Oxford (BL P8, BL227). One of the latter is attributed to Macdonald.

COOPER 1914 and 1915

The botanist R.E.Cooper made two trips to Bhutan in the years 1914 and 1915, touring the country very extensively. The first expedition took him by way of Buxa, Chukha, Chapcha, Thimphu, Lingshi, Punakha, Wangdü Phodrang, Tongsa, Bumthang, and back to Thimphu, Lingshi, Paro and thence back to India the way he had come. On the second trip he proceeded by way of Buxa, Chukha, Paro, Gasa, Tremo La, Thimphu, Punakha, Wangdü Phodrang, Tongsa, Bumthang, Kurtö, Senge Dzong, Tashiyangtse, Tashigang, Dramitse, Mongar, Ura, Tongsa, Wandu Phodrang and south by way of Chukha, Murichom and Sinchu La. It is clear from the Cooper MSS preserved in the archives of the **RBG**, Edinburgh, that he took a good number of photographs. At the end of the first of three of his Bhutan notebooks there is recorded a "Photographic Negative Index for Season 1915", listing the contents of 24 boxes of (glass-plate?) negatives, each containing twelve items. It is a matter of great regret that neither these negatives, nor those dating from his earlier trip of 1914, have yet been located despite a thorough search in the **RBG**, Edinburgh, and enquiries made in all other likely places. His widow died in 1983 without issue, and attempts to trace other relatives have so far failed. Eight miscellaneous prints of very poor quality are kept alongside his notebooks at the **RBG**, Edinburgh, also two maps of Bhutan showing his itineraries of 1914-15. Although most of his photographs deal with botanical subjects, it is clear from his lists that he also took a fair number of landscapes and portraits. R.E. Cooper Notebook 1 contains (d) "Bhutan. 1914" (notes on his travels, 20 pages), (f) "Itinerary of Road from Biaka Pumthang to Tawang Border" (journey of 1915, 38 pages), and the index of negatives referred to above (6 pages). R.E. Cooper Notebook 2 contains "Notes of Itinerary in Second Tour in Bhutan, 1915" (70 pages). R.E. Cooper Notebook 3 contains (a) "Notes on Topography and Vegetation of W. Bhutan" (written in?1915, 4 pages). See also R.E. Cooper, "Botanical Tours in Bhutan", *Notes, R.B.G., Edin.,* lxxxvii (1933), pp. 647-121; R.E. Cooper,

"'Daktas: People with a Tail in the East Bhutanese Himalaya", *Man*, xxxiii (1923), pp. 125-8; D.G. Long, "The Bhutanese Itineraries of William Griffith and R.E. Cooper", *Notes, R.B.G., Edin.*, xxxvii (1979), pp. 355-68.

RONALDSHAY 1921

While he was posted as Governor of Bengal, Lord Ronaldshay (later 2nd Marquess of Zetland) paid a visit to Bhutan accompanied by W.R. Gourlay, Lt. C.B. Lyon, David Macdonald, and the latter's son. Their route took them by way of Tremo La, Drugyel Dzong, Paro and Ha. Unfortunately, it has not been possible to trace any of the original prints or negatives from this mission. In a letter dated 10 July 1985 the present Marquess of Zetland wrote "We do have a number of large photographs of temples and scenes from that part of the world, though regrettably I do not know if they are actually of Bhutan". The Zetland papers are preserved at the County Record Office, Northallerton, Yorkshire, and copies of four negatives were found there; only two deal with Bhutan (a view of Paro Dzong and a camp scene). Other photographs were published in Ronaldshay's *Travels in the Lands of the Thunderbolt: Sikhim , Chumbi and Bhutan* (London, 1923). Ronaldshay's private papers preserved at Northallerton contain miscellaneous notes and drafts, also four original letters in Bhutanese addressed to him by the king and queen of Bhutan together with translations. Also found among his papers is a privately printed and very rare work by W. R. Gourlay, who was Ronaldshay's private secretary and accompanied him on this trip. It is entitled *Letters from Bhutan* (printed at the B.S. Press [Calcutta?], n.d.), 42 pages, dedicated to the author's wife. A copy was located recently at the Indian Institute Library, Oxford. It is clear from these letters that Gourlay also took photographs on this trip (see, for example, his comments on p. 17), but it has not been possible to trace any of them. He died in 1938 leaving no issue. His last address was Kenbank, Dalry, Galloway.

BAILEY 1922

In 1922 F.M. Bailey visited Bhutan to present the insignia of the G.C.I.E. to King Ugyen Wangchuk. He was accompanied by his wife, the Hon. Mrs. Irma Bailey, his mother-in-law, Lady Cozens-Hardy, and also by Capt. H.R.C. Meade of the Survey of India and J.C. Dyer, Civil Surgeon, Gangtok. Their route took them by way of Ha along the main lateral road to Bumthang, and thence north by the Mönla Karchung pass into Tibet. All of Bailey's negatives, not only from his Bhutan trips but also from all his travels, appear to be preserved at the OIOC, London, where they are found in the Bailey Collection along with his and his family's papers (MSS. Eur. F. 157). They are in the process of being duplicated and it will be some years before indexing will be completed. To do this it will be necessary not only to take account of the captions written on the reverse of the duplicate prints also in the collection, but also the detailed captions in the collection of albums formerly in the possession of the Hon. Mrs. Irma Bailey at Stiffkey, Wells-next-Sea, Norfolk. It is not clear where these albums were deposited after her death. The typescript catalogue of the Collection notes that "many of the photographs taken in Tibet and India [and Bhutan] by Lt-Col Frederick Marsham Bailey were duplicated, and copies of them sent home to be arranged in albums by his mother, Mrs. F.A. Bailey". One such album, which includes photographs taken on the 1922 trip, is MSS. Eur. F. 157/486. A great number of prints were never arranged into albums by Bailey's mother, and these are still found in the original envelopes and bundles; one such bundle from the 1922 trip to Bhutan is MSS. Eur. F. 157/491. See F.M. Bailey, "Report on the Presentation of the G.C.I.E. to His Highness the Maharaja of Bhutan in Bumthang and of a Journey thence to Gyantse" (Dyer's medical report is appended): OIOC, L/P&S/12/2225; F.M. Bailey, Diary of Visit to Bhutan, 1922: OIOC, MSS. Eur. F. 157/211 (three typescript copies); F.M. Bailey, three unbound notebooks relating to Bhutan trip of 1922: OIOC, MSS. Eur. F. 157/212. See also OIOC, MSS. Eur. F. 157/290-1; F.M. Bailey, "Travels in Bhutan", *Journal of the Central Asian Society*, xvii (1930), pp. 206-20; F.M. Bailey, "Bhutan: A Land of Exquisite Politeness", *Geographical Magazine*, 1 (1935). Eight prints of Bailey's Bhutan photographs are found in the RGS, but it is likely that some of them may date from his later trips. They are catalogued as 071826, 071828-36.

MEADE 1922

Capt. H.R.C. Meade, who accompanied the above mission as surveyor, took numerous photographs. Apart from his official survey photographs (which are presumably still with the Survey of India), he took some two hundred topographical and cultural scenes, the best of which were later arranged into albums and presented to the RGS, London, the Alpine Club, the Dalai Lama and the king of Bhutan. See H.R.C. Meade, "Narrative Report of the Bhutan and South Tibet Survey Detachment, 1922", *Records of the Survey of India*, xxi (1925), pp. 27-49, esp. p.47. A further album of Meade's photographs used to be in the possession of the Hon. Mrs. Irma Bailey in Norfolk, and there are also prints in the OIOC, London: MSS. Eur. F. 157/491 (see above). Those at the RGS, London, are indexed variously between 071840 and 071906.

BAILEY 1924

In 1924 Bailey, accompanied by the same party as in the previous trip (but minus the doctor) made a trip to Punakha. The details are not yet clear, but it seems he went to attend the installation of Raja Sonam Topgye Dorji's very young son, Jigme Dorji, as Ha Drungpa (governor of the Ha valley). Photographs of the trip are found in the Bailey Collection at the OIOC, London, and the albums formerly with Mrs. Bailey (see above). The principal interest, however, lies in Bailey's black and white film of the installation procession at Punakha, probably the first film ever made in Bhutan. This is preserved at the NFA, London, where it appears in a reel (Bailey no. 4 (203004A) silent positive black and white) which also contains shots of Bailey's 1928 visit to the second king at Dewangiri (see below).

BAILEY 1927

In 1927 Bailey attended the coronation of the second king, Jigme Wangchuk, at Punakha. He was accompanied by his wife, Major R.L. Vance and Lt. D.B. Sangster, also by Dr. D.J.A. Graham (of Dr. Graham's Homes, Kalimpong). As above, Bailey's photographs are in the Bailey Collection at the OIOC, London (the negatives are designated as "Album", and these make up No. 20, containing approximately 47 items; prints are in the bundle referred to above).

Other prints are to be found in an album formerly with Mrs. Bailey (album inscribed "Oct 1925 - Oct 1928"). Particularly interesting was the role played in the coronation by the Shabdrung incarnation: there are two photographs of him taken on 22 March 1927, also one of the king, seated and crowned, with his bodyguard standing behind, also his younger brother Dasho Dorje: **OIOC**, MSS. Eur. F. 157/491/ 8560108.

BAILEY 1928

In 1928 Bailey visited King Jigme Wangchuk in southeast Bhutan at Dewangiri. He seems to have been accompanied by the botanist Frank Ludlow (see below). Bailey's photographs are located as above at the **OIOC**, London (the negatives from this trip are in Album No. 4), and prints are found in the same album formerly in the possession of Mrs. Bailey referred to above. The **NFA** Bailey film noted above starts with scenes taken during this trip.

LUDLOW 1928

Frank Ludlow's photographs of the 1928 trip to Dewangiri are, like all his Bhutan photographs, divided in London between the Botanical Library of the **NHM**, where his negatives are preserved ("Tibet, Sikkim and Bhutan" [no date]), and the **OIOC**, where his negatives are kept (Photo 743/5, and 743/6, album inscribed "Bhutan, January, February 1928 / Manas, Darrang"). Ludlow's papers are at the **OIOC**, MSS Eur D 979.

WEIR 1931

In 1931 Lieut.-Col. J.L.R. Weir travelled by way of Ha on the usual route to Bumthang to invest King Jigme Wangchuk with the K.C.I.E. He was accompanied by his wife Thyra, his daughter Joan Mary, his sister-in-law (name not known), and by Lt. M.R. Sinclair of the Indian Medical Service. The party left Bhutan by way of Dewangiri in the southeast. Weir's films and photographs taken during this trip are still in the possession of his daughter Joan Mary Jehu. The films are numbered in reels 1 to 5, but are out of sequence (the proper order should perhaps be 1, 2 pt. i, 4, 3, 2 pt ii, 5). The still photographs of Weir are also in the possession of his daughter Joan Mary Jehu. The negatives are stored in three wallets (two large, one small), indexed in Weir's own hand. Some prints from the Weir negatives are to be found at the **RGS**, listed variously between 071825 and 072042.

MORRIS 1933

Major C.J. Morris entered Bhutan via Sarbhang and visited Chirang Dzong. He re-entered the country at Chamurchi and proceeded north via Dorkha, Denchuka, Raplika and over the Sele La to Ha and Paro, before leaving by way of Ha to Yatung in Tibet's Chumbi valley. Many of his photographs from this trip are preserved at the **RGS**, London, listed variously between 071909 and 072009. Twelve photographs accompany his report "A Journey in Bhutan", *The Geographical Journal*, lxxxvi no. 3 (1935), pp. 201-17.

WILLIAMSON 1933

Frederick Williamson, Political Officer in Gangtok, travelled to Bumthang on the usual route from Ha to present another medal to the king. He was accompanied by his wife Margaret ("Peggy") and Dr. D. Tennant. At Ha they were joined by the botanists Frank Ludlow and George Sherriff, who went with the party as far as Bumthang. From Bumthang the Williamson party went on north to Lhasa, while Ludlow and Sherriff made their way east to Bhutan by way of Kurtö and Tashiyangtse, and thence to Tibet. See, Margaret D. Williamson, *Memoirs of a Political Officer's Wife* (London: Wisdom, 1987), pp. 65-78. The Ludlow and Sherriff material from this expedition is described below. The Williamson material, including films, negatives and albums also Bhutanese artefacts, now form the Williamson Collection of the **MAA**, Cambridge, and five photograph albums have been catalogued by Dr. Krystina Cech. The relevant photographs from this trip are in Williamsom Album 2, nos. 41-147. Negatives await sorting and cataloguing. The original Williamson films were donated to the **NFA**, London, but have not yet been copied and so are not yet in viewable form. A copy of the films formerly in the possession of Mrs. Williamson was left to the **MAA**, Cambridge.

LUDLOW 1933

Frank Ludlow and George Sherriff went on their first major botanical expedition to Bhutan in 1933. Their route took them by way of Ha, Paro, Wangdü Phodrang, Tongsa, Bumthang, Kurtö, Tashiyangtse and the Me La pass. See Fletcher, *Quest of Flowers*, ch. 1. Two negative wallets are preserved at the **NHM**, London, inscribed "Bhutan and Tibet 1933" and "Bhutan-Tibet 1933". The relevant albums at the **OIOC**, London, are Photo 743/9 and 743/10. Some of Ludlow's photographs from this trip are found at the **MAA**, Cambridge, Williamson Album 3, nos. 1-18.

SHERRIFF 1933

All of George Sherriff's negatives are preserved at the **MM**, London, where they are slowly being copied, arranged and indexed. Sherriff's own index does not seem to cover his Bhutan photographs and consequently it is not easy to date them. Moreover, some of the photos seem to be exact copies of those found in Ludlow's collection at the **NHM**, London, so it is not yet clear to whom they should be attributed. At present some 111 negatives in the Sherriff Collection at the **MM** have been identified as having been taken in Bhutan. The negatives are either (1) colour glass slides (most of them "Lumiere" and "Finlay", and possibly "Agfa"; (2) black and white glass slides ("Lantern slides") and negatives made from these; (3) black and white film negatives, stored in wallets. The whole relationship between this collection and the Ludlow Collections at the **OIOC** and the **NHM** will take much time and care to establish. Sherriff's film of this trip of 1933 is preserved at the **NFA**, London, where it is held on two reels: Sherriff Reel No. 1 (2006002A) and Sherriff Reel No. 2 (2006002B), both 16 mm silent positive black and white.

LUDLOW 1934

This year Ludlow and Sherriff made a trip through eastern Bhutan to southeast Tibet, entering Bhutan through Dewangiri and proceeding by way of Tashigang to Sakden, and visiting Tashiyangtse and Tashigang again on their return. See Fletcher, *Quest of Flowers*, ch. 2. The negatives from this trip are in a wallet at the **NHM**, inscribed "Natural History and 1934". Prints are preserved at the **OIOC**, Photo 743/10, section inscribed "Bhutan-Tibet, 1934".

WILLIAMSON 1934-5

In October 1934 Frederick ("Derick") Williamson visited Ha together with his wife and Major W. Hailey (British Trade Agent at Gyangtse and a future bursar of St. Antony's College, Oxford) and Dr. S. St J. Hendricks. The king and senior queen of Bhutan visited Calcutta and Gangtok in the winter of 1934-5 accompanied by the Williamsons. See Williamson, *Memoirs of a Political Officer's Wife*, pp. 168-9, and ch. 13. (Scenes of the visit to Calcutta are contained in Davie's missing film, on which see next entry). The Williamson albums (and uncatalogued negatives) covering this visit, including the Bhutanese royal visits to Calcutta and Gangtok, are at the **MAA**, Cambridge: Album 4, nos. 173-205; Album 5 nos. 1-5, 13-35. See also **MCM**, Liverpool, 50.31.142: framed photograph of the king and queen of Bhutan taken during this visit to Calcutta, brown monochrome print, signed in English by the king and in Bhutanese by the queen, formerly in the possession of Col. and Mrs. F.M. Bailey.

DAVIE 1935

Lt. J.E.J. Davie accompanied the Governor of Bengal Sir John Anderson (later Viscount Waverley) to Bhutan as his ADC. They visited Paro, entering and leaving the country by way of Ha. It is clear from Davie's publications that he took photographs and made a film during his visit, but so far all attempts to trace these have failed. See J.E.J. Davie, "A Visit to Bhutan", *Asiatic Review*, xxxiv (1938), pp. 249-52; J.E.J. Davie, "Forbidden Bhutan", *Journal of the Manchester Geographical Society*, xlix (1938-9), pp. 57-63.

LUDLOW 1936

This year the Ludlow and Sherriff team was joined by K. Lumsden and entered Bhutan by way of Dewangiri and proceeded through east Bhutan to Tashigang and Mera. From there the party entered southeast Tibet, separately returning again through east Bhutan to Dewangiri. See Fletcher, *Quest of Flowers*, ch. 3. The Sherriff photographs from this trip are presumably in his collection at the **MM**, where they await sorting and identifying. Besides three negative wallets inscribed "Views 1936" and one inscribed "1 views and Types - Colour", there are at least two packets of loose, unindexed Ludlow negatives from this trip at the **NHM**, where they are found among an indefinite number of similar packages (containing both negatives and prints) presently stored in seventeen new plastic envelopes. Prints are preserved in **OIOC**, Photo 743/10, section inscribed "Bhutan-Tibet 1936". Some prints from this trip are deposited at the **RGS**, London, though it is not clear if they are Ludlow's or Sherriff's: PR/030399, PR/030400, PR/030404 (wrongly attributed to Sir George Taylor who deposited them there).

SHERRIFF 1936

A few scenes taken in Bhutan at the end of the 1936 trip are contained in Reel 6 of Sherriff's films as listed in his typescript shot list (photocopy at the **MCM**, Liverpool). The film is deposited at the **NFA**, London (65140) and is entitled "Bhutan and Tibet 1936". Unfortunately it is not yet in viewable form. The relevant entries in

the shot list are: "Trashiyangsi bridge", "Clematis simulacfolia", "Tashigong Dz.", "Sunset near Yonpu La", "Khamba dancers at Bhutan House, Kalimpong".

SHERRIFF 1937

This year Sherriff made a journey by himself to central Bhutan, approaching by way of the Galey Chu river, and proceeding by way of Phrumzur and Dungshing Gang (The Black Mountains) to Adao and Chendebji. From there he made a trip north, then west to Domkhar and finally east to Phobsikha and along the usual route to Ha. See Fletcher, *Quest of Flowers*, ch. 4. Besides the unsorted Sherriff Collection at the **MM**, some of his negatives (or duplicate negatives) are found among Ludlow's negatives at the **NHM** in the negative wallet inscribed "1 Views and Types - Colour", nos. 92-5, also in the wallet inscribed "2 Views and Types - Colour". Nos. 6-8 are missing from the wallet and have yet to be located elsewhere. There are seven Sherriff prints from this trip at the **RGS**, attributed to Sir George Taylor (who deposited them there): PR/030396, PR/030401 - 7. A film taken by Sherriff during his 1937 trip is deposited at the **NFA** (65110AE), but it is not yet in viewable form. It finds no mention in the typescript shot list of Sherriff's films deposited at the **MCM**, Liverpool.

SHERRIFF 1938

On this trip Ludlow and Sherriff were joined by G. (later Sir George) Taylor, entering a corner of east Bhutan on a return journey to India from the Tsangpo drainage area in S.E. Tibet. Their route took them from Trashiyangtse south to Dewangiri. Ludlow does not appear to have taken any photographs on this trip, and Sherriff's own still photographs are presumably among his unclassified collection at the **MM**. Sir George Taylor's photographs were formerly in his own possession but their present location since his death is not known. The main record of the Bhutan portion of their trip is therefore the section of Sherriff's film contained in Reel no. 6 (**NFA**, "S.E. Tibet and E. Bhutan", 16mm st. pos. col. 412ft).

GOULD 1938

B.J. (later Sir Basil) Gould visited Bhutan this year to meet the king at Bumthang, proceeding along the main lateral route in company with one Capt. J.F. Morgan of the Indian Medical Service. See the account in Sir Basil Gould, *The Jewel in the Lotus: Recollections of an Indian Political* (London, 1957), ch. 13, esp. pp. 184, 187-91. A few stills taken by Gould himself are now in the possession of his son, Dick Gould, who writes (3 July 1985): "I regret that we have very little in the way of still photographs but we do have some. They are not, however, well organised!". The main record of the trip is therefore contained in Gould's film, now deposited at the **NFA**, London. It is divided into two reels, only the second of which is unambiguously devoted to the 1938 trip. The first of the two reels indicates that Betty Sherriff was also a member of the party, at least as far as the Ha valley (my dating of this reel to 1938 rests on the fact that Gould is shown being carried in a litter, which accords with his own written description in the account cited above). The reels may be in the wrong containers at present since the labels do not match the documentation contained in the catalogue entries prepared by D.G. Swift, former Assistant Cataloguer at the **NFA**, on the basis of several differing transcriptions of a tape recording made by Gould during a screening in the early 1950s. There may therefore be some confusion in regard to reel numbers): Gould Reel no. 10 (Bhutan 1) location no. 603896A; Gould Reel no. 12 (Bhutan 3) location no. 603898A.

GOULD 1941

This year Sir Basil Gould visited Bhutan on his return journey from Tibet to Sikkim. He was accompanied by Hugh Richardson as far as Ha. Betty Sherriff too appears to have joined the party. Apart from the photographs which may still be with his son, the following Gould film at the NFA deals with this trip, though there is some doubt whether the second reel actually dates from 1941: Gould Reel no. 8 (Bhutan 1941) location no. 603897A; Gould Reel no. 11 (Bhutan 2) location no. 603899A.

HENDERSON 1943

William Henderson, who was attached to the viceregal household in a private capacity as ADC at this time, took what are perhaps the best photographs of Bhutan surviving from this period. He was a member of a party that included Doreen Marchioness of Linlithgow (the vicereine), Vivian Countess of Hopetoun (daughter-in-law), Mrs Joy Wilson (later Mrs Cagiari, friend), Sir Basil Gould (Political Officer, Sikkim), Col. Henry Elliot (medical officer), and Prince Thondup of Sikkim. Henderson's main album is destined eventually for the OIOC, London, where his watercolour paintings from this trip have already been deposited (WD 3828-3839). A duplicate set of Henderson's Bhutan photographs was given to the author in 1985.

WILSON 1943

Mrs Joy Wilson (later Mrs Cagiari, of Beverley Downs, Massachusetts, USA) was a friend of the Linlithgow family and joined them on the 1943 trip to Bhutan. She kept a diary entitled "Bhutan: A Memory", which survives in two versions, both still in her possession. The first version was prepared for Lady Linlithgow but was returned to Mrs. Wilson on her death. The second, less polished version, was intended by Mrs Wilson only for herself. It consists of 28 typewritten pages interspersed with 35 photographs opposite.

HOPKINSON 1947

The party this year consisted of Arthur John Hopkinson (Political Officer, Gangtok), his wife Eleanor, and a medical officer, Col. Lloyd Ledger, and his wife Cecily. The king of Bhutan travelled to Ha to meet the party and to receive the insignia of the K.C.S.I. This was the last official British mission to Bhutan before Indian independence. One colour film, an album of black and white photographs, and the negatives are all still with Mrs Eleanor Hopkinson. It is likely that the Hopkinson film will eventually be deposited at the NFA, and the still photographs at the OIOC where his papers are preserved as MSS Eur D 998. A typescript of Col. Ledger's diary entitled "Tour to Bhutan from Gangtok in Sikkim, by L.K. & C.B. Ledger, September 1947" and photographs of this trip are still in the possession of his family.

SHERRIFF 1947

This year the botanists included George and Betty Sherriff, Frank Ludlow and Col. Henry Elliot, but as it turned out only the Sherriffs entered Bhutan on the return from India from the gorges of the Tsangpo in Tibet. They took their usual route through E. Bhutan to Dewangiri. See Fletcher, *Quest of Flowers*, ch. 6. No photographs of Bhutan taken during this trip have yet come to light. However, there may be some in the unsorted Sherriff Collection at the MM. At the NFA, London, one reel is believed to be of the 1947 trip: Sherriff Reel no. 10 ("S.E. Tibet - 5", 16mm silent positive colour 300ft).

LUDLOW and SHERRIFF 1949

The final trip of the botanists to Bhutan, also the final journey made by any British in the period covered by this survey, was the most ambitious of all their Bhutan expeditions. The group was composed of both Sherriffs, Frank Ludlow and Dr. J.H. Hicks. Ludlow began separately, proceeding by way of Ha, Drugyel Dzong, Lingshi, Laya, Gasa, Lunana and Kangla Karchu La to Dur, Bumthang and Tongsa. Meanwhile the Sherriffs and Hicks travelled up the Mangde Chu valley to Kunga Rabden, Bumthang and Lhuntse Dzong, from where they split into two groups. Sherriff proceeded to central Bhutan, while his wife and Hicks went east to the Me La region. On 26 July the whole expedition was reunited in Bumthang. From there the Sherriffs travelled to Ha, Betty Sherriff departing from there to Calcutta to recover from an accident and George retracing his steps to Bumthang and then heading north. From Bumthang, Hicks went back to the Me La and Ludlow returned to Lunana and ultimately to Ha. Sherriff and Hicks were reunited at Bumthang, where they had a final meeting with the king during which plans were discussed for the crown prince Jigme Dorji Wangchuk and the future prime minister Jigme Dorje to go to England. From Bumthang Sherriff and Hicks took the usual lateral route west to Ha, and from there back to England by way of Chumbi, Sikkim and India. See fletcher, *Quest of Flowers*, ch. 7. The main photographic collection is presumably to be found with Sherriff's other negatives at the MM, London. Some of these appear to be duplicated in Ludlow's collection at the NHM, where there is a box marked "Bhutan 1949". There is no list enclosed, but some of the negatives are titled, including one marked "Kinga Rapden 7/4/49" showing Betty Sherriff posing with the royal family. The negatives corresponding to a number of prints held at the RBG, Edinburgh, are also found in this box. Another print from 1949 wrongly attributed to Sir George Taylor is found in the RGS (PR/030393): "Changala at Denchung, Bhutan 29/4/49". The most valuable record of the 1949 trip is provided in Sherriff's colour films, which are held at the NFA, London. The typescript shotlist at the MCM, Liverpool, shows that there are five reels devoted to the 1949 trip: Sherriff Reel Nos. 2 ("Bhutan - 1", 422ft), 3 ("Bhutan - 2", 155ft), 4 ("Bhutan - 3", 421ft), 5 ("Bhutan - 4", 425ft) and 18 ("Bhutan - 5", 320ft); the NFA shotlists correspond to the respective MCM shotlists, with the exception of "Bhutan - 2" of which substantial sections are missing.

Bibliographies

Bhutanese sources

BRDK 'Brug dkar-po / 'brug rgyal-khab-kyi chos-srid gnas-stangs ["The White Dragon: The Nature of Religion and State in the Kingdom of Bhutan"] by Lobpön Nado (Slob-dpon gNag-mdog) (Tharpaling and New Delhi, 1986)

BRGI 'Brug-gi rgyal-rabs slob-spon padma tshe-dbang-gis sbyar-ba / 'brug gsal-ba'i sgron-me ["A History of Bhutan Assembled by Lobpön Pema Tsewang: The Lamp which Illuminates Bhutan"] (Thimphu and New Delhi, 1994)

BRTU 'Brug-tu 'od-gsal lha'i gdung-rabs 'byung-tshul brjod-pa smyos-rabs gsal-ba'i me-long ["An Discourse on the Coming to Bhutan of a Lineage of the Gods of Clear: The Mirror which Illuminates the Generations of the Nyö (Clan)"] by Lama Sangak (Bla-ma gSang-sngags) (Thimphu and New Delhi, 1983)

LCB II dPal-ldan 'brug-pa'i gdul-zhing lho-phyogs nags-mo'i ljongs-kyi chos-'byung blo-gsar rna-ba'i rgyan ["A Religious History of the Field of Conversion of the Glorious Drukpa, the Southern Land of Forests: The Ear Ornament for New Minds"] by Gendun Rinchen (dGe-'dun Rinchen) (blockprint, Tango, 1972)

PGLR Pad-gling lo-rgyus drang-gtam ["An Account of Pemalingpa: The True Story"] by Pema Tsewang (Padma Tshe-dbang) (Thimphu, 1991)

SMLJ sMan-ljongs 'brug rgyal-khab chen-po'i sde-srid khri-rabs dang brgyud-'dzin-gyi rgyal-po rim-par byon-pa'i rgyal-rabs deb-ther gsal-ba'i me-long ["A History of the Incumbents to the Throne of the Regents and the Successive Hereditary Monarchs of the Land of Medicine, the Great Kingdom of Bhutan: The Mirror which Illuminates the Annals"] (draft history mimeographed in Bhutanese cursive and submitted for approval to the National Assembly of Bhutan in the 3rd month of the Year of the Fire Horse, 1966, but never published)

English sources and secondary works

Anon. 1865. "Bootan and the Booteeas", *Once a Week*, ccxciv, pp. 205-10.

Aris, Michael. 1979. *Bhutan: The Early History of a Himalayan Kingdom* (Warminster: Aris and Phillips; and New Delhi: Vikas)

Aris, Michael. 1982. *Views of Medieval Bhutan: The Diary and Drawings of Samuel Davis, 1783* (London and Washington, D.C.: Serindia and Smithsonian Inst. Press).

Aris, Michael. 1986. *Sources for the History of Bhutan* (Wiener Studien zur Tibetologie und Buddhismuskunde, Heft 14, Vienna).

Aris, Michael. 1987. "'The Boneless Tongue': Alternative Voices from Bhutan in the Context of Lamaist Societies", *Past and Present*, no. 115, pp. 131-64.

Aris, Michael. 1988. "New Light on an Old Clan of Bhutan: The *sMyos-rabs* of Bla-ma gSaṅ-sṅags", in Helga Uebach and Jampa L. Panglung (eds.), *Tibetan Studies: Proceedings of the 4th Seminar of the International Association for Tibetan Studies, Schloss Hohenkammer — Munich, 1985* (Munich: Kommission fur Zentralasiatische Studien, Bayerische Akademie der Wissenschaften, Studia Tibetica, Quellen und Studien zur Tibetische Lexicographie, Band II)

Aris, Michael. 1994. "Conflict and Conciliation in Traditional Bhutan", in Hutt 1994.

Aris, Michael, and Michael Hutt (eds.). 1994. *Bhutan: Aspects of Culture and Development* (Gartmore: Kiscadale).

Bailey, F.M. 1930. "Travels in Bhutan", *Journal of the Central Asian Society*, xvii, pp. 206-20.

Bailey, F.M. 1934. "Through Bhutan and Southern Tibet", *Geographical Journal*, lxiv.

Bailey, F.M. 1935. "Bhutan: A Land of Exquisite Politeness", *Geographical Magazine*, 1.

Bell, Sir Charles. 1924. *Tibet: Past and Present* (Oxford: OUP)

Bell, Sir Charles. 1928. *The People of Tibet* (Oxford: OUP)

Cooper, R.E. 1933. "Botanical Tours in Bhutan", *Notes, R.B.G., Edin.*, lxxxvii, pp. 647-121.

Cooper, R.E. 1923. "Daktas: People with a Tail in the East Bhutanese Himalaya", *Man*, xxxiii, pp. 125-8.

Collister, Peter. 1987. *Bhutan and the British* (London: Serindia).

Davie, J.E.J. 1938. "A Visit to Bhutan", *Asiatic Review*, xxxiv, pp. 249-52.

Davie, J.E.J. 1938-9. "Forbidden Bhutan", *Journal of the Manchester Geographical Society*, xlix, pp. 57-63.

Deb, Arabinda. 1976. *Bhutan and India: A Study in Frontier Political Relations* (Calcutta: Firma KLM).

Dogra, Ramesh C. 1990. *Bhutan* (Oxford: Clio, World Bibliographical Series, cxvi).

Eden, Ashley. 1864. "Report on the State of Bhutan and on the Progress of the Mission of 1863-64", in *Political Missions to Bootan*, pp. 1-137.

Fletcher, Harold R. 1975. *The Quest for Flowers: The Plant Explorations of Frank Ludlow and George Sheriff Told from their Diaries and Other Occasional Writings* (Edinburgh: Edinburgh University Press).

Forbes Watson, J. and John William Kaye (eds.). 1868. *The People of India: A Series of Photographic Illustrations with Descriptive Letterpress* (London, India Museum).

Godwin Austin, H.H. 1894. "Bhutan and the Himalayas East of Darjeeling", *Scottish Geographical Magazine*, x, pp. 635-40.

Gould, Sir Basil. 1957. *The Jewel in the Lotus: Recollections of an Indian Political* (London).

Grey, F. and C. (eds.). 1912. *Tales of Our Grandfather [L.J.H. Grey]: or, India Since 1856* (London: Smith, Elder).

Gupta, S.S. 1974. *British Relations with Bhutan* (Jaipur: Panchsheel Prakashan).

Hutt, Michael (ed.). 1994. *Bhutan: Perspectives on Conflict and Dissent* (Gartmore: Kiscadale).

Illustrated London News, no. 46, 1865: 28 Jan., 29 Apr., 6 May, 24 June; no. 47, 1865: 30 Sept.

Imaeda, Yoshiro. 1986. "La théocratie bhoutanaise du XVIIe au XIXe siècle: une lecture critique des récits des Européens", in *Chibetto no bukkyô to shakai* [Tibetan Buddhism and Society] (Tokyo: Shunjû-sha), pp. 647-82.

Imaeda, Yoshiro. 1987. "La constitution de la théocratie 'Brug pa au dix-septième siècle et les problèmes de la sucession du premier *Zhabs drung*" (Doctorat d'Etat es lettres et sciences humaines, Université Paris 7, 2 vols.).

Kohli, Manorama. 1982. *India and Bhutan: A Study in Interrelations, 1772-1910* (New Delhi: Munshiram Manoharlal).

Labh, Kapileshwar. 1974. *India and Bhutan* (New Delhi: Sindhu).

Long, D.G. 1979. "The Bhutanese Itineraries of William Griffith and R.E. Cooper", *Notes, R.B.G., Edin.*, xxxvii, pp. 355-68.

MacGregor, C.M. 1866. *A Military report of the Country of Bhutan: Containing All the Information of Military Importance which Has Been Collected up to the Present Day, 12th July 1866* (Calcutta: QMG's Dept.)

Markham, Clements Robert (ed.). 1879. *Narrative of the Mission of George Bogle to Tibet and of the Journey of Thomas Manning to Lhasa* (London: Trubner; repr. New Delhi: Mañjuśrī, 1971).

Marshall, Julie. 1977. *Britain and Tibet, 1765-1947: The Background to the India-China Border Dispute* (Bundoora: La Trobe University Library, Pubn no. 10).

Meade, H.R.C. 1925. "Narrative Report of the Bhutan and South Tibet Survey Detachment, 1922", *Records of the Survey of India*, xxi, pp. 27-49.

Morris, C.J. 1935. "A Journey in Bhutan", *The Geographical Journal*, lxxxvi no. 3, pp. 201-17.

Myers, Diana K. and Bean, Susan S. (eds.). 1994. *From the Land of the Thunder Dragon: Textile Arts of Bhutan* (London: Serindia Publications, and Salem: Peabody Essex Museum).

Papers Relating to Bootan; Presented to Parliament by Her Majesty's Command (London: House of Commons, 1865, xxxix 47); *Further Papers Relating to Bootan* (London: House of Commons, 1866, lii 13).

Political Missions to Bhootan, Comprising the Reports of the Hon'ble Ashley Eden, 1864; Capt. R.B. Pemberton, 1837, 1838, with Dr. W. Griffiths's Journal [1837-8]; and the Account of Baboo Kishen Kant Bose [1815] (Calcutta: Bengal Secretariat Office, 1865; repr. New Delhi, Mañjuśrī, 1972).

Rahul, Ram. 1971. *Modern Bhutan* (New Delhi: Vikas).

Rennie, D.F. 1866. *Bhotan and the Story of the Dooar War* (London: John Murray; repr. New Delhi: Mañjuśrī, 1970).

Report on the Explorations of Lama Serap Gyatsho 1856-69, Explorer K-P 1880-84, Lama UG 1883, Explorer RN 1885-86, Explorer PA 1885-86, in Sikkim, Bhutan and Tibet (Dehra Dun, 1889).

Ronaldshay, L.J.L.D. (Earl of, later 2nd Marquess Zetland). 1923. *Travels in the Lands of the Thunderbolt: Sikhim, Chumbi and Bhutan* (London).

Rustomji, Nari. 1971. *Enchanted Frontiers: Sikkim, Bhutan and India's North-East Borderlands* (New Delhi: OUP).

Rustomji, Nari. 1978. *Bhutan: The Dragon Kingdom in Crisis* (New Delhi: OUP).

Sandberg, Graham. 1896. "Bhotan: The Unknown Indian State". *Calcutta Review*, cvii, pp. 14-41.

Singh, Amar Kaur Jasbir. 1988a. *Himalayan Triangle: A Historical Survey of British India's Relations with Tibet, Sikkim and Bhutan, 1765-1950* (London: The British Library).

Singh, Amar Kaur Jasbir. 1988b. *A Guide to Source Materials in the India Office Library and Records for the History of Tibet, Sikkim and Bhutan, 1765-1950* (London: The British Library).

Todd, Burt. 1952. "Bhutan, Land of the Thunder Dragon", *National Geographic Magazine*, cii, pp. 713-54.

Turner, Samuel. 1800. *An Account of an Embassy to the Court of the Teshoo Lama in Tibet; Containing a Narrative of a Journey through Bootan and part of Tibet* (London: Bulmer; 2nd edn. 1806; repr. New Delhi: Mañjusrī, 1971).

Van Driem, George. 1994. "Language Policy in Bhutan", in Aris and Hutt 1994.

Warren, F.G.E. 1867. "My Journal During the Bhootan Campaign, 1864-5", *Minutes of Proceedings of the Royal Artillery Institution*, v, pp. 116-60.

White, J.C. 1907. "Across Unknown Bhutan", *Wide World Magazine*, xix, pp. 322-7.

White, J.C. 1909a. "My Journey in Bhutan", *Wide World Magazine*, xxiii, pp. 13-23, 179-85.

White, J.C. 1909b. *Sikhim and Bhutan: Twenty-one Years on the North-East Frontier, 1887-1908* (London).

White, J.C. 1914. "Castles in the Air: Experiences and Journeys in Unknown Bhutan", *The National Geographic Magazine*, xxv, pp. 365-453.

Williamson, Margaret D. 1987. *Memoirs of a Political Officer's Wife* (London: Wisdom).

Index

Bhutanese and Tibetan names, titles and terms as rendered in this book are followed by brackets containing their transliterated spellings according to the Wylie System. Unknown or doubtful transliterations are indicated.

Abors, 148
Adang, Adao (A-thang), 71, 152
Adap Sangye, Chözim (A-dang-pa Sangs-rgyas, Chos-gzim), 142
Ahom, 42
Agi Hap (A-rgas Had-pa), 71, see Tsultrim Namgyel
Alo Dorje (A-lo rDo-rje), 73, 78, 80-1, 84, 103, 111
Amban, 40, 48, 99-100
Amlah, 111
Amochu (A-mo-chu), 88
Anderson, Sir John (later Viscount Waverley), 152
Angdruk (Ang-'brug), 69-70
Anglo-Bhutan war of 1773-4, 42
Anglo-Bhutan war of 1864-6, 15, 42, 62-6, 81
Anglo Bhutanese War of 1864-5, 148
Arunachal Pradesh, 12
Ashi (A-zhe), 71
Asoka, 144
Assam, 14, 42, 49, 56, 133
Assam Duars, 60, 72
Aung San, 136
Avalokitesvara, 27
Bagen ('Ba-'gan), 95
Bailey, F.M., 8, 90, 107-10, 116-17, 120, 123, 127, 134, 142-3, 148, 150, 152
Bailey, Irma, 8, 109, 150
Bala (sp?), 64
Balpö Lama (Bal-po'i Bla-ma), 42, 49
Beling (? sBas-gling), 118
Bell, Sir Charles, 20-1, 28, 34, 88, 99-100, 102-4, 111, 134, 142, 148-9
Benchen (Ban-chen), 118
Bengal, 42-3, 62, 73
Bhotanta, 24
Bhutan, 86
Bhutan House, 110, 133
Bidung (sBis-gdung), 22
Bogle, George, 43-4, 49
Bönbzhi (Bon-sbis), 22, 51
Brokpa ('Brog-pa), 120
Buli (Bu-li), 51
Bumthang (Bum-thang), 7, 13, 16, 18, 32, 40, 48, 51-2, 58, 66-8, 71-2, 77, 83, 93, 106-9, 113, 118-19, 121,

128, 135, 137, 140-2, 148-51, 153
Burmiak Kazi, 94
Buxa, see Pasakha
Buxa Duar, 64
Byagar (Bya-dkar), 32, 53, 68, 77
Byagar Dung (Bya-dkar gDung), 52
Byagar Dzong (Bya-dkar rDzong), 40, 52, 58
Byagar Dzongpön (Bya-dkar rDzong-dpon), 55-6, 76, 78
Byagar Pönlop (Bya-dkar dPon-slob), 62
Calcutta, 94, 102, 133, 135, 137, 152-3
Campbell, W.L., 97, 112, 149
Central Bodish, 12
Chakpa Sangye (lCags-pa Sangs-rgyas), 53-4, 147
Chaksam (lCags-zam), 88
Chakzampa (lCags-zam-pa), 20
Chamkhar (lCam-mkhar), 73
Chamurchi, 64, 151
Changgap ('Chang-sgar-pa), 52
Chapcha (sKyabs-khra), 48, 149
Chasipangkheb (Phyag-bsil spang-kheb), 117
Chendebji, 152
Chibu Lama (sp?), 58-1
Chichacotta, 42
Chila (sPyi-bla), 34
Chimey Dorje ('Chi-med rDo-rje), 50
China, 15, 42, 49, 92, 99, 122, 143
Chinese, 87-8, 99-100, 124, 129, 140
Chirang Dzong, 151
Chögyel (Chos-rgyal) of Sikkim, 94
Chögyel Zangpo (Chos-rgyal bZang-po), 76, 147
Chöjé (Chos-rje), 51-2
Chökhor (Chos-'khor), 16, 116
Chökhor Rabtentse (Chos-'khor Rab-brtan-rtse), 38, see also Tongsa Dzong
Chökyi (Chos-skyid), 50, 125, 128
Chökyi Gyeltsen (Chos-kyi rGyal-mtshan), 121
Chökyi Nyima, Panchen Lama (Chos-kyi Nyi-ma, Paⁿ-chen Bla-ma), 122

Chökyi Wangchuk (Chos-kyi-dBang-phyug), 8
Cholé Namgyel (Phyogs-las rNam-rgyal), 40
Cooper, R.E., 149
Chowringhee, 135
Chöying Wangmo, Rani (Chos-dbyings dBang-mo, Ra-ṇi), 50, 86, 106, 110, 117, 133-6
Chukha (Chu-kha), 43, 149
Chumbi (sp?), 84, 103, 112, 135, 148, 151, 153
Chumé (Chu-smad), 51, 73, 116, 125
Chuméchu (Chu-smad-chu), 67
Chuni, Rani, see Chöying Wangmo
Cozens Hardy, Lady, 109, 150
Curzon, Lord, 86-7, 90, 144
Daga (Dar-dkar), 34, 46, 48
Daga Dzong (Dar-dkar rDzong), 28
Daga Pönlop (Dar-dkar dPon-slob), 53, 76, 111
Daganang (Dar-dkar-nang), 40
Dakpa (Dwag-pa), 120
Dalai Lama (Da-la'i Bla-ma), 11, 40
Dalai Lama, 5th, 24, 32, 37, 40, 48
Dalai Lama, 13th, 86-8, 124, 143
Daling Dzong (brDa-gling rDzong), 64
Dalingcote, 64, 148
Dalingkha, (brDa-gling-kha), 42
Damchö Lhundrup (Dam-chos lHun-sgrub) alias Barchung (Bar-chung, 55, 70, 147
Damchö Rinchen (Dam-chos Rin-chen), 68, 111
Damtsik (Dam-tshig), 36
Damtsik tsangma (Dam-tshig gtsang-ma), 36
Dangchu (Dwangs-chu), 36
Darjeeling (rDo-rje-gling), 20, 60-2, 73, 84, 106, 133, 148
Darlung Topgye (Dar-lung sTobs-rgyas), 58, 61, 67, 72
Darpön (Dar-dpon), 52
Dasho (Drag-shos), 71
Davie, J.E.J., 152
Davis, Samuel, 43, 49
Daw Khin Kyi, 136
Dawa (Zla-ba), 22, 116

Dawa, Chözim (Zla-ba, Chos-gzim), 69
Dawa Penjor (Zla-ba dPal-'byor), 20, 50, 78-80, 97, 106, 130
Deb Raja, 11, 46, 48, 90, 99, 102, 147
Deb Zimpön (sDeb gZim-dpon), 91, 97, 102, see also Gongzim
Dechen Phodrang (bDe-chen Pho-drang), 34
Dechen Wangmo (bDe-chen Wang-mo), 50
Dechen Zangmo (bDe-chen bZang-mo), 78, 82-4
Deki Yangdzom (bDe-skyid dByangs-'dzom), 50, 125
Delhi, 99, 105, 138, 149
Demcho (bDe-mchog), 50, 115
Denchuka (sp?), 151
Depa (sDe-pa), 48
Desi (sDe-srid), 48
Desi Tsangpa (sDe-srid gTsang-pa), 27
Dewa Zangpo (bDe-ba bZang-po), 21
Dewangiri or Dewathang (bDe-ba-thang), 62-4, 66, 117-18, 140, 150-3
Dharma Raja, 11, 40, 58, 72, 76, 87, 90, 95, 102, 123
Dichu (sp?), 88
Dochen (? mDo-chen, rDo-chen), 13
Dogna Dzong, 149, see Dungnak
Dombu (lDom-bu), 72
Domchung (Dom-chung) alias Kun-zang Norbu (Kun-bzang Nor-bu), 99
Domkhar (Dom-mkhar), 125, 152
Döndrup Zangpo (Don-sgrub bZang-po), 22
Dongkheb (gDong-kheb), 126
Dongön Dzong (rDo-rngon rDzong), 32
Donyuk Dzong (rDo-snyug rDzong), 32
Doring (rDo-ring), 128
Dorje (rDo-rje), 28, 50, 86, 107, 109, 112, 117
Dorje Drolö (rDo-rje Gro-lod), 16
Dorje Namgyel (rDo-rje rNam-rgyal), 48, 68, 73, 147

Dorje Norbu (rDo-rje Nor-bu), 53-4, 147

Dorje Rabden (rDo-rje Rab-brtan), 50, 82, 84, 92, 106, 116, 125, 142

Dorje Wangmo (rDo-rje dBang-mo), Queen of Bhutan, 50

Dorje Wangmo (rDo-rje dBang-mo), sister of Shabdrung Jigme Dorje, 125

Dorjelingpa (rDo-rje Gling-pa), 52

Dorkha (sp?), 151

Doshong Gönpa (rDo-gzhong dGon-pa), 111

Drakpa Gyelpo (Grags-pa rGyal-po), 22

Dralha (dGra-lha), 56

Dramitse (sGra-mi-rtse), 22, 58, 119, 149

Dramitse Chöjé (sGra-mi-rtse Chos-rje), 51, 54, 80

Dranang (Grwa-nang), 40

Drap (Grwa-pa), 125

Drepung ('Bras-spungs), 106

Drikhungpa ('Bri-khung-pa), 23

Driknamzhak (sGrig rnam-gzhag), 146

Drimélingpa (Dri-med Gling-pa), 16

Drönyer (mGron-gnyer), 36, 53, 56, 61, 106, 115, 129, 140, 146

Dröphu (Drod-phu), 22

Drugyel Dzong ('Brug-rgyal rDzong), 31, 150, 153

Drugyel Dzongpön ('Brug-rgyal rDzong-dpon), 31

Druk ('Brug), 24

Druk Desi ('Brug-sDe-srid), 11, 28, 37, 40, 87, 102, 147

Druk Gyelpo ('Brug rGyal-po), 22, 95, 147

Druk Namgyel ('Brug rNam-rgyal), 44, 49

Druk Tendzin ('Brug bsTan-'dzin) alias Sangye Tendzin (Sangs-rgyas bsTan-'dzin), 44

Drukpa ('Brug-pa), 15, 20-1, 24, 27-8, 31-2, 34, 55, 80

Drukpa Kagyü ('Brug-pa bKa'-rgyud), 38

Drukpa Kunley ('Brug-pa Kun-legs), 20-1

Drukyul ('Brug-yul), 24, 145

Drupa (sGrub-pa), 82

Duars, 14, 56, 64, 79, 140

Dung (gDung), 18, 116

Dungkar (Dung-dkar), 22, 51

Dungkar Chöjé (Dung-dkar Chos-rje), 40, 51, 78, 80, 82, 86, 144

Dungkar Gyeltsen (Dung-dkar rGyal-mtshan), 50, 66, 68, 76, 111, 118

Dungnak (gDung-nag), 84

Dungsam (gDung-bsam), 48, 53

Dungshing Gang (Dung-shing sGang), 25, 152

Dünjom Rinpoche (bDud-'joms Rin-po-che), 128

Dur (Dur), 153

Durwai Dung (Dur-ba'i gDung), 142

Dyer, J.C., 150

Dzigar ('Dzi-sgar), 106

Dzokchen (rDzogs-chen), 20, 106, 118

Dzongkha (rDzong-kha), 12

Dzongpön (rDzong-dpon), 34, 36, 46, 53, 55, 58, 71, 76

East Bodish, 13

Eden, Ashley, 58, 60-3, 71-2, 93, 111, 148

Elliot, Henry, 132, 153

Fentook (? Phan-thog), 68

Galey Chu (sp?), 152

Gandhi, 121-22

Gangri Lama (sGang-ri Bla-ma), 42

Gangphu (sGangs-phu), 14

Gangteng Tulku (sGangs-steng sPrul-sku), 50

Gangtok (sGang-tog), 100, 133, 135, 152

Gap (rGed-pa), 36

Gasa (sGar-sa), 28, 48, 55, 84, 149, 153

Gasa Dzongpön (sGar-sa rDzong-dpon), 111

Gauhati, 133

Gawa Zangpo (dGa'-ba bZang-po), 79, 147

Gelong (dGe-slong), 46

Gelpa Wangdü (Gal-pa dBang-'dus), 119

Gelukpa (dGe-lugs-pa), 23, 27, 32, 42, 106, 120

Gendun Rinchen (dGe-'dun Rin-chen), 21

Genja ('Gan-rgya), 95

George, Prince of Sikkim, 139

George V, 102-3

Giwang (Gi-dbang, Gri-dbang), 111

Godwin-Austin, H.H., 148

Gongzim (Gong-gzim), 47, 82, 102, 140-1

Gorina (sGo-ra-nang), 71

Gorkha, 42

Gould, Sir Basil, 8, 132-3, 138, 143, 152-3

Gould, Dick, 8, 152

Gourlay, William R., 105, 113, 150

Graham, D.J.A., 104, 150

Gurkha, 138

Guru (Gu-ru), 22

Gyadrung (rGya-drung), 53

Gyangathang (? rGyang-ga-thang), 14

Gyangtse (rGyal-rtse), 88

Gyeltsap (rGyal-tshab), 38

Gyurmé Dorje ('Gyur-med rDo-rje), 50, 129

Ha (Had, Has), 23, 28, 71, 84, 99, 102, 104, 113, 137, 139, 148-53

Ha Drung or Drungpa (Had Drung, Drung-pa), 28, 102, 107, 140, 150

Hailey, W., 152

Hamilton, Alexander, 43, 49

Hastings, Warren, 42-3

Hastings House, 94

Henderson, William, 8, 18, 131-3, 153

Hicks, J.H., 153

Holland, D.E., 94

Hopetoun, Vivian Countess of, 132

Hopkinson, Arthur J., 8, 23, 28, 139-40, 153

Hopkinson, Eleanor, 8, 153

Humrel Dzong (Hūṃ-ral rDzong), 32

Hyslop, Henry, 16, 31, 94-5, 97, 100, 112, 149

India, 11, 16, 28, 68, 70, 75, 86, 88, 93, 122, 124, 132, 138, 140, 142-4, 149, 152-3

Indo-Aryan, 13, 24

Jaigaon, 149

Jami Tsewang Pedrön (rGya-mi Tshe-dbang dPal-sgron), 112

Jampa, Ashang (Byams-pa, A-zhang), 78

Jampai Lhakhang (Byams-pa'i lHa-khang), 16, 66, 72, 109

Jampai Tobzang (Byams-pa'i sTobs-bzang), 21

Jampel Dorje ('Jam-dpal rDo-rje), 37

Jampel Shenyen ('Jam-dpal bShes-gnyen), 95

Jamtrül Jamyang Tendzin ('Jam-sprul 'Jam-dbyangs bsTan-'dzin), 55, 147

Jamyang, Dasho ('Jam-dbyangs, Drag-shos), 50, 116, 135

Jangchub Tsöndrü (Byang-chub brTson-'grus), 52, 55-6, 71-2

Jangdü (Byang-bdud), 56

Jangsa (Gyang-gsar), 51

Je khenpo (rJe mKhan-po), 27, 36, 87

Jehu, Joan Mary, 8, 151

Jehu, Maybe, 8

Jigme Dorje Wangchuk ('Jigs-med rDo-rje dBang-phyug), 3rd King of Bhutan, 7, 11, 47, 50, 86, 128, 135, 139-41, 143, 147, 153

Jigme Drakpa, Shabdrung ('Jigs-med Grags-pa, Zhabs-drung), 40

Jigme Drakpa, Shabdrung, the Second ('Jigs-med Grags-pa, Zhabs-drung), 49

Jigme Gesar Namgyel Wangchuk ('Jigs-med Ge-sar rNam-rgyal dBang-phyug), heir apparent, 50

Jigme Namgyel ('Jigs-med rNam-rgyal), 28, 44, 50-73, 76, 147

Jigme Norbu, Shabdrung ('Jigs-med Nor-bu, Zhabs-drung), 49, 54, 58, 80

Jigme Palden Dorje ('Jigs-med dPal-ldan rDo-rje), Prime Minister, 86, 107, 110, 116, 135, 140-1, 150, 153

Jigme Senge ('Jigs-med Seng-ge), 44, 49

Jigme Senge Wangchuk ('Jigs-med Seng-ge dBang-phyug), 4th King of Bhutan, 7, 11, 50, 86, 147

Jigme Wangchuk ('Jigs-med dBang-phyug), 2nd King of Bhutan, 11, 50, 115-43, 147, 150-1

Jomolhari (Jo-mo lHa-ri), 13

Jowo Dungshing (Jo-bo Dung-shing), 25

Kacharis, 14

Kadröp (bKa'-sgrub-pa), 145

Kagyüpa (bKa'-rgyud-pa), 20-1, 23-4, 128-9

Kailash, 42

Kalacakra, 66

Kalimpong (Ka-spungs), 32, 60, 84, 106, 109-110, 113, 130, 133, 138

Kangla Karchu La (? sGang-la mKhar-chu-la), 153

Karbjisa (dKar-sbis(spe)-sa), 55

Kargyü Wangchuk (dKar-brgyud dBang-phyug), 58, 147

Karma Trinley (Karma 'Phrin-las), 50

Karmapa (Karma-pa), 106, 126-7

Karsapani, 27

Kasha, Kalön (Ka-shar, bKa'-blon), 55

Kashag (bKa'-shag), 143

Kathmandu, 42

Kathogpa (Ka-thog-pa), 23

Kawang Dorje (Ka-wang rDo-rje), 111

Kawang Mangkhel (Ka-wang Mang-khel), 67-8

Kennedy, Robert, 149

Kesang Chödrön Dorje [Wangchuk] (bsKal-bzang Chos-sgron rDo-rje [dBang-phyug]), Queen Mother of Bhutan, 7-8, 50, 86, 135, 141

Kezang Wangmo (bsKal-bzang dBang-mo), 50

Khaling (Kha-gling), 48

Kham (Khams), 108

Khamsum Yongdröl (Khams-gsum Yongs-sgrol), 84

Khangmar (Khang-dmar), 122

Khasar Topgye (Kha-gsar sTobs-rgyas), 58, 67

Kheng ('Khan, Kheng), 48

Khenpalung (mKhan-pa-lung), 16

Kheri (Khe-ri), 22

Khöma (Khol-ma), 84

Khouchung (mKho-chung), 22

Khouchung Chöjé (mKho-chung Chos-rje), 51

Khyikha Ratö (Khyi-kha Ra-thod), 16

Kishen Kant Bose, 46

Könchok Zangpo (dKon-mchog bZang-po), 22

Könchok Wangdü (dKon-mchog dBang-'dus), 80

Kuch Bihar, 42, 44

Kujé (sKu-rjes), 16, 52, 58, 84, 107, 109, 118

Kujé Lhakhang (sKu-rjes lHa-khang), 107-8, 121

Kumarkatra, 72

Kunga Drakpa (Kun-dga' Grags-pa), 81

Kunga Pelden (Kun-dga' dPal-ldan) alias Sonam Topgye (bSod-nams sTobs-rgyas), 72, 147

Kunga Rabden (Kun-dga' Rab-brtan), 118-19, 127-8, 141, 153

Kunga Wangpo (Kun-dga' dBang-po), 22, 51

Kunley Dorje (Kun-legs rDo-rje), 67

Kunzang Tenpai Nyima, Peling Sungtrül (Kun-bzang bsTan-pa'i Nyi-ma, Pad-gling gSung-sprul), 50, 52, 84

Kunzang Trinley (Kun-bzang 'Phrin-las), 50, 77, 82, 84, 88, 91, 97

Kunzang Tsering (Kun-bzang Tshe-ring), 91, 97

Kurtö (sKur-stod), 40, 48, 51-2, 82, 84, 149, 151

Kurtö Drung (sKur-stod Drung), 99

Kurtöpa Kolong (sKur-stod-pa Ko-long), 56-8

Kushütara (Ku-shud-'thag-ras), 82

Kutsap (sKu-tshab), 87

Kyerchu Lhakhang (sKyer-chu lHa-khang), 16

Kyiduk (sKyid-sdug), 146

Kyikyila (sKyid-skid-la), 66

Kyirong (sKyid-grong), 49

Ladakh (La-dwags), 42

Lahul (? lHo-yul, lHa-yul), 42

Lam Pelri (Blam dPal-ri), 77

Lamé Gönpa (Bla-med dGon-pa), 77, 108, 109

Lamgong (Lam-gong), 84

Lance, W.H.J., 148

Landon, Perceval, 112

Langdarma (Glang-dar-ma), 18

Langmalung (Glang-ma-lung), 52

Laushong (Sla'u-gzhong), 55

Laya (La-yag), 153

Ledger, Cecily B., 153

Ledger, Lloyd K., 153

Legön Jarok Dongchen (Las-mgon Bya-rog gDong-can), 56

Lemo (Las-mo), 50, 82-4, 108, 111, 115, 142

Lepcha, 112

Lhadrön (lHa-sgron), 50, 82

Lhalung (lHa-lung), 22, 52, 56, 66, 71, 75, 84, 93, 128

Lhalung Thuksé (lHa-lung Thugs-sras), 22

Lhapa (lHa-pa), 23, 28

Lhasa (lHa-sa), 37, 40, 48, 66, 83-4, 88, 100, 107, 151

Lhengye tsokpa (lHan-rgyas Tshogs-pa), 36, 47

Lho (lHo), 24

Lhodrak (lHo-brag), 93

Lhodruk (lHo-'brug), 24

Lhomön Khazhi (lHo-mon Kha-bzhi), 24

Lhuntse (lHun-rtse), 32, 71

Lhuntse Dzong (lHun-rtse rDzong), 40, 153

Lhuntse Dzongpön (lHun-rtse rDzong-dpon), 52

Lingshi (Gling-bzhi), 28, 84, 148-9, 153

Lingtu (sp?), 86

Linlithgow, Doreen Marchioness of, 18, 131-2, 153

Lobpön (Slob-dpon), 36

Lobsang Chöden (Blo-bzang Chos-don?), 94

Lochak (Lo-phyag/Lo-chag), 40

Lome La (sp?), 149

Lönchen (Blon-chen), 140

Longchenpa (Klong-chen-pa), 20-1

Lucknow, 62

Ludlow, Frank, 16, 77, 130, 151-3

Ludrong Drölma (Klu-grong sGrol-ma), 76

Lumsden, K., 152

Lunana (Lung-nag-nang), 153

Luntenzampa (Lung-bstan Zam-pa), 75

Lyon, C.B., 150

Macdonald, David, 104, 149-50

Machen zimpön (Ma-chen gzim-dpon), 38

Mahakala, 27, 56, 62-3

Mahasammata, 144

Manchus, 40, 48, 100

Mangdé (Mang-sde), 48

Mangde Chu (Mang-sde Chu), 153

Mangdelung (Mang-sde-lung), 25, 51, 53-4, 118-19, 127

Marchang (? Mar-chang), 146

Maurya, 144

Me La (Me-la), 151, 153

Meade, H.R.C., 107, 109, 150

Mechis, 14

Meerut, 62

Mera, 152

Mikthöm (Mig-thol-ma), 54

Milarepa (Mi-la-ras-pa), 20-1

Mindruk, Geshé (sMin-drug, dGe-bshes), 84, 115, 142

Mingyur Tenpa (Mi-'gyur brTan-pa), 28, 32, 38, 42

Minto, Lord, 99

Mishmis, 148

Mochu (Mo-chu), 34, 45

Mön (Mon), 24

Mön Drubdé (Mon sGrub-sde), 38

Mongar (Mong-sgar), 149

Mongol, 23

Mönla Karchung (Mon-la Khar-chung), 150

Mönpa (Mon-pa), 120

Mönyul (Mon-yul) Corridor, 32

Morgan, J.F., 152

Morris, C.J., 151

Mughal emperor, 62

Muktsen (rMugs-btsan), 54

Murichom (sp?), 149

Nado, Lobpön (Nag-mdog, Slob-dpon), 7

Nadzi Pasang (gNag-rdzi Pa-sangs) alias Döndrup (Don-grub) alias Püntso Namgyel (Phun-tshogs rNam-rgyal), 58, 147

Nagas, 148

Nakhu (Nag-ku) alias Karma Trinley Lhundrub (Karma 'Phrin-las lHun-sgrub), 107, 109, 117, 129

Namdröl (rNam-sgrol), 99

Namgyel (rNam-rgyal), 50

Namgyel Wangchuk (rNam-rgyal dBang-phyug), 50, 125, 128

Nangsi Zilnön (sNang-srid Zil-gnon) , 84

Narthang (sNar-thang), 56

Naru (rNa-ru), 51

Nauché (sNa'u-che), 16

Nawab of Bengal, 42

Nepal, Nepali, Nepalese, 11-14, 28, 42, 49, 58, 62, 87-8, 90, 99, 107, 130, 133, 142, 145

Ngagi Wangchuk (Ngag-gi dBang-phyug), 38

Ngalong (sNga-slong), 12-13

Ngödrup (dNgos-sgrub), Punakha Dzongpön, 68

Ngödrup (dNgos-grub), 125, neice of Cholé Tulku, 125

Ngödrup Pemo (dNgos-sgrub dPal-mo), 84

Norbu (Nor-bu), 45

Norbhu Dhondup (Nor-bu Don-grub), Rai Sahib, 109

Norbu Drölma (Nor-bu sGrol-ma), 52

North-East Frontier Agency, 148

Nyagö (gNya'-rgod), 53

Nyamai Zampa (Nyal-mig Zam-pa), 32, 63

Nyerchen (gNyer-chen), 36

Nyima Dorje (Nyi-ma rDo-rje), 68, 73

Nyimalung (Nyi-ma-lung), 128

Nyingmapa (rNying-ma-pa), 21, 23, 106-7, 128

Nyö (gNyos, sMyos), 25, 116

Nyötön Trülshik Chöjé (gNyos-ston 'Khrul-zhig Chos-rje) alias Demchok (bDe-mchog), 22

Pa-chu, 105

Padmasambhava, 16, 84, 133, 144

Padshah Raja, 62

Pakhi (sp?), 43

Pakistan, 16

Pala Gyeltsen (Pa/P›/dPa'-la rGyal-mtshan), 50-1, 84, 86

Palden Wangchuk (dPal-ldan dBang-phyug), 91, 97

Panchen Lama (Paṇ-chen Bla-ma), 42, 94

Pangkheb (sPang-kheb), 121

Pangtey Gompa (sp?), 113

Parasmani Pradhan, 113

Paro (sPa-gro), 16, 18, 20, 28, 31-2, 34, 46-8, 54, 60, 63, 68-70, 73, 75, 78, 83-4, 86, 104-5, 110, 131, 133, 141, 148-52

Paro Dzong (sPa-gro rDzong), 27, 68, 70

Paro Pönlop (sPa-gro dPon-slob), 20, 47, 54-5, 67-9, 71, 73, 75, 78, 79-80, 83, 87, 97-100, 104, 106, 109, 116, 119, 122, 130-3, 141-2

Paul, A.W., 148

Pasakha (dPag-bsam-kha) or Buxa, 42, 64, 73, 87, 122, 149

Pasang (Pa-sangs), 56

Pedong (sPos-sdong), 20

Pedrön (dPal-sgron), 50, 83-4, 106, 126

Peking, 40, 100

Peling Sungtrul (Pad-gling gSung-sprul), 22, 93

Pelpung (dPal-spungs), 106

Pema, Geshé (Padma, dGe-bshes), 128

Pema Chödrak (Padma Chos-grags), 45

Pema Chödrön (Pema Chos-sgron), 50, 125

Pema Chökyi (Pema Chos-skyid), 50, 52, 56, 77

Pema Dechen (Padma bDe-chen), 7, 50, 58, 125, 127-8, 135

Pema Karpo (Padma dKar-po), 27

Pema Lhadrön (Padma lHa-sgron), 50

Pema Ösel Gyurmé Dorje, Peling Sungtrül (Padma 'Od-gsal 'Gyur-med rDo-rje, Pad-gling gSung-sprul), 128

Pema Trinley (Padma 'Phrin-las), 142

Pema Tendzin (Padma bsTan-'dzin), 50, 52, 66, 68, 76-8, 111

Pema Tsewang (Padma Tshe-dbang), 7, 93, see Pemala

Pemala (Padma-la), 7, 9, 49, 111

Pemalingpa (Padma Gling-pa), 21-2, 25, 51-2, 56, 73, 75, 78, 84, 93, 128, 144

Pesha (Pad-zhwa), 126

Phajo (Pha-jo), 24

Phari (Phag-ri), 56, 83, 104, 112

Phentok (Phan-thog), 68, see Fentook

Phobsikha, 152

Phochu (Pho-chu), 34

Phochu-Mochu (Pho-chu Mo-chu), 36

Phrumzur (? Phur-btsugs), 152

Phurgyel (Phur-rgyal) alias Chökyi Gyeltsen (Chos-kyi rGyal-mtshan), 48, 53

Pila Gönpo Wangyel (Pi/Pɪ-la mGon-po dBang-rgyal), 50-1, 86

Pon, Pön (dPon), 146

Pönlop (dPon-slob), 34, 36, 46, 58, 71, 98

Portuguese Jesuit, 28

Potala, 96

Prince of Wales, 94, 102, 115

Puna Dromchö (sPu-na sGrub-mchog), 21

Punakha, 28, 34, 36, 38, 45-6, 48, 52, 54, 58, 60, 67, 69-70, 75, 78, 80-1, 84, 91, 96-8, 100-1, 106-7, 109, 116, 120, 135, 145, 147-50

Punakha Dzong (sPu-na-kha, sPungs-thang rDzong), 21, 27, 34, 37-8, 44, 53-5, 70, 87, 91, 95-6, 107, 117-18, 123

Punakha Dzongpön (sPu-na-kha rDzong-dpon), 44, 46-7, 67-8, 73, 91

Punjab, 62

Püntso Chödrön (Phun-tshogs Chos-sgron), 7, 16, 50, 99, 115-16, 125-8, 134-5

Püntso Dorje (Phun-tshogs rDo-rje), 73, 78, 80-2

Püntso Wangdü (Phun-tshogs dBang-'dus), 50, 71, 109

Purgyel (Phur-rgyal) alias Chökyi Gyeltsen (Chos-kyi rGyal-mtshan), 48, 53, 147

R. N., 111

Pusola (sPu-so-la), 111

Rahula, 62

Rakshi , 22

Ralung (Ra-lung), 24, 27

Ram, Bansi, 109

Ranjit Singh, 62

Raplika (sp?), 151

Raven Crown, 56, 72, 75, 88, 90, 106, 116-17, 142, 145, 148

Reading, Lord, 143

Rennick, F.W., 91-2, 97, 148-9

Richardson, Hugh, 8, 133, 143, 153

Rigdzin Nyingpo (Rig-'dzin sNying-po), 91

Rinchen (Rin-chen), 50, 84

Rinchen Terdzö (Rin-chen gTer-mdzod), 107

Rinpung Dzong (Rin-spungs rDzong), 18, 20, 32, 63, 100, 131, 133, see also Paro Dzong

Ronaldshay, Lord (later Marquess of Zetland), 105, 113, 150

Rustomji, Nari, 143

Sakden (Sa-stengs), 152

Sakya (Sa-skya), 18, 71

Samada (sp?), 122

Samardzingkha (Sa-dmar-rdzing-kha), 75

Samdrup (bSam-grub), 71

Samdrup Chöling (bSam-grub Chos-gling), 118-19

Sampa Lhundrup (bSam-pa lHun-grub), 16

Samten Özer (bSam-gtan 'Od-zer), 31

Samtengang (bSam-gtan-sgang), 78, 82

Samvara, 53, 55

Samyé (bSam-yas), 16, 66

Sangak, Lam (gSang-sngags, Bla-ma), 7

Sangak Zabdön Phodrang (gSang-sngags Zab-don Pho-brang), 28, see also Simtokha, Simtokha Dzong

Sangdak (gSang-bdag), 22

Sangster, D.B., 150

Sangye Chödrön (Sangs-rgyas Chos-sgron), 50

Sangye Dorje (Sangs-rgyas rDo-rje), 82, 99, 147

Sangye Gyamtso (Sangs-rgyas rGya-mtsho), 48

Sangye Penjor (Sangs-rgyas dPal-'byor), 7, 113

Sangye Tendzin (Sangs-rgyas bsTan-'dzin), regent, 44

Sangye Tendzin, brother-in-law of Shabdrung Jigme Dorje, 125

Sarbhang, 151

Sele La (? Se-le-la), 151

Senge Dzong (Seng-ge rDzong), 149

Senge Namgyel (Seng-ge rNam-rgyal), 76-8

Shab (Zhabs), 146

Shabdrung (Zhabs-drung), 11, 24, 54-6, 58, 62, 71, 82, 84, 87, 90, 96, 98, 100-2, 115-16, 120-2, 124-5, 138, 144-6

Shabdrung Jigme Chögyel (Zhabs-drung 'Jigs-med Chos-rgyal), 71, 76, 81, 111

Shabdrung Jigme Dorje (Zhabs-drung 'Jigs-med rDo-rje), 81, 102, 123-5, 151

Shabdrung Jigme Drakpa (Zhabs-drung 'Jigs-med Grags-pa), 28, 45, 51

Shabdrung Jigme Drakpa (Zhabs-drung 'Jigs-med Grags-pa) the Second, 44

Shabdrung Jigme Norbu (Zhabs-drung 'Jigs-med Nor-bu), 71, 147

Shabdrung Ngawang Namgyel (Zhabs-drung Ngag-dbang rNam-rgyal), 15, 24, 27-40, 87

Shabdrung Tsultrim Drakpa (Zhabs-drung Tshul-khrims Grags-pa), 46

Shakya Dorje (Shākya rDo-rje), 119

Shakya Namgyel (Shākya rNam-rgyal), 51

Shakyashri (Shɔkya-shrɪ), 107

Shamkhar (gSham-mkhar), 58

Shar (Shar), 36, 48, 79

Shar Sigye (Shar Srid-rgyas), 67

Sharchop (Shar-phyogs-pa), 13

Sharpa Pünchung (Shar-pa sPun-cung), 86

Shedra (bShad-grwa), 128

Shemgang (gZhal-sgang), 32

Shengo (Zhal-ngo), 116

Sherab Wangchuk (Shes-rab dBang-phyug), 42

Sherriff, Betty, 128, 152-3

Sherriff, George, 8, 14, 25, 40, 45, 119, 126-8, 140, 151-3

Shillong, 138

Shongar (gZhong-sgar), 32, 48, 53

Shongar Dzongpön (gZhong-sgar rDzong-dpon), 99

Shung Drönyer (gZhung mGron-gnyer), 36, 45, 73, 91

Shung Kalön (gZhung bKa'-blon), 36

Sikh, 62

Sikkim, 40, 42, 49, 60-1, 73, 90, 93-4, 98-9, 103, 106, 112, 116, 132-3, 135-6, 139-40, 145, 149, 153

Simpson, Benjamin, 61, 148

Simtokha (Srin-mo-rdo-kha), 28, 69, 80

Simtokha Dzong (Srin-mo-rdo-kha rDzong), 68, 70

Sinchula (? Srin-chu-la), 64, 149

Sinclair, M.R., 151

Sindhu Raja, 16

Sino-Nepalese war of 1792, 43

Sino-Tibetan, 12

Sithub (Sri-thub), 99

Sölpön (gSol-dpon), 146

Sombrang (Sum-phrang), 22

Sonam Chödrön (bSod-nams Chos-sgron), 50

Sonam Döndrub (bSod-nams Don-grub), 62

Sonam Drugye (bSod-nams 'Brug-rgyas), 46, 52

Sonam Pedzom (bSod-nams dPal-'dzom), 50-1

Sonam Thayé (bSod-nams mTha'-yas), 67, 72

Sonam Topgye Dorje, Gongzim and Raja (bSod-nams sTobs-rgyas rDo-rje, Gong-gzim), 50, 86, 109-10, 117-18, 130, 133, 135-6, 140, 142-3, 150

Songtsen Gampo (Srong-brtsan sGam-po), 15, 84

Surmang (Zur-mang), 106, 129

Swat, 16

Swayambhunath, 42, 107

Ta Dzong (lTag rDzong), 32, 63, 69

Taktsang (sTag-tshang), 16, 21

Talo (rTa-log), 54, 81, 120, 122, 124

Tamdrin Ngödrup (rTa-mgrin dNgos-grub), 111

Tamshing (gTam-zhing), 22

Tamshing Chöjé (gTam-zhing Chos-rje), 16, 52, 78, 80

Tang (sTang), 15, 51

Tango (rTa-mgo), 81

Tango Tulku (rTa-mgo sPrul-sku), 81

Tangpa Rabgye (lTang-pa Rab-rgyas), 71

Tangun, 42

Tapön (rTa-dpon), 54

Tashi (bKra-shis), 136

Tashi the Bastard (Brang bKra-shis), 67

Tashi Dorje (bKra-shis rDo-rje), 86, 110, 135

Tashi Dorje (bKra-shis rDo-rje), regent, 53-4, 147

Tashi Namgyel, Chögyal (bKra-shis rNam-rgyal, Chos-rgyal), 135, 137

Tashi Namgyel (bKra-shis rNam-rgyal) alias Sonam Gyeltsen (bSod-nams rGyal-mtshan), 44, 139

Tashichö Dzong (bKra-shis Chos-rdzong), 32, 67, 116

Tashigang (bKra-shis-sgang), 32, 48, 53, 66, 149, 152

Tashigang Dzong (bKra-shis-sgang rDzong), 45

Tashiyangtse (bKra-shis-yang-rtse), 32, 48, 53, 149, 151-2

Tawang (rTa-wang), 120, 124

Taylor, Sir George, 8, 152

Tazik Drönma (sTag-gzig sGron-ma), 54

Teesta, 64

Tekha (Te-kha, gTer-kha), 111, 118

Temple, Sir Richard, 73

Tendzin Chökyi Gyeltsen, Peling Sungtrül (bsTan-'dzin Chos-kyi rGyal-mtshan, Pad-gling gSung-sprul), 50, 93

Tendzin Drugye (bsTan-'dzin 'Brug-rgyas), 37

Tendzin Drukdra (bsTan-'dzin 'Brug-sgra), 47-8

Tendzin Namgyel (bsTan-'dzin rNam-rgyal), 49

Tendzin Özer (bsTan-'dzin 'Od-zer),

7, see Nado, Lobpön

Tendzin Rabgye (bsTan-dzin Rab-rgyas), 28, 40, 44

Tennant, D., 130, 151

Tenpa Rinchen, Geshé (bsTan-pa Rin-chen, dGe-bshes), 128

Tenpai Nyima (bsTan-pa'i Nyi-ma), 116, 142

Tessla, 86, see Tsering Yangdzom

Thangtong Gyelpo (Thang-stong rGyal-po), 20-1

Tharpaling (Thar-pa-gling), 128

Thed, 48

Thimphu (Thim-phu), 28, 32, 46, 48, 58, 67-8, 73, 75-6, 78, 80, 83-4, 109, 141, 147-9

Thimphu Dzongpön (Thim-phu rDzong-dpon), 46, 48, 54-5, 58, 67, 69, 82, 88, 91, 97, 111, 148

Thimphu Zimpön (Thim-phu gZim-dpon), 99

Thondup Namgyel (Don-grub rNam-rgyal), Prince (later Chögyel) of Sikkim, 131-2, 139, 153

Thuksé (Thugs-sras) 116

Thutop Namgyel (mThu-stobs rNam-rgyal), Chögyel of Sikkim, 94, 103

Tibet, 11-12, 15, 18, 20, 23-5, 32, 40, 42-4, 49, 56, 66, 71, 75, 81, 93-4, 99, 106, 108, 112, 120, 122, 129, 132, 142, 149-51, 153

Tibetan, 124

Tibeto-Burman, 12-13

Tingkhab (mThing-khab), 126

Tongsa (Krong-sar), 25, 32, 34, 46, 51-3, 55-6, 58, 62, 64, 70-2, 83, 92, 106, 111, 115, 119, 122, 141, 148-9, 151, 153

Tongsa Drönyer (Krong-sar mGron-gnyer), 141-2

Tongsa Dzong (Krong-sar rDzong), 51-3, 55, 62, 64

Tongsa Pönlop (Krong-sar dPon-slob), 38, 40, 44, 47-8, 51, 53-6, 58, 67, 70, 76-8, 87, 90, 94, 96, 115, 118, 141

Topga Rinpoché (sTobs-dga' Rin-po-che), 8

Topgye Dorje (sTobs-rgyas rDo-rje), 84

Tozen (lTo-gzan), 52

Trakhar (sPra-mkhar) or Prai, 22, 116

Trashichodzong, 116, see Tashi Chödzong

Tremo La (sp?), 149-50

Tridé Songtsen (Khri-lde Srong-brtsan), 18

Trinley ('Phrin-las), 147

Trinley Dorje, Gangteng Tulku ('Phrin-las rDo-rje, sGangs-steng sPrul-sku), 142

Trinley Namgyel ('Phrin-las rNam-rgyal), 113

Trinley Topgye ('Phrin-las sTobs-rgyas), 50, 71-2, 78

Trinley Zangpo ('Phrin-las bZang-po), 67

Tritrül Jigme Senge (Khri-sprul 'Jigs-med Seng-ge), 44

Tritrül Tsultrim Drakpa (Khri-sprul Tshul-khrims Grags-pa), 45, 49

Tsakaling (Tsakakling), 22

Tsamang (rTsa-mang), 45

Tsang (gTsang), 24, 122

Tsangma (gTsang-ma), 18

Tsangpa Gyaré (gTsang-pa rGya-ras), 55

Tsangpo (gTsang-po), 152-3

Tsangyang Gyamtso (Tshangs-dbyangs rGya-mtsho), 22

Tsaphukpa Tsewang (Tsha-phug-pa Tshe-dbang), 54

Tsaphukpa Dorje (Tsha-phug-pa rDo-rje), 44

Tsarong (Tsha-rong), 86

Tsendong (bTsan-stong), 84, 86

Tsendong Namgyel (bTsan-stong rNam-rgyal), 142

Tsering Dröma (Tshe-ring sGrol-ma), 50

Tsering Pema (Tshe-ring Padma), 50

Tsering Penjor (Tshe-ring dPal-'byor), 50, 83, 106, 109, 116, 130, 133

Tsering Yangdzom (Tshe-ring dByangs-'dzom), 86

Tsewang (Tshe-dbang), 84

Tsewang, Lama (Tshe-dbang, Bla-ma) alias Sonam Gyeltsen (bSod-nams rGyal-mtshan), 147, 68-9, 76

Tsewang Norbu (Tshe-dbang Nor-bu), 68

Tsewang Penjor (Tshe-dbang dPal-'byor), 91

Tsewang Sithub (Tshe-dbang Sri-thub), 58, 68, 99, 147

Tshangla (sp?), 13, 18, 52

Tsokye Dorje (mTsho-skyes rDo-rje), 52, 56, 72

Tsöndrü Gyeltsen (brTson-'grus rGyal-mtshan), 52-3, 55, 56, 58, 62

Tsöndrü Pekar (brTson-'grus Pad-dkar), 58, 147

Tsongpön (Tshong-dpon), 52

Tsukphü Namgyal (gTsug-phud rNam-rgyal), Chögyel of Sikkim, 61

Tsultrim Namgyel (Tshul-khrims rNam-rgyal) alias Agi Hap (A-rgas Had-pa), 54, 71

Tsultrim Yönten (Tshul-khrims Yon-tan), 58, 147

Tubby, 143, see Sonam Topgye Dorje

Turner, Samuel, 43-4, 49

Ü (dBus), 40

Ugyen Chöling (U-rgyan Chos-gling), 52

Ugyen Dorje, Gongzim (U-rgyan rDo-rje, Gong-gzim), 50, 84, 87, 91, 94-5, 97-104, 106, 112, 135, 148

Ugyen Dorje, Phodrang Rinpoche (U-rgyan rDo-rje, Pho-brang Rin-po-che), 86

Ugyen Dorje (U-rgyan rDo-rje), father of the queens of Bhutan, 125

Ugyen Pelri (U-rgyan dPal-ri), 8, 130-3

Ugyen Püntso, 16, 50-2, 56

Ugyen Wangchuk (U-rgyan dBang-phug), 1st King of Bhutan, 11, 16, 28, 31-2, 50, 56, 58, 69-70, 72, 75-116, 125-6, 141-2, 144-5, 147-50

Ugyen Zangmo (U-rgyan bZang-mo), 22

Ugyen Zangpo (U-rgyan bZang-po), 22

Ula ('U-lag), 32

Umadewa alias Sherab Tharchin (U-ma-de-ba), 55, 58, 67, 147

Umdzé Chapchapa (dBu-mdzad sKyabs-khra-pa), 44

Umdzé Parop (dBu-mdzad sPa-gro-pa), 44

Umtengkha (Um-steng-kha), 103

United Nations, 140, 143

Ura (U-ra), 149

Urukpa Döndrup (U-rug-pa Don-grub), 51

Vance, R.L., 150

Vajravarahi, 55

Wang (Wang), 28, 44, 46, 48

Wangchuk (dBang-phyug), 11, 22, 50

Wangchuk Gyelpo (dBang-phyug rGyal-po), 54, 147

Wangdü Chöling (dBang-'dus Chos-gling), 8, 58, 66, 73, 77-8, 82-3, 125, 128

Wangdü Phodrang (dBang-'dus Pho-brang), 28, 36, 46, 48, 53, 67, 70-1, 78, 148-9, 151

Wangdü Phodrang Dzongpön (dBang-'dus Pho-brang rDzong-dpon), 54, 58, 61, 69, 78, 87, 99

Wangmo (dBang-mo), 50, 107, 109, 126-7

Wangya, Kalön Ashang (dBang-rgya, bKa'-blon A-zhang), 76

Wangyön (dBang-yon), 32

Wawel Wangdrak (Wa-wal dBang-grags), 50

Weir, Leslie J., 8, 36, 38, 47, 69, 106, 110, 121-2, 142-3, 151

Weir, Thyra, 151

West Bengal, 14, 20, 60

White, John Claude, 31-2, 34, 38, 79, 81-3, 87, 90-2, 94-5, 97, 99-100, 105, 112, 148, 149

Williamson, Frederick (Derick), 8, 135, 137, 151-2

Williamson, Margaret, 8, 130, 135

Wilson, Joy, 132, 153

Yagang (g.Yag-sgang), 22

Yangdön Tsering (dByangs-sgron Tshe-ring), 50

Yangdzom (dByang-'dzom), 50, 83

Yarlung (Yar-lung), 66

Yatung (sp?), 151

Yeshé Chödrön (Ye-shes Chos-sgron), 50, 78, 82-3, 125, 128

Yeshé Drölma (Ye-shes sGrol-ma), 94

Yeshé Gyeltsen (Ye-shes rGyal-mtshan), 46, 49

Yeshé Ngödrup, Cholé Tulku (Ye-shes dNgos-grub, Phyogs-las sPrul-sku), 49, 58, 87, 91, 94, 101-2, 125, 147

Yongla Gompa (Yong-la dGon-pa), 66

Yönten Gyeltsen (Yon-tan rGyal-mtshan), 58

Yönten Rinchen (Yon-tan Rin-chen), 71, see Tazik Drönma

Younghusband, Francis, 87-8, 90, 112, 148

Yudrön (g.Yu-sgron), 50

Yung Cheng, 100

Yungdrung Chöling (g.Yung-drung Chos-gling), 118

Zangskar (Zangs-dkar), 42

Zhidar (bZhi-dar), 44

Zhudrel (bZhugs-gral), 91

Zimgap, 122, see Zingap

Zimnang (gZim-nang), 52

Zimpön (gZim-dpon), 36, 146

Zingap (gZim-'gag-pa), 52, 122, 142